TEPS in
TEPS

800청해

박기혁

서울대학교 졸
(현) 메가스터디 어학센터 TEPS 강사
(현) SLA 학원 TEPS 대표 강사
(현) 중앙일보 영자 신문 중앙 데일리 교육 분야 객원 논설위원
(현) 한국 생산성 본부 영어 전임 강사
(현) PTT(Park's TEPS Teacher's Group) 대표 강사
-TEPS의 최고를 지향하는 강사들의 모임

송승룡

성균관대학교 졸업, 경희대학교 대학원 석사과정
영국 Wimbledon School of English 어학과정 이수
(현) 중앙데일리 영자 신문 객원 해설위원
(현) 민중에센스 아동영어/실용영어 연구센터 연구위원
(현) 한국생산성본부 영어 지도위원
(현) PTT(Park's TEPS Teacher's Group) 강사
-TEPS의 최고를 지향하는 강사들의 모임

TEPS in TEPS 800 청해

저자 | 박기혁 · 송승룡
초판 1쇄 발행 | 2009년 5월 25일
초판 4쇄 발행 | 2014년 2월 10일

발행인 | 박효상
편집장 | 강성실
기획 · 편집 | 박운희, 박혜민, 박문정
디자인 책임 | 손정수
마케팅 총괄 | 이종선
마케팅 | 이태호, 이전희
디지털콘텐츠 | 이지호, 김정숙
관리 | 남채윤

Special Staff

표지 | 장선숙
내지 | 홍수미
편집 | 정선영
조판 | 조지연

출판등록 | 제10-1835호
발행처 | 사람in
주소 | 121-839 서울시 마포구 양화로11길 14-10(서교동 378-16) 4F
전화 | 02) 338-3555(代)   팩스 | 02) 338-3545
e-mail | saramin@netsgo.com
Homepage | www.saramin.com

:: 책값은 뒤표지에 있습니다.
:: 파본은 바꾸어 드립니다.

ⓒ박기혁 · 송승룡 2009

ISBN 978-89-6049-124-3 18740
    978-89-6049-116-8 (세트)

사람이 중심이 되는 세상, 세상과 소통하는 책 **사람in**

TEPS in TEPS

800 청해

박기혁 · 송승룡

사람in

Preface

영어 시험을 둘러싼 여러 가지 환경 변화에 의해서 TEPS의 중요성은 나날이 강조되고 있고 그 특징 또한 뚜렷이 변화를 겪고 있다.

첫째, 갈수록 문제가 다양화되고 있고 더욱더 세련되어지고 있다.
둘째, 시험을 치르는 대상 연령층이 자꾸 낮아지고 있다.
셋째, 특목고나 외고, 로스쿨이나 의학전문대학원 진학 등 그 쓰임새가 더욱 광범위해졌다.

이러한 세 가지 변화에 발맞추어, TEPS 교재도 다양화되고 진화되어야 하는데, 현재의 교재 시장은 그러한 가시적인 변화에 능동적으로 대처하지 못하는 것이 사실이다. 이에, 이번 TEPS in TEPS 시리즈를 통해서 진화하는 TEPS에 가장 적합한 패러다임을 제시하고자 한다.

TEPS는 참으로 복잡하고 미묘한 시험이다. TOEFL처럼 학문적인 점에 초점을 맞추는 것도 아니고, TOEIC처럼 실용 언어적인 측면만을 강조하는 시험도 아니다. 어쩌면 이 둘의 장점만을 모아 놓은 시험이라 할 수 있겠다.

학문적인 내용들을 풀어가되 좀 더 현실성을 부여하여 실용적으로 쓰이는 영어들을 묻는 것이다. TEPS가 최근 시험 시장에 지각 변동을 일으키고 있는 이유는 이런 장점이 토대가 되었다고 볼 수 있다.

TEPS는 실제로 회화를 하다가 혹은 네이티브가 보는 외국 신문 등을 읽다가 느끼는 애로사항을 잘 해결해 줄 수 있는 시험이다. 어휘력의 측면에서 보아도 실생활에서 우리는 이런 어려움을 겪는다. '단어 하나하나의 해석은 되는데 왜 전체적으로는 독해가 안 되고 해석이 안 될까?', '이 상황에서 저 말은 대체 무슨 뜻으로 쓰이는 걸까?'

그것은 바로 간단한 단어라도 초보적으로 배웠던 사전적 지식 외에 실생활에서는 다양한 뜻으로 활용되기 때문이다.

이처럼 네이티브와의 가장 적절한 의사소통에 초점을 둔 TEPS는 지극히 영어수험과 영어실용의 접목이라는 공인영어시험의 목적에 가장 합당한 인증시험이라 하겠다.

TOEIC이 점수 인플레로 상위권 수험생의 변별력을 상실했다는 비판이 많다. TEPS는 TOEIC과 같은 패턴의 지속적인 반복만으로는 해결할 수 없는 시험이다. 이에 학습자들도 이런 TEPS에 대한 관심과 욕구가 더욱 늘어나고 있는 현실이다.

필자는 좀 더 실용적이고 영어 실력 향상에 도움이 되는 TEPS에 대한 관심이 높아지고 있는 것은 고무적인 일이라 생각한다. 그리고 그런 TEPS를 연구하고 학습하는데, 이 'TEPS in TEPS 시리즈'가 선구자적인 역할을 하길 진심으로 바라는 마음으로 문제 하나 설명 하나에 세심한 신경을 쓰면서 작업에 임하였다.

혼자서는 할 수 없었던 작업에 언제나 도움이 되었던 분들께 감사의 마음을 전할까 한다. 늘 미안한 마음이 드는 가족들과, 사람in 출판사의 박효상 사장님, 김상호 팀장님, 조승주 대리님 그리고 이 책의 출간에 물심양면으로 도움을 주신 류건 선생님, 신일섭 조교, 윤이랑 조교에게도 아울러 감사의 뜻을 표하고 싶다.

PTT(Park's TEPS Teacher's Group) 대표 강사

박 기 혁

TEPS in TEPS

학생들의 자습서와 학원 교재의 성격을 둘 다 가질 수 있게 만들었다. 그래서 학원에서의 강의는 물론 독학용으로 사용하도록 준비했다.

1. 상세한 해설을 통해 정답을 공략하는 법과 함께 오답을 피할 수 있는 Skill들을 제시하여 좀 더 높은 점수로의 도약이 가능하게 하였다.

2. TEPS의 4대 영역(독해, 어휘, 청해, 문법)과 기준 점수대별로 학습 목표와 가장 효율적인 방법들을 제시하여 좀 더 전문적이고 체계적인 학습자 맞춤형 학습이 가능하도록 하였다.

3. 애매모호한 이론이나 군더더기 설명을 최대한 배제하여 학습 시간 대비 효율성을 극대화하도록 구성하였다.

TEPS in TEPS

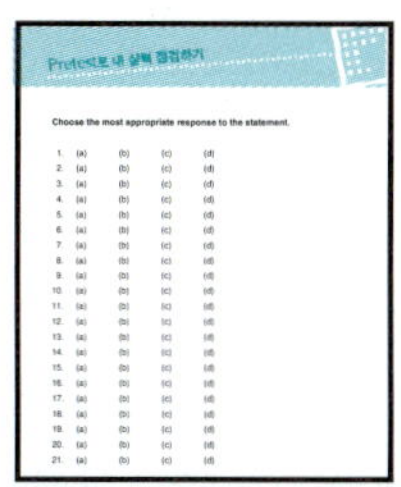

1. 내 실력을 미리 점검하는 Pretest

실제 시험 문제와 가장 가까운 형태의 각 Part별 Pretest를 통해 현재의 내 실력을 점검하고, 보강해야 할 부분에 관한 평가와 처방을 들어본다.

2. TEPS 청해의 해결법을 제시한 Pretest Clinic

Pretest의 문제를 상세한 해설과 함께 정답 포인트를 짚어봄으로써, TEPS 중요 출제 포인트를 짚는다.

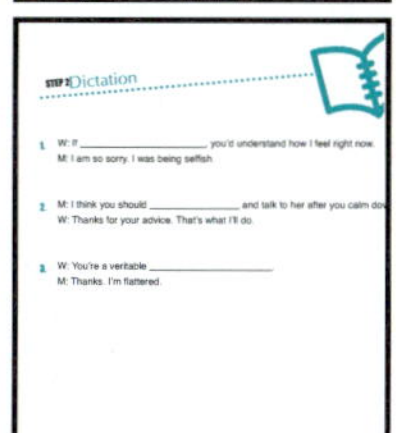

3. 핵심 단어와 표현을 캐치하는 Dictation

Clinic에 나오는 핵심 단어와 표현을 음성을 들으면서 캐치하는 훈련을 한다.

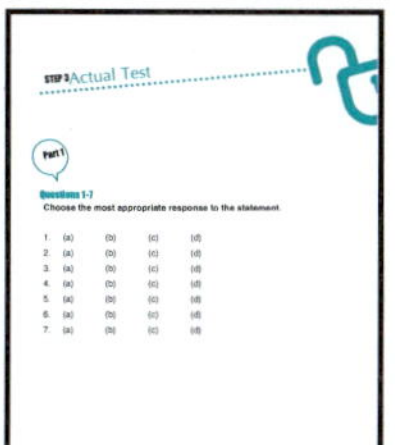

4. 자신만의 해결 노하우를 만들어가는 Actual Test

실전 연습 문제를 통해 실전에 대한 감각을 극대화하도록 한다. 영문 스크립트와 지문의 해석 및 해설은 정답과 해설에서 확인하며 충분한 보충 학습이 될 수 있도록 하였다.

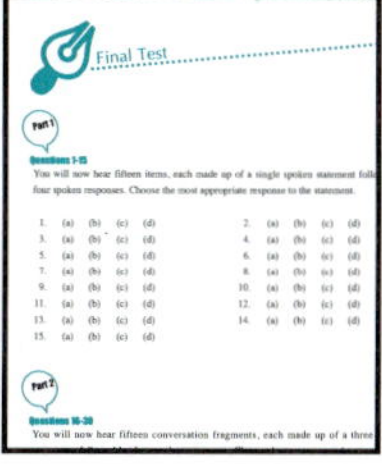

5. 실전보다 더 실전 같은 Final Test

청해 1회분의 모의고사를 실었다. 난이도는 정기시험과 동일하다. 실전 문제를 통해 정확한 자기 실력을 파악할 수 있다.

TEPS in TEPS

TEPS의 구성

TEPS는 청해, 문법, 어휘, 독해 4개 영역에 걸쳐 총 200문항으로 구성되어 있으며 시험 시간은 140분이다. 만점은 문항 반응 이론(IRT)에 따라 채점하기 때문에 전부 맞아도 990점이고 모두 틀려도 10점은 나온다.

영역	PART별 내용	문항 수	시간/배점
청 해 Listening Comprehension	Part Ⅰ : 문장 하나를 듣고 이어질 대화 고르기 Part Ⅱ : 3문장의 대화를 듣고 이어질 대화 고르기 Part Ⅲ : 6-8문장의 대화를 듣고 질문에 해답하는 답 고르기 Part Ⅳ : 단문의 내용을 듣고 질문에 해당하는 답 고르기	15 15 15 15	55분/396점
문 법 Grammar	Part Ⅰ : 대화문의 빈칸에 적절한 표현 고르기 Part Ⅱ : 문장의 빈칸에 적절한 표현 고르기 Part Ⅲ : 대화에서 어법상 틀리거나 어색한 부분 고르기 Part Ⅳ : 단문에서 어법상 틀리거나 어색한 부분 고르기	20 20 5 5	25분/99점
어 휘 Vocabulary	Part Ⅰ : 대화문의 빈칸에 적절한 단어 고르기 Part Ⅱ : 단문의 빈칸에 적절한 단어 고르기	25 25	15분/99점
독 해 Reading Comprehension	Part Ⅰ : 지문을 읽고 지문의 빈칸에 들어갈 내용 고르기 Part Ⅱ : 지문을 읽고 질문에 가장 적절한 내용 고르기 Part Ⅲ : 지문을 읽고 문맥상 어색한 내용 고르기	16 21 3	45분/396점
총계	13개 PART	200	140분/990점

청해(Listening Comprehension) 60문항

정확한 청해 능력을 측정하기 위하여 문제와 보기 문항을 문제지에 인쇄하지 않고 들려줌으로써 자연스러운 의사소통의 인지과정을 최대한 반영하였다. 다양한 의사소통 기능(Communicative Functions)의 대화와 다양한 상황(공고, 방송, 일상 업무 상황, 대학 교양 수준의 강의 등)을 이해하는 데 필요한 전반적인 청해력을 측정하기 위해 대화문(dialogue)과 담화문(monologue)의 소재를 균형 있게 다루었다.

PART 1	15문항

Listen and choose the most appropriate response.

W: How about talking over lunch on Wednesday?
M: ___________________________________

(a) Sounds good She'd love it.
(b) Tell me about it.
(c) Sorry. I have an appointment. What about Friday?
(d) Fine. Thanks.

Part 1은 질의응답 문제를 다루며 한 번만 들려준다. 내용 자체는 단순하고 기본적인 수준의 생활 영어 표현으로 구성되어 있지만 교과서적인 지식보다는 재빠른 상황 판단 능력을 요구한다. 따라서 이 파트에서는 속도 적응 능력뿐만 아니라 순발력 있는 상황 판단 능력이 요구된다.

PART 2	15문항

Listen and choose the most appropriate response.

M: How come you know so much about fashion?
W: Actually, my sister is a model.
M: Wow! How long has she been in the industry?
M: ___________________________________

(a) She wants to be a fashion designer.
(b) About two years.
(c) Last year she did.
(d) Modeling is a tough job.

Part 2는 짧은 대화 문제로 두 사람이 A-B-A-B 순으로 보통 속도로 대화하는 형식이며 소요 시간은 약 12초 전후로 짧게 구성되어 있다. Part 1과 마찬가지로 한 번만 들려주는 부분이다.

Listen and choose the correct answer to the question.

M: Hello. I'd like to file a complaint with the city.
W: What is the complaint in regards to?
M: About the condition of Canal Street. I drove down the road this morning, and my car sustained a large amount of damage.
W: Did you run into something?
M: No, I drove through an unavoidable pothole and my car got two flat tires.
W: Okay, you're going to have to fill out this form. Someone will call you next week about compensation for the damages.
M: I have to wait one week!

Q. What can be inferred from the conversation?

(a) The man works for the city.
(b) The man is upset about the situation.
(c) Many of the city's streets are in bad condition.
(d) The man is a bad driver.

Part 3는 앞의 두 파트에 비해 다소 긴 대화를 들려 준다. 대신 대화 부분과 질문을 들려 준 뒤 다시 한 번 대화 부분을 들려 주기 때문에 길이가 긴 데 비해 많이 어렵다고는 할 수 없다.

Listen and choose the correct answer to the question.

This year the University has enrolled 25% more foreign students than it has any year in the past. The administration hopes that this will help diversify campus life and activities, as well as participation. We would remind all students to welcome foreign students and make them feel at home on campus and in the city. As with any foreign visitors, our foreign students will be bringing with them pieces of their own cultures, and they may be unaware of certain aspects of our culture. Teach them and learn from them and then this year promises to offer many exciting opportunities for students of all ethnicities.

Q. What can be inferred from the announcement?

(a) The foreign students will not integrate well into campus life.
(b) The administration does not support campus activities.
(c) All students can grow from multicultural experiences if they work together.
(d) The administration concerns itself only with academics.

Part 4는 담화문을 다룬다. 영어권 나라에서 영어로 뉴스를 듣거나 강의를 들을 때와 비슷한 상황을 설정하여 얼마나 잘 이해하는지를 측정하는 부분이다. 이야기의 주제, 목적, 화제, 세부 사항 및 이를 근거로 한 추론 등을 다룬다. 직청 직해 실력, 즉 들으면서 곧바로 내용을 이해할 수 있는지를 잘 평가해 주는 부분이다.

Part I

Choose the most appropriate response to the statement.

1. (a)   (b)   (c)   (d)
2. (a)   (b)   (c)   (d)
3. (a)   (b)   (c)   (d)
4. (a)   (b)   (c)   (d)
5. (a)   (b)   (c)   (d)
6. (a)   (b)   (c)   (d)
7. (a)   (b)   (c)   (d)
8. (a)   (b)   (c)   (d)
9. (a)   (b)   (c)   (d)
10. (a)   (b)   (c)   (d)
11. (a)   (b)   (c)   (d)
12. (a)   (b)   (c)   (d)
13. (a)   (b)   (c)   (d)
14. (a)   (b)   (c)   (d)
15. (a)   (b)   (c)   (d)
16. (a)   (b)   (c)   (d)
17. (a)   (b)   (c)   (d)
18. (a)   (b)   (c)   (d)
19. (a)   (b)   (c)   (d)
20. (a)   (b)   (c)   (d)
21. (a)   (b)   (c)   (d)

1. 1~3번 문제에 약한 경우

평서문 유형의 문제에 취약하다고 볼 수 있다. 특히 세 문제 모두 틀린 경우 평서문에 대한 대비책을 세워야 한다. Chapter 1의 문제들을 풀어 보면서 잘 학습해 두자.

2. 4~6번 문제에 약한 경우

정답이 (a)인 경우 확신을 가지지 못하고 어설픈 오답을 고르는 경우에 해당한다. Chapter 2의 문제들을 통해 충분히 연습하면서 자신감을 갖도록 하자.

3. 7~9번 문제에 약한 경우

의문사 의문문 유형의 기본적인 문제들로 Part 1에서 반드시 맞춰야 하는 영역이다. Chapter 3의 문제들을 잘 풀어 보고 특히 복합의문사에 대해 중점적으로 학습해 두자.

4. 10~12번 문제에 약한 경우

대인 관련 주제 표현에 약하다고 볼 수 있다. 누군가와 만나서 인사하고 헤어지고 약속할 때의 표현들, 또는 제안/권유, 충고, 부탁/허락, 칭찬/축하, 격려/위로, 항의/불평에 관한 표현들을 유형별로 외워 두어야 한다. Chapter 4를 통해 꼼꼼히 학습해 두자.

5. 13~15번 문제에 약한 경우

대인 관련 주제 중 전화, 질의응답에 대한 동의/반대, 그리고 취미 관련 표현들에 대해 아직까지 정리가 안 됐다고 볼 수 있다. 특히 전화 관련 문제는 한 문제 이상 꼭 출제되므로 Chapter 5를 통해 확실히 정리해 두자.

6. 16~18번 문제에 약한 경우

일상생활과 관련하여 직장 및 학교생활, 쇼핑, 음식점, 여행 등 다양한 주제의 문제들이 출제되므로 Chapter 6을 통해 충분히 연습해 두자.

7. 19~21번 문제에 약한 경우

길찾기, 공공안내, 교통, 병원, 건강에 관한 것으로 자주 나오는 내용들이므로 Chapter 7을 참고하며 꼼꼼히 학습해 두자.

평서문 유형 익히기

Chapter 1

Part 1에 나오는 문제 유형은 크게 ❶ 의문사 의문문 ❷ 의문사 아닌 의문문 ❸ 평서문으로 분류할 수 있다. 이 중 가장 중요하고 어려운 부분이 바로 평서문이다. 특별한 요령이 통하지 않기 때문에 구어체 표현이라든지 주제별 대화 내용, 특히 관용어구들을 되도록 많이 익혀 둘 필요가 있다. 또한 들을 때 주어 부분과 시제에 특히 유의하자.

1. W: If the tables were turned, you'd understand how I feel right now.

M: ___________________________________

(a) The table was completely upside-down.
(b) Over my dead body! That's my table.
(c) Don't pull my leg. I'm not in a good mood.
(d) I am so sorry. I was being selfish.

🐞 해설

여기서 the tables were turned는 '테이블이 뒤집혔다' 는 뜻이 아니라 '형세가 역전됐다', '상황이 바뀌었다' 란 관용표현으로 쓰였다. 즉 네가 내 입장이라면 지금 내 심정을 이해할 수 있을 거라고 말하고 있으므로 (d)가 이어지는 것이 적절하다. (a)와 (b)는 table을 이용해 오답을 유도하려는 선택지로 이런 함정에 유의해야 한다.

어휘

upside-down 거꾸로 Over my dead body! 절대 안 돼! pull one's leg ~를 놀리다

2. M: I think you should pocket your pride and talk to her after you calm down.

W: ___________________________________

(a) I talked to her yesterday.
(b) Thanks for your advice. That's what I'll do.
(c) I'm flat broke. I need to borrow some money.
(d) You are in your prime. You should be looking for Miss Right.

🐞 해설

충고를 해주고 있으므로 이를 고맙게 받아들인 (b)가 적절한 응답이다.

어휘

pocket one's pride 자존심을 억누르다 flat broke 무일푼의 in one's prime 인생의 한창때에
Miss Right 이상적인 여자 *cf.* Prince Charming 이상적인 남자

3. W: You're a veritable walking encyclopedia.
 M: ____

(a) Thanks. I'm flattered.
(b) Yes, I've got an encyclopedia.
(c) I'll let you off this time.
(d) No sweat.

해설

walking encyclopedia는 '걸어다니는 백과사전', 즉 다방면에 상식을 많이 갖추고 있는 사람을 뜻하는 표현으로, 남자에게 모르는 게 없다며 칭찬하고 있으므로 이에 대한 답례가 담긴 선택지를 고르면 된다. (b)는 encyclopedia의 의미를 이용한 함정이므로 주의하자.

어휘

veritable 실제의, 정말의 walking encyclopedia 박식한 사람 flatter 아첨하다, 추켜세우다 let ... off (~에게 일·벌 따위를) 면제해 주다 No sweat. 괜찮다, 쉬운 일이다

1. W: If ________________________, you'd understand how I feel right now.

   M: I am so sorry. I was being selfish.

2. M: I think you should ________________ and talk to her after you calm down.

   W: Thanks for your advice. That's what I'll do.

3. W: You're a veritable ____________________.

   M: Thanks. I'm flattered.

STEP 3 Actual Test

Questions 1-7

Choose the most appropriate response to the statement.

1. (a)   (b)   (c)   (d)
2. (a)   (b)   (c)   (d)
3. (a)   (b)   (c)   (d)
4. (a)   (b)   (c)   (d)
5. (a)   (b)   (c)   (d)
6. (a)   (b)   (c)   (d)
7. (a)   (b)   (c)   (d)

☞ 역사

anecdote	일화
archaeology	고고학
atrocity	포악, 잔학
barbarian	야만인, 미개인
Bronze Age	청동기 시대
chivalry	기사도
coronation	대관식
cromlech	환상 열석(環狀列石)
decadence	쇠미, 타락
emancipation	해방
the feudal age	봉건 시대
feudalism	봉건 제도
flowering	전성기
fossil	화석
hierarchy	서열
hominoid	유인원
homo erectus	직립 원인
monument	기념비
mound	고분
primeval	원시 시대의, 태고의
progenitor	(동식물의) 원종(原種), 조상
regal	제왕의, 제왕다운
relics	유물
ruins	유적
slavery	노예 제도
specimen	표본
Stone Age	석기 시대
stratum	층, 계급

선택지 (a)
유형 익히기

Chapter 2

청해에 자신이 없거나 기초가 부족한 학습자들의 경우, 특히 정답이 (a)인 문제에 약한 경우가 많다. 따라서 이 경우엔 정답을 마음속으로 분류해 놓는 것이 효과적이다. 예를 들어 확실한 정답은 (O), 확실한 오답은 (x), 불확실한 정답이나 오답은 (/), 잘 못 들었을 경우엔 (?), 이런 식으로 분류해 나가면 문제를 해결할 수 있을 것이다.

4. M: This is really a big favor you're doing for me.

W: ________________________________

(a) Think nothing of it. You would do the same for me, wouldn't you?
(b) What a nerve!
(c) That'll be the day.
(d) You are my life savior.

🐞 해설

은혜에 대한 고마운 마음을 전하고 있으므로 이에 답례하는 내용의 선택지를 골라야 한다. Think nothing of it.은 감사에 대한 응답 표현으로 '별말씀을요', '천만에요', '별거 아니에요' 라는 뜻의 정중하고 친근감을 주는 표현이다.

> **어휘**
>
> do ... a favor ～에게 은혜를 베풀다   What a nerve! 배짱 한번 좋군!   That'll be the day. 해가 서쪽에서 뜰 일이다, 어림도 없는 일이다   life savior 생명의 은인

5. W: I'm sorry. I know I'm the one who goofed it up.

M: ________________________________

(a) Don't be so hard on yourself. It's not just your fault.
(b) Back me up.
(c) Get real.
(d) I already apologized. What else do you want me to do?

🐞 해설

일을 망쳐놓은 것에 대해 사과하고 있으므로 자책하지 말라며 위로하는 (a)가 적절하다.

> **어휘**
>
> goof up 실수하다, (일을) 망치다   back ... up ～를 지지[후원]해 주다

6. M: I should apologize for jumping to conclusions.

W: _______________________________________

(a) Forget it.
(b) You're a penny pincher.
(c) You're an old woman.
(d) Don't get so technical on me.

🐝 **해설**

여자에게 사과를 하고 있으므로 (a)가 정답이다. Forget it.은 '신경 쓰지 마라', '잊어라'의 뜻으로 사과를 하는 상대에게 해줄 수 있는 말에 해당된다. 특히 가까운 사이에서 쓸 수 있는 표현.

어휘

jump to conclusions 속단하다 **penny pincher** 깍쟁이, 구두쇠 **an old woman** 깐깐한 사람
get technical 어려운 말을 쓰다

4. M: This is really a big favor you're doing for me.

W: _________________. You would do the same for me, wouldn't you?

5. W: I'm sorry. I know I'm the one who goofed it up.

M: _______________________________. It's not just your fault.

6. M: I should apologize for jumping to conclusions.

W: _________________.

Questions 1-5

Choose the most appropriate response to the statement.

1. (a) (b) (c) (d)
2. (a) (b) (c) (d)
3. (a) (b) (c) (d)
4. (a) (b) (c) (d)
5. (a) (b) (c) (d)

☞ 문학/언어

dialect	방언, 지방 사투리
phonetics	음성학
platitude	평범한 의견, 상투어
rhyme	각운
syntax	구문론
allegory	우화; 풍유; 상징
antagonist	적수
anthology	명시 선집
bibliography	저서 목록, 서지학
biography	전기
censorship	검열
copyright	판권, 저작권
crib	표절
epic	서사시
epistolary	서간체의, 서간문에 알맞은
epitome	발췌, 개요
euphuism	미사여구
excerpt	발췌록, 인용구
fable	우화, 꾸며낸 이야기
literati	문학자들
lyrical	서정적인
piracy	불법복제
protagonist	(이야기 등의) 주인공
synopsis	줄거리
virtuoso	(예술의) 거장
pseudonym	(작가의) 필명, 아호, 익명

의문사
의문문
유형 익히기

Chapter 3

Who, Where, What, Why, When 등의 의문사 의문문 문제 유형은 반드시 맞추고 넘어가야 하는데, 복합의문사로 물어보는 경우 틀리기 쉽기 때문에 대답 유형과 함께 충분히 학습해 두어야 한다.

7. W: What's wrong with this weekend's travel plans?

M: ______________________________________

(a) You must be feeling jet lagged.
(b) The catch is that my car needs to be repaired.
(c) I got a bit airsick.
(d) The plane has been delayed.

🔦 해설

여자가 여행 계획에 무슨 문제가 생겼는지 묻고 있으므로 이에 관한 내용이 담긴 선택지를 고르면 된다.

> **어휘**
>
> **jet lagged** 시차로 피곤한   **the catch** (계획·일 등의) 결함   **airsick** 비행기 멀미를 하는

8. M: Where should I pull over?

W: ______________________________________

(a) I want this pullover.
(b) Would you mind backing up?
(c) It will be good if you park over there.
(d) You shouldn't jaywalk.

🔦 해설

차를 어디에 대는 게 좋을지 묻고 있으므로 (c)가 정답이다. (a)의 pullover는 '스웨터'의 뜻으로, 동일한 발음을 이용해 오답을 유도하려는 함정이므로 주의해야 한다.

> **어휘**
>
> **pull over** (길가에) 차를 대다   **pullover** (머리부터 뒤집어써 입는) 스웨터   **back up** 후진시키다
> **jaywalk** 무단 횡단하다

9. M: How are you getting on with your new friend, Christina? I heard she's kind of boring.

W: _______________________________________

(a) Yes, she's witty and humorous.
(b) Well, she's not the most stimulating conversationalist.
(c) No, quite the opposite. She's very dull.
(d) Not at all. My boss and I are on great terms.

🐛 **해설**

그녀가 지루한 사람이라고 들었다고 했으므로 이에 동의하거나 부정하는 내용의 선택지를 고르면 된다. (a)는 Yes가 아니라 No 라고 해야 맞고, (c)는 앞부분에서 정반대 성격이라고 했으므로 dull이 아닌 exciting(재밌는)과 같은 표현이 와야 맞다.

어휘

witty 재치 있는 humorous 유머러스한 stimulating 활기를 띠게 하는 conversationalist 이야기하기 좋아 하는 사람 quite the opposite 정반대 dull 지루한, 따분한 on great terms 사이가 아주 좋은

7. W: What's wrong with this weekend's travel plans?

M: _______________________ my car needs to be repaired.

8. M: Where should I pull over?

W: _______________________________________.

9. M: How are you getting on with your new friend, Christina? I heard she's kind of boring.

W: Well, ____.

Part 1

Questions 1-8

Choose the most appropriate response to the statement.

1. (a)   (b)   (c)   (d)
2. (a)   (b)   (c)   (d)
3. (a)   (b)   (c)   (d)
4. (a)   (b)   (c)   (d)
5. (a)   (b)   (c)   (d)
6. (a)   (b)   (c)   (d)
7. (a)   (b)   (c)   (d)
8. (a)   (b)   (c)   (d)

☞ 예술

accompaniment	반주
adagio	느리게
chamber music	실내악
choir	합창단
chord	(악기의) 현, 줄
composition	작문, 작곡
execution	(미술 작품의) 제작, 수법; 연주, 연주 솜씨
fiddle	(특히 재즈나 컨트리 음악에 쓰는) 바이올린
largo	아주 느리게
percussion	타악기
prelude	전주곡, 서곡
recital	독주회
refrain	후렴, 반복구
strings	현악기
undertone	배경음, 반주음; 저음
abstract painting	추상화
caricature	풍자화
choromatic	색채의
formative arts	조형미술
lucent	빛을 내는, 투명한
profile	옆얼굴, 반면상
sculptor	조각가
sculpture	조각
motif	주제

주제별 유형 익히기: 대인관계 Ⅰ

Chapter 4

Part 1에서는 일상생활에서 벌어지는 상황들이 빠짐없이 등장하므로, 다른 사람과의 만남, 작별, 약속, 제안/권유, 충고, 부탁/허락, 칭찬/축하, 격려/위로, 항의/불평 등 갖가지 상황들을 잘 정리해 익혀 두자.

---

10. W: Things have been icy between Jane and I since we had that argument last week.

M: ________________________________

(a) You're walking on thin ice with me, mister.
(b) It has been oddly cold recently.
(c) Jane broke the ice with an amusing story.
(d) You should try to have a heart to heart talk with her.

🐸 해설

제인과 싸운 후 사이가 냉랭해졌다고 말했으므로 이에 관해 조언이나 충고를 해주는 내용이 이어져야 자연스럽다. 남에게 충고를 해줄 때 사용하는 조동사 should를 기억한다면 (d)가 정답임을 금방 알 수 있을 것이다.

> **어휘**
>
> **mister** 이봐, 이 양반아　**oddly** 이상하게　**break the ice** 어색한 분위기를 깨다　**have a heart to heart talk with** ~와 마음을 터놓고 이야기하다

---

11. M: How about a second helping?

W: ________________________________

(a) Let me fix you a drink.
(b) It's not right to call him that.
(c) No, thanks. I've had enough.
(d) I don't need your help.

🐸 해설

한 그릇 더 먹으라는 권유에 대한 응답을 고르는 문제로, 충분히 먹었다며 사양을 하는 (c)가 정답이다.

> **어휘**
>
> **a second helping** 두 그릇째, 추가분　**fix ... a drink** ~에게 음료를 갖다주다　**call** 비난하다

12. M: May I come home past my curfew tonight? It's my friend's birthday.

W: ___________________________________

(a) I have to be back by 10 p.m.
(b) Well, in that case, you need to call me. I'll pick you up.
(c) That's easier said than done.
(d) What are friends for?

🐙 **해설**

집에 늦게 와도 되는지 허락을 구하고 있으므로 (b)가 적절한 응답이다.

어휘

curfew 통금시간 That's easier said than done. 행동보다 말이 쉽다. What are friends for? 친구 좋다는 게 뭐니?

10. W: Things have been icy between Jane and I since we had that argument last week.

M: ____ with her.

11. M: How about a second helping?

W: _________________________________.

12. M: May I come home past my curfew tonight? It's my friend's birthday.

W: Well, _________________________________. I'll pick you up.

Questions 1-5

Choose the most appropriate response to the statement.

1. (a) (b) (c) (d)
2. (a) (b) (c) (d)
3. (a) (b) (c) (d)
4. (a) (b) (c) (d)
5. (a) (b) (c) (d)

☞ 교육/대학

alumnus	졸업생, 동창생
application form	입학원서
curriculum	교육과정
diploma	졸업 증서, (학위·자격) 증서
Doctor	박사 (학위)
Master	석사 (학위)
dormitory	기숙사
drop-out	중퇴자
monograph	모노그래프, 특수 연구서, 전공논문
optional subject	선택과목
required subject	필수과목
postgraduate	대학원의; 대학원 학생
repeater	유급생
roll	출석부
scholarship	장학금
tuition	학비
tutor	가정교사
undergraduate	대학생
pedagogy	교육학, 교수법

주제별 유형 익히기: 대인관계 II

Chapter 5

대인 관련 주제 중 전화, 질의응답에 대한 동의/반대, 그리고 취미에 관한 표현들도 잘 알아 두어야 한다. 특히 전화 관련 문제는 한 문제 이상 꼭 출제되므로 확실히 정리해 두자.

13. W: What's bugging you?
M: ___________________________________

(a) Nothing. I'm just backlogged with work.
(b) Don't lose your cool.
(c) I don't mean to be a pest.
(d) I'm thrilled for you.

🐙 해설

걱정거리가 있는지 묻고 있으므로 이에 답한 (a)가 정답이다. (d)는 '참 잘됐다'는 뜻으로, Good for you!, I'm happy for you!와 마찬가지 표현으로 쓸 수 있다.

어휘

bug 귀찮게 굴다, 괴롭히다   **backlog** (미처리된 채) 쌓이다   **lose one's cool** 흥분하다, 화내다   **a pest** 성가신 사람, 골칫거리

14. W: I'm on my last legs. I can't work anymore.
M: ___________________________________

(a) You let the cat out of the bag.
(b) Good fortune comes only to the brave.
(c) You're kidding. You didn't even lift a finger.
(d) You need crutches.

🐙 해설

I'm on my last legs.는 '정말 피곤하다', '갈 때까지 갔다'라고 말할 때 쓸 수 있는 표현이다. 따라서 힘들어서 더 이상 일을 못하겠다고 불평을 하고 있는 상황이므로 이에 어울리는 응답은 (c)다. not lift a finger는 '손가락 하나 까딱하지 않다'란 뜻으로, 즉 한 것도 없으면서 뭐가 힘드냐며 어이없다는 말을 하고 있다.

어휘

be on one's last legs 힘이 거의 없다, 궁지에 빠지다   **let the cat out of the bag** 비밀을 폭로하다
good fortune 행운   **the brave** 용감한 사람   **crutch** 목발

15. M: I'm not big into music.

W: _______________________________

(a) Are you a musician?
(b) I'm tone deaf.
(c) He likes rock while she likes jazz.
(d) Tastes differ.

🐙 **해설**

음악을 그다지 좋아하지 않는다는 말에 이어질 적절한 응답은 (d)로, 사람마다 취향이 제각각이니 그럴 수 있다는 뜻이 담겨 있다.

어휘

tone deaf 음치의 Tastes differ. 사람마다 취향이 다르다.

13. W: What's bugging you?

M: Nothing. ____.

14. W: I'm on my last legs. I can't work anymore.

M: You're kidding. _____________________________________.

15. M: ____.

W: Tastes differ.

Questions 1-6

Choose the most appropriate response to the statement.

1. (a)   (b)   (c)   (d)
2. (a)   (b)   (c)   (d)
3. (a)   (b)   (c)   (d)
4. (a)   (b)   (c)   (d)
5. (a)   (b)   (c)   (d)
6. (a)   (b)   (c)   (d)

☞ **철학/윤리**

abnegation	금욕, 자제
aesthetic	미의, 심미적인, 미적 감각이 있는
altruistic	이타주의의
awareness	자각
epistemology	인식론
hypothesis	가설, 가정
idealism	관념주의
induction	귀납(법)
inference	추론
metaphysics	형이상학
motivation	동기 부여
repression	억압 (본능)
resistance	저항
skeptic	회의론자
sophism	궤변, 억지 이론
stereotype	고정관념
amoral	도덕성이 없는
decency	품위, 예의 바름
immoral	부도덕한
naughty	외설적인
obsession	강박관념
precept	교훈, 권고

주제별
유형 익히기 :
사회관계

Chapter 6

사회 관계 영역에서는 일상생활에서 많은 부분을 차지하는 직장 및 학교생활, 쇼핑, 음식점, 여행 등에 관한 주제들로 대화 내용이 이루어진다.

16. W: Why did he get axed?

M: _______________________________________

(a) I don't know exactly what happened, but he was quite lazy.
(b) Put it on ice.
(c) He had to chop some firewood.
(d) I'm so glad I could be of help.

해설

그가 해고당한 이유를 묻고 있으므로 이에 관해 언급한 (a)가 정답이다.

어휘

get axed 해고당하다　put ... on ice ~을 뒤로 미루다　chop 자르다, 패다　firewood 장작　be of help 도움이 되다

17. M: They're selling at rockbottom prices.

W: _______________________________________

(a) They're so greedy.
(b) This floor is uncomfortable.
(c) Don't even bring that up.
(d) Let's go get some.

해설

최저가에 팔리고 있다는 말을 들었으므로 가서 사자는 (d)가 적절한 응답이다.

어휘

rockbottom prices 최저가　greedy 욕심 많은, 탐욕스러운　bring up (이야기 등을) 꺼내다

18. W: I'll buy the lunch today.

M: ___________________________________

(a) I usually tip 10% of the check.
(b) Let's go dutch.
(c) It's the most exclusive restaurant in this area.
(d) I have a sweet tooth.

해설

점심값을 내겠다는 여자에게 각자 부담하자고 제안하는 (b)가 적절하다. Let's split the bill.도 마찬가지 표현으로 함께 알아 두자.

어휘

tip 팁을 주다 go dutch (비용을) 각자 부담하다 exclusive 고급의 have a sweet tooth 단 것을 좋아하다

16. W: ____________________________?
M: I don't know exactly what happened, but he was quite lazy.

17. M: They're ____.
W: Let's go get some.

18. W: ________________________________.
M: Let's go dutch.

Questions 1-9

Choose the most appropriate response to the statement.

1.   (a)   (b)   (c)   (d)
2.   (a)   (b)   (c)   (d)
3.   (a)   (b)   (c)   (d)
4.   (a)   (b)   (c)   (d)
5.   (a)   (b)   (c)   (d)
6.   (a)   (b)   (c)   (d)
7.   (a)   (b)   (c)   (d)
8.   (a)   (b)   (c)   (d)
9.   (a)   (b)   (c)   (d)

☞ 종교

Advent	그리스도의 강림
atheism	무신론
baptism	세례
benediction	축복, 감사 기도
confucianism	유교
contemplation	명상, 묵상
demon	악마
eschatology	종말론
fairy	요정
foresight	선견지명
funeral	장례식
heterodox	이단의
icon	성화상
immolation	희생, 제물
martyrdom	순교
mission	전도, 포교
mundane	세속적인
Muslim	이슬람교도
nirvana	열반, 해탈
omnipotent	전능한, 절대력을 가진
orthodox	정설의, 정통파의
penitent	회개하는
persecution	박해, 학대
pilgrim	순례자, 성지 참배자
Protestant	신교도
Puritan	청교도
resurrection	그리스도의 부활
Sabbath	안식일
sacrilege	신성 모독
worship	예배(하다), 숭배(하다)

주제별 유형 익히기: 공공관계

Chapter 7

공공관계에 관한 내용은 길 찾기, 공공안내, 교통, 병원, 건강에 관한 사항들이다. 자주 등장하는
내용들이므로 충분히 연습해 두자.

19. W: Why are you limping, Adam?

M: ______________________________

(a) He is in critical condition.
(b) She's exhausted from overwork.
(c) My leg is asleep.
(d) You look out of shape.

🐛 해설

다리를 절뚝거리고 있는 이유를 묻고 있으므로 이에 관해 언급한 (c)가 정답이다. '다리가 저리다'라고 할 때 쓸 수 있는 표현으로
잘 기억해 두자.

> **어휘**
>
> limp 절뚝거리다　be in critical condition 중태다　overwork 과로　out of shape 몸 상태가 안 좋은

20. M: I think we should get a head start to beat traffic.

W: ______________________________

(a) Then, take a detour here.
(b) They repaved the road.
(c) Don't worry. This car is very fuel-efficient.
(d) I can't agree with you more.

🐛 해설

일찍 출발하자고 제안하고 있으므로 이에 동의하는 (d)가 정답이다. 상대방의 제안에 '대찬성이다', '전적으로 동의한다'라고 말
할 때 쓸 수 있는 표현이다.

> **어휘**
>
> get a head start 일찍 출발하다　beat traffic 교통혼잡을 피하다　take a detour 우회하다　repave (도로를)
> 다시 포장하다　fuel-efficient 연비가 좋은

21. W: How would you like your hair done?

M: ___________________________________

(a) She's got split ends.

(b) How about having bangs?

(c) I want it layered.

(d) Pull your socks up.

🎙 **해설**

미장원에서 미용사가 손님에게 머리 모양을 어떻게 해주길 원하는지 묻고 있는 상황이다. 따라서 원하는 스타일을 제시한 선택지를 고르면 된다. (d)는 직역하자면, '네 양말을 치켜 올리라'는 말로, '정신을 바짝 차리고 다시 뭔가를 시작해라', '기운을 내라'의 뜻으로 쓰이는 관용 표현이다.

어휘

split ends 갈라진 머리끝 bangs 앞머리 layer 층을 내다 pull one's socks up 기운 내다

19. W: Why are you limping, Adam?

    M: _________________________________.

20. M: I think _________________________________.

    W: I can't agree with you more.

21. W: _________________________________?

    M: I want it layered.

Questions 1-8

Choose the most appropriate response to the statement.

1. (a)   (b)   (c)   (d)
2. (a)   (b)   (c)   (d)
3. (a)   (b)   (c)   (d)
4. (a)   (b)   (c)   (d)
5. (a)   (b)   (c)   (d)
6. (a)   (b)   (c)   (d)
7. (a)   (b)   (c)   (d)
8. (a)   (b)   (c)   (d)

☞ **정치/외교**

ballot box	투표함
by-election	보궐선거
candidate	후보자
plurality	과반수
poll	투표
referendum	국민투표
suffrage	참정권; 투표
administration	행정
anarchy	무정부상태
autarchy	독재권, 전제 정치
autocracy	독재 정치
bicameral	양원제의
cabinet	내각
commonwealth	국가, 공화국, 연방
delegate	대표자
overthrow	뒤엎다, 쓰러뜨리다, 전복시키다
parliament	의회, 국회
ratify	비준하다
regent	섭정
regime	정권
reign	통치 기간
secession	탈당
treaty	조약, 협정
aristocracy	귀족 정치
aristocrat	귀족
bourgeois	유산 계급
proletariat	무산 계급
bureaucracy	관료 (정치)
chauvinism	국수주의
communism	공산주의
stopgap	미봉책
theocracy	신정(神政)

Part Ⅱ

Choose the most appropriate response to complete the conversation.

1. (a) (b) (c) (d)
2. (a) (b) (c) (d)
3. (a) (b) (c) (d)
4. (a) (b) (c) (d)
5. (a) (b) (c) (d)
6. (a) (b) (c) (d)
7. (a) (b) (c) (d)
8. (a) (b) (c) (d)
9. (a) (b) (c) (d)
10. (a) (b) (c) (d)
11. (a) (b) (c) (d)
12. (a) (b) (c) (d)

Part 2는 대화 마지막 부분을 잘 들으면 답을 찾을 수 있다. 문제 유형은 Part 1과 유사하며, 대화 한 세트가 추가되어 있기 때문에 오히려 Part 1보다 쉬울 수 있다. 상황에 따라 자주 쓰이는 표현들을 꼼꼼히 학습해 두도록 하자.

1. 1~6번 문제에 약한 경우

Chapter 8, 9를 중점적으로 학습하면서 대인 관련 주제에 나온 대화 내용과 표현들을 정리하자.

2. 7~9번 문제에 약한 경우

Chapter 10을 중점적으로 학습하면서 사회 관련 주제에 나온 대화 내용과 표현들을 정리하자.

3. 10~12번 문제에 약한 경우

Chapter 11을 중점적으로 학습하면서 공공 관련 주제에 나온 대화 내용과 표현들을 정리하자.

주제별
유형 익히기:
대인관계 I

Chapter 8

STEP 1 Pretest Clinic

Part 1에서 다뤘던 주제 중 인사, 초대, 제안/권유, 충고, 부탁/허락, 칭찬/축하, 격려/위로와 관련해 대인 간에 자주 발생하는 상황의 대화 내용으로 구성된다.

1. W: I think I'll wear my new spring dress for the party next week.
M: You'd better wait. It's still very cold.
W: For me, I'd be able to suffer for the sake of fashion.
M: _______________________________

(a) Don't take it out on me.
(b) That dress looks really good on you.
(c) Does it hurt much?
(d) It's up to you. But you might catch a cold.

🦑 **해설**

날씨가 아직 많이 춥다는 충고에도 생각을 바꾸지 않고 있으므로 알아서 결정하라는 (d)가 적절하다.

> **어휘**
>
> for the sake of ~을 위해서 take it out on ~에게 화풀이하다

2. M: Jane doesn't seem to enjoy the meal. She is just playing with her food.
W: Yeah, she's a picky eater. I'm really worried about her eating habits.
M: Come over to my house sometime? I can cook something nice for her.
W: _______________________________

(a) That's because she snacks late up at night.
(b) You should watch what you eat.
(c) This is delicious!
(d) Thanks for the offer. You are so kind.

🦑 **해설**

밥을 잘 안 먹는 아이를 위해 요리를 해주겠다며 집에 초대하고 있으므로 이에 대한 감사의 뜻이 담긴 선택지를 고르면 된다.

> **어휘**
>
> picky 까다로운 snack 가벼운 식사를 하다, 간식을 하다

3. M: You know? You are one of the nicest people I know.

W: Thanks, but what's the catch?

M: Nothing. I really mean it.

W: ___________________________________

(a) That's rude of you to say so.

(b) I'm sorry but I can't help you.

(c) Okay. I'll take it as a compliment.

(d) I wish you'd trust me on this.

🦑 해설

왜지 순수한 뜻으로 칭찬해 준 게 아닌 것 같아 속셈이 뭔지 묻는 질문에 남자가 진심이라고 했으므로 칭찬으로 받아들이겠다는 (c)가 적절하다.

어휘
What's the catch? 속셈이 뭐야? rude 무례한, 버릇 없는 compliment 칭찬

1. W: I think I'll wear my new spring dress for the party next week.

M: You'd better wait. It's still very cold.

W: For me, I'd be able to ________________________.

M: ________________________. But you might catch a cold.

2. M: Jane doesn't seem to enjoy the meal. She is just playing with her food.

W: Yeah, ________________________. I'm really worried about her eating habits.

M: ________________________? I can cook something nice for her.

W: Thanks for the offer. You are so kind.

3. M: You know? You are one of the nicest people I know.

W: Thanks, but ________________________?

M: Nothing. I really mean it.

W: Okay. I'll ________________________.

STEP 3 Actual Test

Questions 1-9

Choose the most appropriate response to complete the conversation.

1. (a) (b) (c) (d)
2. (a) (b) (c) (d)
3. (a) (b) (c) (d)
4. (a) (b) (c) (d)
5. (a) (b) (c) (d)
6. (a) (b) (c) (d)
7. (a) (b) (c) (d)
8. (a) (b) (c) (d)
9. (a) (b) (c) (d)

☞ 사회

census	인구 조사
ethnic	인종의, 민족의
gregarious	군거하는, 군집의
kinship	친척관계, 혈족관계
throng	군중
underpopulated	인구 밀도가 낮은
confederacy	연합, 동맹(국)
donation	기부
alienation	소외
capitalism	자본주의
colony	식민지
communism	공산주의
exploitation	착취
facilities	설비, 시설
functionalism	기능주의
generalization	일반화
imbalance	불균형
panic	공황
paradigm	패러다임, 이론적 틀
social integration	사회통합
sociology	사회학
sovereignty	주권, 통치권
totalitarianism	전체주의

주제별 유형 익히기: 대인관계 II

STEP 1 Pretest Clinic

Part 1에서 다뤘던 주제 중 감사, 사과, 항의/불평, 질의응답 및 동의/반대하기에 관련해 대인
간에 자주 발생하는 상황의 대화 내용으로 구성된다.

4. M: How much would you like?

W: I'd like ten bucks worth, please.

M: O.K. And what kind? Regular or premium?

W: ________________________________

(a) Both would be great.

(b) Fill it up, please.

(c) Shall I check your oil?

(d) Regular unleaded, please.

🐙 해설

기름의 종류를 묻고 있으므로 이를 언급한 선택지를 고르면 된다. 참고로, 기름의 종류에는 regular unleaded(보통 무연 휘발
유), plus unleaded(중급 무연 휘발유), premium[super] unleaded(고급 무연 휘발유)가 있다.

어휘

buck 달러   fill up 가득 채우다

5. M: Look out! Watch where you're going for God's sake!

W: Calm down. It wasn't that close.

M: What? We cut her off and could have almost hit her.

W: ________________________________

(a) She'll get better soon.

(b) It's just a scratch.

(c) Okay, I'll ease off the gas. Stop nagging me.

(d) I got a kick out of it.

🐙 해설

남자가 운전 중인 여자에게 다른 차량에 끼어들어 사고가 날 뻔했다고 나무라고 있으므로 속도를 줄이겠다는 (c)가 이어져야 적절
하다.

6. W: What happened on my computer?

M: It seems there's been a complete hard drive failure.

W: Oh, no. What do you think I should do?

M: ________________________________

(a) How do I know what you're thinking about?

(b) Is it still under warranty?

(c) Give me your cellphone number.

(d) Stop asking me for help.

해설

고장 난 컴퓨터를 두고 어떡해야 할지 남자의 생각을 묻고 있으므로 (b)가 가장 적절하다.

4. M: How much would you like?

W: _____________________________, please.

M: O.K. And what kind? Regular or premium?

W: _____________________________, please.

5. M: Look out! Watch where you're going for God's sake!

W: Calm down. It wasn't that close.

M: What? _______________ and could have almost hit her.

W: Okay, _____________________. Stop nagging me.

6. W: What happened on my computer?

M: It seems ____.

W: Oh, no. What do you think I should do?

M: ____?

Questions 1-6

Choose the most appropriate response to complete the conversation.

1. (a)   (b)   (c)   (d)
2. (a)   (b)   (c)   (d)
3. (a)   (b)   (c)   (d)
4. (a)   (b)   (c)   (d)
5. (a)   (b)   (c)   (d)
6. (a)   (b)   (c)   (d)

☞ **법률**

administration of justice	사법	arson	방화(죄)
civil law	민법	blackmail	공갈 협박하다
code	법전	bugging	도청
constitution	헌법	delude	속이다
criminal law	형법	embezzle	횡령하다
the executive	행정부	ex-convict	전과자
judiciary	사법부	fraud	기만, 사기
legislature	입법부	holdup	노상 강도
complaint	고소	homicide	살인
conviction	유죄 판결	kidnap	유괴하다
court	법정	larceny	절도(죄)
cross-examine	반대 심문하다	misdemeanor	경범죄
culprit	범죄자, 형사 피고인	phony	사기꾼
custody	구류, 감금	racketeering	공갈
defendant	피고(인)	smuggle	밀수하다
fine	벌금	swag	장물
indict	기소하다	swindler	사기꾼, 협잡꾼
iniquity	부정[불법] 행위	promulgate	선포하다, 공포하다
innocence	무죄	shackle	수갑을 채우다, 구속하다
invalidity	무효		
jury	배심원		
lawsuit	소송, 고소		
life imprisonment	무기징역		
lose a case	패소하다		
parole	가석방		
penalty	형벌, 벌금		
perjury	위증(죄)		
plaintiff	원고		
plea	탄원, 진술		
practitioner	변호사		
prosecution	기소, 고발		
prosecutor	검사		
abduct	유괴하다		

주제별
유형 익히기:
사회관계

Chapter 10

STEP 1 Pretest Clinic

Part 1에서 다뤘던 주제 중 학교/직장, 쇼핑, 식당, 여행과 관련된 주제들로 구성된다. 학습하면서 자주 나오는 표현들을 잘 정리해 익혀 두도록 하자.

7. M: Yesterday was graduation, wasn't it?

W: Yes. My teacher and all my classmates cried at the graduation ceremony.

M: What for? Graduation is a happy occasion.

W: _______________________________________

(a) Everyone had really bonded over the year.

(b) I happened to see my teacher in the store.

(c) The occasion was on February 28th.

(d) The teacher was touched by our song.

🦑 **해설**

졸업식에서 운 까닭을 묻고 있으므로 이에 관해 언급한 선택지를 고르면 된다.

어휘

graduation ceremony 졸업식   bond 친밀한 관계를 맺다

8. M: Excuse me, ma'am. What can I do for you?

W: I'd like to change my steak order from well-done to medium.

M: Sorry. Your dishes have already been made.

W: _______________________________________

(a) Oh well. That's alright.

(b) I had a medium steak a few days ago.

(c) That's ok. I'll have a bowl of chicken soup.

(d) Well-done steaks are too tough.

🦑 **해설**

주문한 웰던 스테이크를 미디엄 스테이크로 바꾸고 싶었는데 이미 요리가 다 됐다고 했으므로 체념의 의미가 담긴 (a)가 이어져야 적절하다. Oh well.은 '아 그래, 할 수 없지' 의 뜻으로, 어떤 일에 대한 체념을 나타낼 때 쓰는 감탄사다.

dish (접시에 담은) 요리   tough 질긴

9. M: That is a nice looking watch.

W: This is quite a hot sale item these days.

M: But it's a bit out of my budget.

W: ________________________________

(a) I'm sold. I'll take it.

(b) It cost me a pretty penny.

(c) You won't regret purchasing it. I promise you.

(d) You should keep track of your money.

해설

상점에서 손님과 점원 간에 이루어지고 있는 대화다. 물건이 마음에 들긴 한데 너무 비싸다고 하는 손님에게 점원은 어떻게든 설득해서 물건을 사게 할 것이므로 (c)가 이어지는 게 적절하다.

어휘

hot sale item 아주 잘 팔리는 상품 out of budget 예산을 벗어난 sell 〈구어〉 납득시키다 a pretty penny 꽤 많은 금액 keep track of ~을 계속 알고 있다, ~의 진로를 쫓다

7. M: Yesterday was graduation, wasn't it?

W: Yes. My teacher and all my classmates cried at the graduation ceremony.

M: What for? Graduation is a happy occasion.

W: Everyone _______________________________________.

8. M: Excuse me, ma'am. What can I do for you?

W: _______________________________ from well-done to medium.

M: Sorry. _______________________________.

W: Oh well. That's alright.

9. M: That is a nice looking watch.

W: ____.

M: But it's a bit out of my budget.

W: _______________________________. I promise you.

Questions 1-10

Choose the most appropriate response to complete the conversation.

1. (a) (b) (c) (d)
2. (a) (b) (c) (d)
3. (a) (b) (c) (d)
4. (a) (b) (c) (d)
5. (a) (b) (c) (d)
6. (a) (b) (c) (d)
7. (a) (b) (c) (d)
8. (a) (b) (c) (d)
9. (a) (b) (c) (d)
10. (a) (b) (c) (d)

☞ **경제/경영**

account	계좌	lucre	이익
bargain	매매 계약, 거래	mischief	손해
bidding	입찰	moratorium	지불 정지
forge	위조하다	mortgage	저당, 저당잡히다
inflation	인플레이션	national treasury	국고
installment	분할 불입(금)	notary	공증인
interest	이자	offset	상쇄하다
monetary system	화폐 제도	remuneration	보수, 보상, 급료
passbook	통장	revenue	세입
principal	원금	stagflation	경기 침체하의 인플레이션
promissory note	약속 어음		
usury	고리대금업		
barter	물물 교환하다		
bond	보증(금)		
clearing house	어음 교환소		
commodity	상품, 일용품		
peddler	행상인		
proprietary	독점의		
retail	소매(상)		
rush	대수요, 주문 쇄도		
speculate	투기하다		
stock-taking	재고 조사		
subcontract	하청 계약		
outlay	지출, 소비		
pumping-priming policy	경기부양책		
recession	경기 후퇴, 불경기		
skyrocket	물가가 치솟다		
slump	물가가 폭락하다		
stagnation	침체, 불경기		
tycoon	실업계의 거물		
indemnity	배상, 변상		
liquidation	(부채의) 청산		

주제별 유형 익히기: 공공관계

Chapter 11

Part 1에서 다뤘던 주제 중 교통, 병원, 미용, 길 안내 등 공공관계에 대한 주제들로 구성된다. 학습하면서 자주 나오는 표현들을 잘 정리해 익혀 두도록 하자.

10. M: I have an appointment at 3:00 with Dr. Shin in minor surgery, but I can't find that department.

W: Take the elevator to the second floor. It'll be on your right side, just past the optometry department.

M: Do I need to register here or do it over at the minor surgery desk?

W: _________________________________

(a) Well, it depends on what kind of coverage you have.

(b) If possible, I'd like to see Dr. Lee.

(c) You can take care of it over there.

(d) I'll do the best I can.

🐸 **해설**

수속을 어디서 하는지 묻고 있으므로 이에 관해 언급한 선택지를 고르면 된다.

> **어휘**
>
> **minor surgery** (중요하지 않은) 작은 수술   **optometry department** 안과   **do over** 다시 하다   **coverage** 보험

11. W: What the hell happened to your hair?

M: This is the hip hairstyle these days.

W: The fashion these days is looking like a clown?

M: _________________________________

(a) I'm joining the circus.

(b) Go back and recolor your hair.

(c) That's not a nice thing to say.

(d) If you shampoo, your curls will straighten out quickly.

🐸 **해설**

헤어스타일이 광대 같다고 하는 여자의 말에 그렇게 말하지 말라고 충고하는 (c)가 적절하다.

12. M: I can't stop hiccupping.

W: Hold your breath for as long as you can.

M: I tried that, but it didn't work.

W: _______________________________________

(a) Then try sipping some water. That'll fix it.

(b) Must be entertaining.

(c) My ankle swelled up.

(d) The cramps are quieting down.

해설

숨을 참아도 딸꾹질이 멈추지 않는다고 했으므로 이에 대한 해결책을 제시하는 선택지를 고르면 된다.

10. M: _________________________ at 3:00 with Dr. Shin in minor surgery, but I
    can't find that department.

    W: Take the elevator to the second floor. It'll be on your right side, ____________
    _________________________.

    M: Do I need to register here or do it over at the minor surgery desk?

    W: _________________________.

11. W: What the hell happened to your hair?

    M: _________________________.

    W: The fashion these days is looking like a clown?

    M: _________________________.

12. M: _________________________.

    W: Hold your breath for as long as you can.

    M: I tried that, but it didn't work.

    W: Then _________________________. That'll fix it.

Part 2

Questions 1-9

Choose the most appropriate response to complete the conversation.

1. (a)   (b)   (c)   (d)
2. (a)   (b)   (c)   (d)
3. (a)   (b)   (c)   (d)
4. (a)   (b)   (c)   (d)
5. (a)   (b)   (c)   (d)
6. (a)   (b)   (c)   (d)
7. (a)   (b)   (c)   (d)
8. (a)   (b)   (c)   (d)
9. (a)   (b)   (c)   (d)

☞ 교통/운송

bales	화물
cargo	선하, 뱃짐
alley	골목, 샛길
avenue	대로
blind alley	막다른 골목
boulevard	넓은 가로수길
bypass	우회로
crosscut	지름길
crosswalk	횡단보도
detour	우회하다
devious	구불구불한
overpass	고가도로
pike	유료 도로, 통행 요금
toll	사용세, 요금
underpass	지하도
armada	함대
dinghy	작은 배
liner	정기선
adrift	(배가) 표류하여
charter	(배·버스·비행기 등의) 전세
depot	역, 버스 터미널 (건물), 공항 (건물)
derailment	탈선
embargo	입출항 금지
manned	사람을 실은
one-way traffic	일방통행

Part Ⅲ

Choose the option that the best answers the question.

1. (a)   (b)   (c)   (d)
2. (a)   (b)   (c)   (d)
3. (a)   (b)   (c)   (d)
4. (a)   (b)   (c)   (d)
5. (a)   (b)   (c)   (d)
6. (a)   (b)   (c)   (d)
7. (a)   (b)   (c)   (d)
8. (a)   (b)   (c)   (d)
9. (a)   (b)   (c)   (d)

1. 1~3번 문제에 약한 경우

주제문을 파악하는 문제 유형에 약한 경우인데, Part 3에서 가장 쉬운 유형에 속하기 때문에 반드시 맞추고 넘어가야 한다. Chapter 12를 통해 충분히 연습하자.

2. 4~6번 문제에 약한 경우

세부 사항을 파악하는 데 약한 경우로, 출제되는 질문 유형을 미리 잘 파악해 두어야 한다. Chapter 13을 통해 충분히 연습하자.

3. 7~9번 문제에 약한 경우

대화문을 통해 추론할 수 있는 내용을 묻는 문제 유형으로 가장 어려운 영역에 해당한다. Chapter 14를 통해 충분히 연습하자.

Chapter 12

대화문 주제 파악하기

대화의 주제는 단지 부분적인 사실만을 강조하는 것이 아니라 대화문 전체 내용을 포괄적으로 함축할 수 있어야 한다. 또 정답은 주제문을 '바꿔쓰기(paraphrasing)' 해서 나오는 경우가 많은데, 오답을 유도하기 위해 대화에 나온 단어를 이용하는 경우가 많으므로 이런 함정들에 특히 유의하자.

1. W: Did you see the March sales figures?

M: Not yet. What about it?

W: Sales increased over the last quarter.

M: Have they? That's good. Do you know why?

W: Getting some new blood helped. In particular, our new sales manager is incredible, and the sales team members also seem to like working with him.

M: That's true, but I think we should keep an eye on him.

W: Are you jealous?

M: No way. I just think we should wait to see how good he really is.

Q. What is the conversation about?

(a) The new employee's behavior

(b) The reason for the sales increase

(c) A briefing on the last meeting

(d) How to treat employees

해설

대화 초반에 지난 분기 동안 판매가 증가했다는 얘기가 나오면서 그 이유에 대한 내용이 이어지고 있다. 따라서 정답은 (b)가 된다.

어휘

sales figure 판매실적 **new blood** 새로운 인재, 젊은 피

2. M: Good afternoon. What can I do for you?

W: Hello. I'd like to fix my laptop.

M: What's the problem?

W: Whenever I turn it on, a black screen pops up suddenly.

M: Alright. It sounds like a problem with the hard disk.

W: How serious is it? I have a lot of important information stored there. Can you recover it?

M: Probably not 100%, but I'll try my best.

Q. What is the main focus of the conversation?

(a) Finding new information via the Internet
(b) Removing a virus on a computer
(c) Repairing a broken computer
(d) Replacing the hard disk

해설

컴퓨터에 문제가 생겨 고치러 온 상황이므로 정답은 (c)가 된다.

어휘

pop up 갑자기 나타나다 via ~을 통해서

3. M: Choose any one you like. Don't worry about the price. It's a gift for you. I thought it'd be better than my choosing one.

W: Really? It's difficult to decide.

M: How about this novel?

W: I've read that one before. Have you ever read this Irish novel?

M: Yes, I did. The first part was hard to understand, but the more I read the more interesting it got.

W: Then, I'll take it. Thank you very much.

M: Not at all.

Q. What is the main point of the talk?

(a) The present for the woman
(b) The woman's favorite book
(c) The man and woman's hobbies
(d) The review of a novel

해설

남자가 여자에게 선물을 사 주려는 상황이므로 정답은 (a)가 된다.

어휘

the more ... the more ~ …하면 할수록 더 ~하다   review 감상평

1. W: Did you see the March sales figures?

M: Not yet. What about it?

W: _______________________________________.

M: Have they? That's good. Do you know why?

W: _______________________________________. In particular, our new sales manager is incredible, and the sales team members also seem to like working with him.

M: That's true, but I think we should keep an eye on him.

W: Are you jealous?

M: No way. I just think _______________________________________.

2. M: Good afternoon. What can I do for you?

W: Hello. _______________________________________.

M: What's the problem?

W: Whenever I turn it on, _______________________________________.

M: Alright. It sounds like a problem with the hard disk.

W: How serious is it? _______________________________________. Can you recover it?

M: Probably not 100%, but I'll try my best.

3. M: _______________________________________. Don't worry about the price. It's a gift for you. I thought it'd be better than my choosing one.

W: Really? It's difficult to decide.

M: How about this novel?

W: _______________________________________. Have you ever read this Irish novel?

M: Yes, I did. The first part was hard to understand, but _______________________________________ _______________________________________.

W: Then, I'll take it. Thank you very much.

M: Not at all.

Part 3

Questions 1-8

Choose the option that the best answers the question.

1. (a)   (b)   (c)   (d)
2. (a)   (b)   (c)   (d)
3. (a)   (b)   (c)   (d)
4. (a)   (b)   (c)   (d)
5. (a)   (b)   (c)   (d)
6. (a)   (b)   (c)   (d)
7. (a)   (b)   (c)   (d)
8. (a)   (b)   (c)   (d)

☞ **물리**

accelerated velocity	가속도
boiling point	비등점
density	밀도, 농도
elasticity	탄성
electromagnetic wave	전자파
flexibility	유연성, 탄력성
freezing point	빙점
friction	마찰
gravity	중력
inertia	관성
mass	질량
melting point	융점, 녹는 점
meson	중간자
sound wave	음파
spatial	공간의, 장소의
vacuum	진공
vibration	진동
volume	부피, 양
wave length	파장

대화문 내용 파악하기

Chapter 13

대화의 내용을 물어보는 문제 유형으로, 대화를 잘 듣고 내용에 맞는 것을 골라야 한다. 대화상으로 정확히 알 수 없는 선택지는 정답이 될 수 없음을 명심하자.

4. W: What was college like for you?

M: Well, many professors and staff supported me through the difficult times and encouraged me to never give up.

W: That sounds so nice. How was your roommate?

M: My roommate was a computer geek. We had a lot of fun together.

W: That's interesting. I bet you had a lot of opportunities to meet lots of people and experience new things. You must have learned a lot from college life.

M: No doubt that I had an amazing time in college. I feel that my time there really prepared me to face the real world.

Q. What is not correct about the man according to the conversation?

(a) He had an amazing time in college.
(b) His roommate was a computer major.
(c) He was helped by the college staff.
(d) He enjoyed his college life.

해설
룸메이트가 컴퓨터광이라고 했지만 그의 전공이 컴퓨터인지는 알 수 없으므로 (b)가 정답이다.

어휘
geek ~광

5. M: Helen, I heard that you are doing journalism these days. Is that true?

W: Well, kind of. I started working at a local broadcasting company.

M: That's amazing. How did you get that job? Wasn't it tough?

W: I had an internship there during my junior year. I got my foot in the door for a full-time job.

M: Wow, that's great. I'm so jealous of you. What's the secret?

W: You should find a field that you really want to work in. I was interning before I got a real job and it helped me to get a first-hand experience.

Q. What is correct according to the conversation?

(a) The woman was an intern during her fourth year of school.

(b) The woman worked as an intern at a different firm.

(c) The competition was tough.

(d) The woman got a chance to work in the company after she finished her internship.

해설

3학년(junior) 때 인턴십을 했고, 인턴십을 한 회사에서 정규직을 얻게 됐다고 했으므로 (a), (b)는 맞지 않다. 또 (c)는 대화 내용상 알 수 없으므로 정답은 (d)가 된다.

어휘

get one's foot in the door (사업이나 어떤 분야에) 처음 발을 들여놓다   **first-hand** 직접적인

6. W: Have you seen the film *Crash*?

M: No. Haven't had the chance to watch it yet.

W: I think it's one of the best movies I have ever seen.

M: Yeah, I heard the soundtrack was great.

W: You should really watch it.

M: What's the story about?

W: It's about racial issues and the stereotypes that affect our society.

M: That's interesting. I gotta see it tonight.

Q. What is correct according to the conversation?

(a) The man has postponed watching the movie.

(b) The man had already heard the music from the movie.

(c) The movie is about racism and related problems.

(d) The woman used to be a racist.

🔦 **해설**

여자의 얘기를 듣고 난 후 영화가 보고 싶어진 것이므로 (a)는 맞지 않다. 그 영화의 음악이 멋지다는 얘기를 들었을 뿐 직접 들어 본 것은 아니므로 (b) 역시 틀리다. (d)는 알 수 없는 내용. 따라서 여자의 마지막 말을 통해 알 수 있는 (c)가 정답이다.

어휘
racial 인종의 stereotype 고정관념 related to ~와 관련된

4. W: ____?

M: Well, many professors and staff supported me through the difficult times and encouraged me to never give up.

W: That sounds so nice. How was your roommate?

M: _______________________________________. We had a lot of fun together.

W: That's interesting. I bet you had a lot of opportunities to meet lots of people and experience new things. You must have learned a lot from college life.

M: No doubt that I had an amazing time in college. I feel that _________________ _______________________________________.

5. M: Helen, I heard that you are doing journalism these days. Is that true?

W: Well, kind of. _______________________________________.

M: That's amazing. How did you get that job? Wasn't it tough?

W: I had an internship there during my junior year. _______________________ _______________________________.

M: Wow, that's great. I'm so jealous of you. What's the secret?

W: You should find a field that you really want to work in. I was interning before I got a real job and _______________________________________.

6. W: Have you seen the film Crash?

M: No. _______________________________________.

W: I think it's _______________________________________.

M: Yeah, I heard the soundtrack was great.

W: You should really watch it.

M: What's the story about?

W: It's about _______________________________________.

M: That's interesting. I gotta see it tonight.

Part 3

Questions 1-10

Choose the option that the best answers the question.

1. (a)   (b)   (c)   (d)
2. (a)   (b)   (c)   (d)
3. (a)   (b)   (c)   (d)
4. (a)   (b)   (c)   (d)
5. (a)   (b)   (c)   (d)
6. (a)   (b)   (c)   (d)
7. (a)   (b)   (c)   (d)
8. (a)   (b)   (c)   (d)
9. (a)   (b)   (c)   (d)
10. (a)   (b)   (c)   (d)

☞ **화학**

acid	산
alkalinity	알칼리성
aluminum	알루미늄
cadmium	카드뮴
carbon	탄소
carbonhydrate	탄수화물
hydrochloric acid	염산
hydrogen	수소
isotope	동위 원소
lead	납
alchemy	연금술
alloy	합금
ammeter	전류계
catalyst	촉매
catalyze	촉매 작용을 하다
fluorescent	형광성의
generate	발생시키다
incandescent	백열의
solidification	응결
solid	고체
sublimation	승화물
vaporization	기화, 증발
volatile	휘발성의
voltmeter	전압계

대화문 내용 추론하기

Chapter 14

대화 내용을 추론하는 문제 유형은 문항 수가 적은 반면, 난이도가 높고 배점이 높은 영역이다. 지문에서 직접적인 힌트가 나오는 경우가 드물기 때문에 대화 내용을 주의 깊게 잘 듣고 선택지를 하나하나씩 소거하는 방식으로 문제를 해결해 나가야 한다.

7. M: What do you think about taking a cruise during this summer vacation?

W: That sounds marvelous. I'd love to sail around the Caribbean.

M: Good. But I was thinking of somewhere a bit further north.

W: You mean the West Indies? But we've already been there.

M: No, not the West Indies. I was thinking about somewhere far north-Alaska.

W: Wow! We could go salmon fishing, pan for gold, and dog sledding!

M: I'll take that as a yes.

Q. What can be inferred from the conversation?

(a) The woman is afraid to go salmon fishing.
(b) The man has already been to the Caribbean.
(c) They want to go on a honeymoon.
(d) They are planning for a trip to Alaska.

🐝 해설

여자의 마지막 대사를 보면 (a)는 맞지 않다. (b)는 대화 내용만으로 정확히 알 수 없고, (c)는 신혼여행이 아니라 방학을 이용해 가는 여행이므로 역시 정답이 아니다. 따라서 정답은 (d)가 된다.

어휘

take a cruise 유람선 여행을 하다   marvelous 멋진, 놀라운   the West Indies 서인도 제도   salmon 연어
pan for gold 사금을 채취하다   dog sledding 개 썰매 타기

8. W: I hope the meeting hasn't already started.

M: I don't think they would start without you since you're giving the main presentation.

W: Maybe you're right, but I'm already nervous enough without being late.

M: It's not your fault. A client had an emergency and no one else could solve it.

W: Because of that I had far less time to prepare.

M: Don't be so worried. Everything will be fine.

Q. What can be inferred about the woman?

(a) She is going to have an important role in the meeting.

(b) She is preparing her presentation.

(c) She started the meeting.

(d) She had an emergency.

해설

남자의 첫 번째 대사에, 여자가 회의에서 주요 발표를 할 것이라는 얘기가 나오므로 (a)가 정답임을 알 수 있다. (b)는 여자가 이미 발표 준비를 끝내고 회의에 참석하려는 상황이기 때문에 맞지 않다.

어휘

emergency 응급 상황

9. M: How would you like your eggs?

W: The same as usual, sunny-side up.

M: How about something different for a change? I was thinking of whipping up an omelet.

W: What are you going to put in it?

M: Ham, cheese, green pepper, carrots.... You know, a traditional Spanish omelet.

W: I thought you were cooking something different.

M: OK. Then, how about olives, cheese, and onions?

W: My mouth is watering, just hearing about it.

Q. What can be inferred from the conversation?

(a) The woman wants to have her eggs poached.
(b) The man is cooking breakfast.
(c) The woman boiled her eggs.
(d) They don't like snacks.

🐛 해설

남자가 여자에게 계란을 어떻게 요리해 주냐고 물었으므로 아침 식사를 준비하고 있음을 짐작할 수 있다. 여자는 한 쪽만 익혀 먹는 달걀 부침을 원했기 때문에 반숙(poach)을 원한다는 (a)는 틀리다.

어휘

sunny-side up 노른자를 터뜨리지 않은 채 한 쪽만 익혀 먹는 달걀 부침   **whip up** (요리 등을) 잽싸게 만들다
My mouth is watering. 군침이 돈다   **poach** 반숙하다   **boil** 삶다

7. M: ____ during this summer vacation?

W: That sounds marvelous. I'd love to sail around the Caribbean.

M: Good. But ____.

W: You mean the West Indies? But we've already been there.

M: No, not the West Indies. I was thinking about somewhere far north-Alaska.

W: Wow! We could go salmon fishing, pan for gold, and dog sledding!

M: ________________________________.

8. W: I hope the meeting hasn't already started.

M: I don't think ____.

W: Maybe you're right, but ____.

M: It's not your fault. A client had an emergency and no one else could solve it.

W: ____.

M: Don't be so worried. Everything will be fine.

9. M: How would you like your eggs?

W: ____.

M: How about something different for a change? ________________________________ ________________________________.

W: What are you going to put in it?

M: Ham, cheese, green pepper, carrots.... You know, a traditional Spanish omelet.

W: I thought you were cooking something different.

M: OK. Then, how about olives, cheese, and onions?

W: ____.

Questions 1-10

Choose the option that the best answers the question.

1. (a)   (b)   (c)   (d)
2. (a)   (b)   (c)   (d)
3. (a)   (b)   (c)   (d)
4. (a)   (b)   (c)   (d)
5. (a)   (b)   (c)   (d)
6. (a)   (b)   (c)   (d)
7. (a)   (b)   (c)   (d)
8. (a)   (b)   (c)   (d)
9. (a)   (b)   (c)   (d)
10. (a)   (b)   (c)   (d)

☞ **생물**

amphibians	양서동물	marsupial	유대류의 포유동물
arthropod	절지동물	membrane	(얇은) 막
assimilation	동화작용	metabolism	신진대사
bacteria	박테리아	metamorphosis	변태
bait	미끼	mollusca	연체동물문(門)
bark	나무껍질	mutation	돌연변이
beak	(새의) 부리	parasite	기생충
biochemistry	생화학	paw	(개 · 고양이 등의 갈고리
botany	식물학		발톱이 있는) 발
zoology	동물학	peck	(부리로) 쪼다
carnivorous	육식성의, 식충성의	perennial	다년생 식물
cellulose	섬유소	petal	꽃잎
chromosome	염색체	primates	영장류
chrysalis	번데기	proliferate	증식하다
claw	(고양이, 매 등의) 발톱	protoplasm	원형질, 세포질
colloid	콜로이드	sponge	해면동물
ecology	생태학	spore	포자(胞子), 홀씨
entomology	곤충학	bough	큰 가지
enzyme	효소	spray	작은 가지
fauna	동물군	sprout	싹트다
ferment	발효시키다	stamen	수술
fermentation	발효	starch	녹말, 전분
fern	양치류	stem	줄기
fin	지느러미	stump	그루터기
fungus	진균류	survival of the fittest	적자생존
generic	속의	web	(물새 등의) 물갈퀴
genetics	유전학	wither	시들다
genus	종류, 속		
gland	선(腺), 분비 기관		
glucose	포도당		
herbivorous	초식성의		
heredity	유전, 유전적 형질		
mammal	포유동물		

Part IV

Choose the option that the best answers the question.

1. (a)   (b)   (c)   (d)
2. (a)   (b)   (c)   (d)
3. (a)   (b)   (c)   (d)
4. (a)   (b)   (c)   (d)
5. (a)   (b)   (c)   (d)
6. (a)   (b)   (c)   (d)
7. (a)   (b)   (c)   (d)
8. (a)   (b)   (c)   (d)
9. (a)   (b)   (c)   (d)

Pretest 평가와 처방

1. 1~3번 문제에 약한 경우

담화문의 주제를 파악하는 문제 유형에 약한 경우다. Part 4에서 가장 쉬운 유형에 속하기 때문에 반드시 맞추고 넘어가야 한다. 대개 첫 문장이나 마지막 문장에 주제가 나와 있기 때문에 이 두 부분을 주의 깊게 듣는 것이 관건이다. Chapter 15를 통해 충분히 연습하자.

2. 4~6번 문제에 약한 경우

담화문의 세부 사항을 파악하는 데 어려움을 겪는 경우다. 따라서 출제되는 질문 유형을 미리 파악하여 잘 익혀 두고, 두 번씩 읽어 주기 때문에 질문을 듣고 마지막으로 한 번 더 들을 때 주의 깊게 들으며 선택지를 하나하나씩 소거해 나가는 방식으로 문제를 해결해 나가야 한다. Chapter 16을 통해 충분히 연습하자.

3. 7~9번 문제에 약한 경우

담화문 내용을 추론하는 문제 유형으로 가장 어려운 영역에 해당한다. 글에 직접적인 힌트가 주어지는 경우가 거의 없기 때문에 잘 듣고 판단하여 추론 가능한 내용을 골라야 한다. Chapter 17을 통해 충분히 연습하자.

담화문 주제 파악하기

Chapter 15

담화문 주제 파악하기는 고득점을 위해 꼭 정복해야 할 문제 유형이다. 주제는 주로 첫 문장이나 마지막 문장에 나와 있으므로 이 두 부분을 놓치지 않고 잘 들어야 한다.

1. An international pilot was arrested as he landed in Sydney yesterday and charged with carrying suitcases stuffed with cash out of Australia in a multimillion-dollar drug-running and money-laundering operation. He is alleged to have picked up suitcases of cash in Melbourne and Sydney and carried them onto planes back to Vietnam, using his privileged status as an airline pilot to bypass customs bag checks.

Q. Which of the following best summarizes the report?

(a) An aviator was arrested for trafficking.
(b) The plane accident occurred in Sydney.
(c) The pilot stole passenger's luggages.
(d) An airplane couldn't take off because of the bad weather.

해설

글 첫 부분에 마약 밀수와 돈세탁을 한 후 현금이 든 가방들을 호주 밖으로 운반한 혐의를 받았다는 내용이 나오므로 정답은 (a)다.

어휘

stuff with ~으로 채우다   multimillion-dollar 수백만 달러의   drug-running 마약 밀수
money-laundering 돈세탁   be alleged to ~으로 알려져 있다   privileged status 특수한 신분[지위]
bypass 회피하다, (단계를) 뛰어넘다   customs bag checks 수하물 검사   aviator 비행사   trafficking 마약 밀수

2. Combine the egg yolk and milk in a bowl and stir until smooth. Roll one sheet of dough out on a lightly floured surface until thin. Place tiny pinches of mozzarella about 3cm apart on the sheet. Top with another sheet of dough. Cut into 2-3cm squares to form ravioli-like parcels of mozzarella. Press edges together with a fork. Repeat with remaining pastry sheets and mozzarella. Shallow fry in hot oil until golden. Drain on a paper towel and season with sea salt.

Q. What is the talk about?

(a) A recipe
(b) An advertisement for the main dish of a restaurant
(c) How to use a gas stove
(d) A way to preserve ingredients

🦑 **해설**

stir, roll out, shallow fry 등의 표현들을 통해 요리법에 대해 설명해 주고 있음을 알 수 있다. 따라서 정답은 (a).

> **어휘**
>
> **yolk** 노른자위 **stir** 휘젓다, 뒤섞다 **roll out** 펴서 판판하게 하다 **dough** 가루 반죽 **floured** 밀가루를 뿌린
> **tiny** 작은 **pinch** 조금, 두 손 끝으로 집을 만한 양 **top with** 위에 놓다 **parcel** 꾸러미, 한 덩어리
> **shallow fry** 살짝 튀기다 **drain** 배수하다, (물기를) 빼다 **season** 양념하다, 간을 맞추다 **sea salt** 천일염
> **preserve** 저장하다 **ingredient** 재료

3. Popular fast foods contain high levels of salt so they are a health danger, a report has found. There is a strong link between salt, high blood pressure and coronary vascular disease, including heart failure, kidney failure and stroke. Children who eat a high sodium diet are at risk of developing obesity, asthma and high blood pressure.

Q. What is the main point the speaker is trying to make?

(a) Salt is the most important ingredient of many dishes.
(b) Salty food contributes to weight loss.
(c) Salty food causes various maladies.
(d) Children should stop having junk food.

해설

패스트푸드에 함유된 다량의 소금이 건강에 위험하다는 연구 결과가 나왔고, 소금이 심장마비, 신부전증, 뇌졸중 등의 질병들과 매우 밀접한 관계가 있다고 했으므로 정답은 (c)가 된다.

어휘

coronary vascular disease 심장혈관 질환 heart failure 심장마비 kidney failure 신부전증 stroke 뇌졸중 sodium 나트륨 obesity 비만 asthma 천식 salty 소금기 있는, 짠 malady 병

1. An international pilot was arrested as he landed in Sydney yesterday and charged
   with _________________________________ out of Australia _______________
   _________________________________. He is alleged to have picked up
   suitcases of cash in Melbourne and Sydney and carried them onto planes back to
   Vietnam, using his ____
   _________________________________.

2. ____ until smooth.
   _________________________________ on a lightly floured surface until thin.
   Place tiny pinches of mozzarella about 3cm apart on the sheet. _______________
   _________________________________. Cut into 2-3cm squares to form ravioli-like
   parcels of mozzarella. Press edges together with a fork. Repeat with remaining
   pastry sheets and mozzarella. _________________________________.
   Drain on a paper towel and season with sea salt.

3. Popular fast foods ____,
   a report has found. _________________________________, high blood
   pressure and coronary vascular disease, including heart failure, kidney failure and
   stroke. ____
   and high blood pressure.

Questions 1-9

Choose the option that the best answers the question.

1. (a)   (b)   (c)   (d)
2. (a)   (b)   (c)   (d)
3. (a)   (b)   (c)   (d)
4. (a)   (b)   (c)   (d)
5. (a)   (b)   (c)   (d)
6. (a)   (b)   (c)   (d)
7. (a)   (b)   (c)   (d)
8. (a)   (b)   (c)   (d)
9. (a)   (b)   (c)   (d)

☞ **의학**

abortion	낙태	bronchus	기관지
barren	불임의	cardiac	심장의
caesarean section	제왕절개 수술	cataract	백내장
contraceptive	피임약	cerebellum	소뇌
delivery	출산, 분만	cerebrum	대뇌
miscarriage	유산	chest	가슴, 흉부
pregnancy	임신	cranium	두개골
acute	급성의	speckle	작은 반점
allergic	알레르기 체질의	spine	척추, 등뼈
amnesia	기억상실	sputum	가래, 담
anemia	빈혈	ward	병동, 병실
arthritis	관절염	anesthesia	마취
brainstorm	정신착란	anesthetic	마취제
breast cancer	유방암	antifebrile	해열제
bump	혹	antiseptic	살균의, 멸균의
chronic	만성의	cerebral death	뇌사
contagion	전염	coma	혼수 상태
diabetes	당뇨병	disinfect	소독하다
dyspepsia	소화 불량	excrement	배설물
epidemic	유행병, 전염병	gastric juice	위액
gastric ulcer	위궤양	hypnosis	최면
hepatitis	간염	hygiene	위생
infectious	전염성의	immune	면역(성)
influenza	독감	injection	주사
insomnia	불면증	olfactory	후각의
leukemia	백혈병	palliate	(병·통증 등을)
malnutrition	영양실조		일시적으로 완화시키다
nausea	구토	palpitate	(심장·맥박이) 뛰다
paralysis	마비, 중풍	sedastive	진정제
pneumonia	폐렴	side effect	부작용
polio	소아마비	transfusion	수혈
scald	화상		
vertigo	현기증		

담화문 내용 파악하기

담화문 내용 파악하기 영역에서는 출제되는 문제 유형들을 충분히 숙지하는 것이 중요하다. 또 두 번씩 들려주므로 첫 번째 들려줄 때 문제를 잘 들은 다음, 두 번째 들을 때는 중요한 세부 사항들을 메모해 가면서 듣는 노력이 필요하다.

4. The mayor of south Island said he's asked county departments to prepare for a 5 percent budget cut to be taken from discretionary spending, not wages and benefits. He said the county will be "OK" this fiscal year, which ends June 30. But he's uncertain about the following fiscal year. The county has been hit by the tourism slowdown. Fewer visitors taking shorter vacations at the island means less tax revenues.

Q. **Why did the mayor ask for the budget cut?**

(a) Because of the decrease in economic profits
(b) Because the mayor decided to invest in the tourist industry
(c) Because of the slow national economy
(d) Because one of the largest companies went bankrupt

해설

글 후반부에서 관광 사업의 침체로 인해 타격을 입었다고 했으므로 (a)가 정답이다.

어휘

cut 삭감 discretionary 임의의, 자유재량의 wage 임금 benefit 수당 fiscal year 회계 연도 tourism 관광 사업, 관광객 slowdown 경기 후퇴, 둔화 tax revenue 세수(稅收) go bankrupt 파산하다

5. Our family watched the news yesterday. I was shocked. The contaminated Chinese protein powder that has sickened some 17,000 American dogs and cats has now turned up in the human food supply. The U.S. Department of Agriculture admits that 6,000 pigs and more than 2.5 million broiler chickens were sold for human consumption after being fed contaminated pet food. How is the toxic Chinese protein powder imported? The government should reinforce international import inspection.

Q. What is the tone of the talk?

(a) Approving
(b) Supportive
(c) Neutral
(d) Critical

해설

미국 개와 고양이를 병들게 한 오염된 중국산 단백질 분말이 우리가 먹는 음식에서도 발견됐고, 오염된 사료를 먹인 돼지와 닭고기가 식용으로 팔렸다는 사실을 언급하며 정부의 국제 수입 검사의 필요성을 주장하고 있다. 따라서 유독성 단백질 분말의 수입에 대해 비판적임을 알 수 있다.

어휘

contaminated 오염된 protein powder 단백질 분말 sicken 병들게 하다 turn up 발견되다
broiler chicken (구이용) 영계 human consumption 식용 pet food 애완동물용 사료 toxic 유독한, 치명적인 reinforce 강화하다 approving 찬성하는

6. The Hawaii High School Athletic Association's executive board voted on Monday to move up the changing of seasons for three sports to the upcoming school year. Starting in the 2008-2009 school year, girls basketball will be moved from spring to winter, softball from winter to spring, and boys volleyball from fall to spring.

Q. **According to the talk, what will change next year?**

    (a) The beginning day of school sports
    (b) The seasons for three sports
    (c) The Athletic Association's executive board
    (d) The basketball team members

해설

첫 부분에 세 가지 스포츠 시즌 변경을 앞당기는 것을 투표로 결정했다는 내용이 나오므로 (b)가 정답임을 알 수 있다.

어휘

executive board 이사회, 임원진　vote 투표하여 결정하다　move up (시일을) 앞당기다　school year 학년

4. The mayor of south Island said he's asked county departments to prepare for
____, not wages and benefits.
He said the county will be "OK" this fiscal year, which ends June 30. But __________
________________________________. The county ____________________
____________________________. Fewer visitors taking shorter vacations at the island
means less tax revenues.

5. Our family watched the news yesterday. I was shocked. ____________________
____________________________________ some 17,000 American dogs and cats
____. The U.S. Department of Agriculture
admits that 6,000 pigs and more than 2.5 million broiler chickens ________________
____________________________ after being fed contaminated pet food. How is the toxic
Chinese protein powder imported? The government ____________________________
________________________________.

6. The Hawaii High School Athletic Association's executive board voted on Monday
____.
Starting in the 2008-2009 school year, ____
________________, softball from winter to spring, and boys volleyball from fall to spring.

Questions 1-9

Choose the option that the best answers the question.

1. (a)   (b)   (c)   (d)
2. (a)   (b)   (c)   (d)
3. (a)   (b)   (c)   (d)
4. (a)   (b)   (c)   (d)
5. (a)   (b)   (c)   (d)
6. (a)   (b)   (c)   (d)
7. (a)   (b)   (c)   (d)
8. (a)   (b)   (c)   (d)
9. (a)   (b)   (c)   (d)

☞ **천문/기상**

acid rain	산성비	equinox	주야평분시(춘분 또는 추분)
atmospheric pressure	기압	galaxy	은하, 은하수
avalanche	눈사태	heat wave	열파
barometer	기압계	heavenly body	천체
blast	돌풍	icecap	만년설
blizzard	눈보라	leap year	윤년
cloudburst	폭우	Jupiter	목성
damp	습기	Mars	화성
downfall	폭우	Mercury	수성
drought	가뭄, 한발	Neptune	해왕성
frigid	몹시 추운	Pluto	명왕성
front	전선(前線)	Saturn	토성
gale	강풍	Uranus	천왕성
glacier	빙하	Venus	금성
hail	우박, 싸락눈	meteor	유성, 운석
haze	아지랑이	nova	신성(新星)
humidity	습도	orbit	궤도
inundation	범람, 침수	planet	행성
drizzle	이슬비	rotation	자전
monsoon	계절풍	satellite	위성
muggy	무더운		
overcast	구름으로 덮다, 흐리게 하다		
sleet	진눈깨비		
tempest	폭풍우		
thermometer	온도계		
weather phenomenon	기상 현상		
weather bureau	기상청		
wind velocity	풍속		
zephyr	서풍, 미풍		
astrology	점성학		
astronomy	천문학		
eclipse	일식, 월식		

담화문 내용 추론하기

Chapter 17

담화문 내용 추론 영역은 문항수가 적은 반면, 난이도와 배점이 높다. 추론하는 문제이기 때문에 지문에 직접적인 힌트가 언급되는 경우가 드물다. 따라서 내용을 잘 듣고 파악하여 선택지를 하나하나씩 소거하는 방식으로 문제를 풀어 나가야 한다.

7. More wind power was installed in the EU than any other electricity generating technology last year. On average, 20 wind turbines were installed for every working day. Statistics released by the European Wind Energy Association show that 43% of all new electricity generating capacity built in the European Union last year was wind energy, exceeding all other technologies including gas, coal and nuclear power.

Q. What can be inferred from the talk?

(a) Wind power is coming into wide use in Europe.
(b) Wind power will soon be an alternative energy source.
(c) Europe wants other countries to install wind power.
(d) Energy resources are insufficient for the future.

🔦 해설

작년에 더 많은 풍력이 유럽에 설치되었고, 모든 새로운 전기 발전 용량 중 43%가 풍력이었다고 했으므로 (a)가 정답임을 알 수 있다. (b)는 풍력이 많이 활용되고 있지만, 그렇다고 대체 에너지원이 될지는 알 수 없으므로 정답이 될 수 없다.

> **어휘**
>
> **on average** 평균적으로 **turbine** 터빈(유수, 증기, 가스 등의 힘으로 회전하는 원동기) **statistics** 통계 (자료) **release** 발표하다 **exceed** 능가하다, 초과하다 **come into** ~의 상태가 되다 **insufficient** 불충분한

8. Four people at the rear of a plane that crashed in a muddy Amazon river managed to open an emergency door and swim to safety as the aircraft sank, dragging 24 others to their death, officials said Sunday. Most victims were members of a single family that had chartered the plane to travel to a birthday party. Seven children died.

Q. What can be inferred from the report?

(a) People on the plane couldn't take part in a birthday party.
(b) An airplane crashed in the Pacific Ocean.
(c) Most of the people survived the accident.
(d) The pilot took a mistaken route.

해설

사고가 난 비행기 탑승객들이 생일 파티를 하러 가기 위해 비행기를 전세 낸 사람들이라고 했으므로 (a)가 정답임을 알 수 있다.

어휘

at the rear of ~의 뒷부분에   muddy 진흙의, 진흙투성이의   emergency door 비상구   aircraft 항공기
sink 가라앉다   drag 끌어내다, 끌어당기다   a single family 편부모 가정   charter 전세 내다

9. President Barack Obama says that for years federal officials have only "talked and tinkered" over health care reform while problems have gone unresolved. Opening his conference on health care, Obama complained that the soaring cost "now causes a bankruptcy in America every 30 seconds." He was speaking Thursday to over a hundred experts and policymakers invited to the White House, including some who opposed the Clinton administration's health-care overhaul.

Q. What can be inferred from the report?

(a) Obama has difficulty resolving the recession in America.
(b) Experts anticipate that the domestic economy will recover in the near future.
(c) The president believes that health care reform hasn't worked well.
(d) The Clinton administration has many enemies everywhere.

🐝 해설

글 첫 부분에 연방 공무원들이 건강보험 개혁에 대해서 단지 떠들기만 하고 처리를 제대로 하지 못했다고 언급한 내용으로 보아 (c)가 정답임을 알 수 있다.

어휘

federal official 연방 공무원 **tinker** 서투르게 일하다 **unresolved** 미해결의 **health care** 건강보험
soaring 치솟는, 급상승하는 **policymaker** 정책 입안자 **overhaul** 철저한 조사 **recession** 경기 후퇴, 불경기

7. More wind power was installed in the EU _________________________________
last year. On average, _______________________________________.
Statistics released by the European Wind Energy Association show that 43% of all
new electricity generating capacity built in the European Union last year was wind
energy, _______________________________________.

8. Four people at the rear of a plane that crashed in a muddy Amazon river _________
_______________________________ as the aircraft sank, ____________
_______________________________, officials said Sunday. Most victims were
_______________________________________ to travel to a
birthday party. Seven children died.

9. President Barack Obama says that for years federal officials have only "talked and
tinkered" over health care reform _______________________________________.
Opening his conference on health care, Obama complained that the soaring cost
"now _______________________________________."
He was speaking Thursday to over a hundred experts and policymakers invited to
the White House, _______________________________________
_______________________.

Questions 1-7

Choose the option that the best answers the question.

1. (a) (b) (c) (d)
2. (a) (b) (c) (d)
3. (a) (b) (c) (d)
4. (a) (b) (c) (d)
5. (a) (b) (c) (d)
6. (a) (b) (c) (d)
7. (a) (b) (c) (d)

☞ **지리/지질/환경**

alluvial	충적(沖積)의
colliery	탄광
delta	삼각주
gorge	골짜기, 협곡
iceberg	빙산
meander	굽이쳐 흐르다
natural levee	자연제방
reef	암초
river basin	유역
rugged	바위투성이의
tributary	(강의) 지류
lava	용암
lime	석회
limestone	석회암
loam	양토
marble	대리석
submarine ridge	해저산맥
subterranean river	지하천
upwarp	곡륭

Final Test

Final Test

Part 1

Questions 1-15

You will now hear fifteen items, each made up of a single spoken statement followed by four spoken responses. Choose the most appropriate response to the statement.

1.	(a)	(b)	(c)	(d)		2.	(a)	(b)	(c)	(d)
3.	(a)	(b)	(c)	(d)		4.	(a)	(b)	(c)	(d)
5.	(a)	(b)	(c)	(d)		6.	(a)	(b)	(c)	(d)
7.	(a)	(b)	(c)	(d)		8.	(a)	(b)	(c)	(d)
9.	(a)	(b)	(c)	(d)		10.	(a)	(b)	(c)	(d)
11.	(a)	(b)	(c)	(d)		12.	(a)	(b)	(c)	(d)
13.	(a)	(b)	(c)	(d)		14.	(a)	(b)	(c)	(d)
15.	(a)	(b)	(c)	(d)						

Part 2

Questions 16-30

You will now hear fifteen conversation fragments, each made up of a three spoken statements followed by four spoken responses. Choose the most appropriate response to the statement.

16.	(a)	(b)	(c)	(d)		17.	(a)	(b)	(c)	(d)
18.	(a)	(b)	(c)	(d)		19.	(a)	(b)	(c)	(d)
20.	(a)	(b)	(c)	(d)		21.	(a)	(b)	(c)	(d)
22.	(a)	(b)	(c)	(d)		23.	(a)	(b)	(c)	(d)
24.	(a)	(b)	(c)	(d)		25.	(a)	(b)	(c)	(d)
26.	(a)	(b)	(c)	(d)		27.	(a)	(b)	(c)	(d)
28.	(a)	(b)	(c)	(d)		29.	(a)	(b)	(c)	(d)
30.	(a)	(b)	(c)	(d)						

Part 3

Questions 31-45

You will now hear fifteen complete conversations. For each item, you will hear a conversation and its corresponding question which will be read twice. Then you will hear four options which will be read only once. Choose the most appropriate response to the statement.

31.	(a)	(b)	(c)	(d)		32.	(a)	(b)	(c)	(d)
33.	(a)	(b)	(c)	(d)		34.	(a)	(b)	(c)	(d)
35.	(a)	(b)	(c)	(d)		36.	(a)	(b)	(c)	(d)
37.	(a)	(b)	(c)	(d)		38.	(a)	(b)	(c)	(d)
39.	(a)	(b)	(c)	(d)		40.	(a)	(b)	(c)	(d)
41.	(a)	(b)	(c)	(d)		42.	(a)	(b)	(c)	(d)
43.	(a)	(b)	(c)	(d)		44.	(a)	(b)	(c)	(d)
45.	(a)	(b)	(c)	(d)						

Part 4

Questions 46-60

You will now hear fifteen spoken monologues. For each item, you will hear a monologues and its corresponding question which will be read twice. Then you will hear four options which will be read only once. Choose the most appropriate response to the statement.

46.	(a)	(b)	(c)	(d)		47.	(a)	(b)	(c)	(d)
48.	(a)	(b)	(c)	(d)		49.	(a)	(b)	(c)	(d)
50.	(a)	(b)	(c)	(d)		51.	(a)	(b)	(c)	(d)
52.	(a)	(b)	(c)	(d)		53.	(a)	(b)	(c)	(d)
54.	(a)	(b)	(c)	(d)		55.	(a)	(b)	(c)	(d)
56.	(a)	(b)	(c)	(d)		57.	(a)	(b)	(c)	(d)
58.	(a)	(b)	(c)	(d)		59.	(a)	(b)	(c)	(d)
60.	(a)	(b)	(c)	(d)						

정답 및
해설

Part 1

Chapter 1 평서문 유형 익히기

STEP 1 Pretest Clinic

1.

해석_ W: 입장이 바뀌면 너도 지금 내 심정을 이해할 거야.

M: _______________________________

(a) 테이블이 완전히 뒤집혔어.

(b) 절대 안 돼! 그건 내 테이블이야.

(c) 놀리지 마. 그럴 기분 아니야.

(d) 정말 미안해. 내가 이기적이었어.

정답_ (d)

2.

해석_ M: 네 마음이 진정되고 나면 자존심을 접고 그녀와 얘기하는 게 좋을 것 같아.

W: _______________________________

(a) 어제 그녀와 얘기했어.

(b) 충고 고마워. 그럴 참이야.

(c) 나 완전 빈털터리야. 돈 좀 빌려야겠어.

(d) 너 한창때잖아. 이상형의 여자를 찾아 봐.

정답_ (b)

3.

해석_ W: 당신은 모르는 게 없군요.

M: _______________________________

(a) 고맙습니다. 과찬이세요.

(b) 네, 저는 백과사전을 가지고 있어요.

(c) 이번만 봐줄게요.

(d) 괜찮아요.

정답_ (a)

STEP 2 Dictation

정답_ 1. the tables were turned

2. pocket your pride

3. walking encyclopedia

STEP 3 Actual Test

1.

M: He is cut out to be a prosecutor.

W: _______________________________

(a) He gave her a pat on the back.

(b) You got a gold star for that.

(c) You hit the nail right on the head.

(d) He cut himself off from the world.

해석_ M: 그는 검사로 적격이에요.

W: _______________________________

(a) 그가 그녀를 칭찬했어요.

(b) 정말 잘했어요.

(c) 내 말이 그 말이에요.

(d) 그는 세상과 등졌어요.

해설_ 그가 검사로 적격이라고 말하고 있으므로 이에 동의나 반대의 의견이 담긴 선택지를 고르면 된다. 따라서 정답은 (c). '바로 맞혔어', '네 말이 절대적으로 맞아'의 뜻으로 상대의 말에 전적인 동감을 나타낸다. (b)는 '정말 잘했어요'라는 뜻으로 상대를 칭찬할 때 쓰는 표현이다.

어휘_ be cut out 적격이다 prosecutor 검사 pat on the back 칭찬의 말[행위] gold star (노력과 성과에 대한) 최고상 hit the nail right on the head 바로 맞히다, 요점을 찌르다 cut oneself off from the world 세상을 등지다

정답_ (c)

2.

W: Oh, I bombed the interview.

M: _______________________________

(a) Any good news?

(b) It's not the end of the world.

(c) What's the damage?

(d) I'm the decision-maker.

해석_ W: 아, 인터뷰를 망쳤어.

M: _______________________________

(a) 어떤 좋은 뉴스?

(b) 그렇다고 세상이 끝난 건 아니야.

(c) 피해 본 게 뭐야?

(d) 결정은 내가 해.

해설_ 인터뷰를 망쳤다고 낙심하고 있으므로 위로의 표현이 담긴 선택
지가 이어져야 적절하다. 따라서 정답은 (b)로, 세상이 끝난 건
아니니 낙심 말라는 뜻이 담겨 있다.

어휘_ bomb 크게 실패하다

정답_ (b)

3.

M: The football coach laughed at me in front of
my teammates.

W: ____

(a) Oh, don't let that get to you.
(b) You can go there by coach.
(c) You'll feel better.
(d) You could've made friends with him.

해석_ M: 축구 감독이 팀원들 앞에서 날 비웃었어.

W: ________________________________

(a) 아, 그 일로 속상해하지 마.
(b) 마차 타고 그곳에 갈 수 있어.
(c) 기분이 더 나아질 거야.
(d) 그와 친해질 수 있었을 텐데.

해설_ 팀원들 앞에서 비웃음을 당해 속상해하고 있으므로 이에 대해
위로해 주는 말이 이어져야 자연스럽다. 따라서 정답은 (a). '그
일로 상심 마', '그 일로 마음 아파하지 마'라는 뜻으로 좋지 않
은 일을 겪은 상대를 위로해 줄 때 쓰는 표현이다. (b)의 coach
는 '마차'의 뜻으로, 동일한 발음을 이용해 오답을 유도한 함정
이므로 주의하자.

어휘_ teammate 팀원 make friends with ~와 친해지다

정답_ (a)

4.

W: Congratulations on your birthday! May your
life prosper in many years to come!

M: ____

(a) Alright, you talked me into it.
(b) I can't help wondering if this is as good as it
gets.
(c) You are always talking my ear off.
(d) So glad to hear that. Thanks.

해석_ W: 생신 축하드려요! 앞으로도 계속 행복하게 잘 사세요!

M: ________________________________

(a) 좋아요, 당신 말대로 할게요.
(b) 이보다 더 좋을 수 있을지 궁금해하지 않을 수가 없어요.
(c) 당신은 항상 수다를 많이 떨어요.
(d) 그 말을 들으니 너무 좋네요. 고마워요.

해설_ 생일 축하 인사를 건네고 있으므로 이에 대한 답례 표현이 담긴
선택지를 고르면 된다.

어휘_ talk ... into ~하도록 …를 설득하다 be as good as it
gets 이보다 더 좋을 수 없다 talk one's ear off 계속 수다
떨다

정답_ (d)

5.

M: The stain didn't come out completely.

W: ____

(a) It's the oldest trick in the book.
(b) I'll be back before you know it.
(c) I'm so sorry. I'll try it again.
(d) You're everybody's friend.

해석_ M: 얼룩이 완전히 안 빠졌어요.

W: ________________________________

(a) 그건 누구나 아는 비법이에요.
(b) 금방 돌아올게요.
(c) 정말 죄송해요. 다시 해볼게요.
(d) 당신은 팔방미인이에요.

해설_ 세탁소에서 접할 수 있는 대화 내용으로, 옷의 얼룩이 다 빠지지
않았다고 항의하고 있으므로 이에 사과하는 표현이 이어져야 적
절하다.

어휘_ stain 얼룩 come out (얼룩 등이) 빠지다 the oldest
trick in the book 누구나 아는 비법 before you know
it 눈 깜짝할 사이에, 금방 everybody's friend 팔방미인

정답_ (c)

6.

W: You've only got yourself to blame.

M: ____

(a) Time hangs heavy on my hands.
(b) What a drag!
(c) Quit your griping.
(d) I heard it through the grape vine.

해석_ W: 네가 탓할 사람은 너뿐이야.

    M: _______________________

    (a) 지루해 죽겠어.

    (b) 아이, 지겨워!

    (c) 불평 좀 그만해.

    (d) 소문을 통해 들었어.

해설_ 남자를 탓하고 있으므로 불평 좀 그만하라고 말하는 (c)가 가장
    적절하다.

어휘_ Time hangs heavy on one's hand. (시간을 주체하지
    못할 정도로) 지루하다.   drag 지겨운 것(사람) gripe 불평하
    다   through the grape vine 소문을 통해서

정답_ (c)

7.

M: Your voice is breaking up.

W: _______________________________

(a) You should recharge your battery.

(b) Can I have extension 321?

(c) Let me hang off and call you back.

(d) Let me check if he's in.

해석_ M: 당신 목소리가 끊겨요.

    W: _______________________

    (a) 배터리를 충전하는 게 좋겠어요.

    (b) 내선 321번으로 연결해 주실래요?

    (c) 제가 끊고 다시 전화할게요.

    (d) 그가 있는지 확인해 볼게요.

해설_ 전화 통화 중 여자의 목소리가 자꾸 끊긴다고 했으므로 끊고 다
    시 전화하겠다는 (c)가 적절하다.

어휘_ break up 중단하다, 부수다   recharge 재충전하다
    extension 내선

정답_ (c)

Chapter 2 선택지 (a) 유형 익히기

STEP 1 Pretest Clinic

4.

해석_ M: 이거 정말 큰 은혜를 입고 있습니다.

    W: _______________________________

    (a) 별말씀을요. 제가 그 처지에 있다면 당신도 그러실 텐데요,
        뭐.

    (b) 배짱 한번 좋군!

    (c) 그렇게 되면 오죽 좋겠어요.

    (d) 당신은 제 생명의 은인입니다.

정답_ (a)

5.

해석_ W: 미안해요. 제가 망쳐놓은 거 알아요.

    M: _______________________________

    (a) 너무 자책하지 마세요. 당신 잘못만은 아니에요.

    (b) 저를 지원해 주세요.

    (c) 현실적이 되세요.

    (d) 이미 사과드렸잖아요. 더 이상 뭘 해주길 바래요?

정답_ (a)

6.

해석_ M: 성급히 결정 내린 거 사과할게.

    W: _______________________________

    (a) 신경 쓰지 마.

    (b) 넌 깍쟁이야.

    (c) 넌 너무 깐깐해.

    (d) 나한테 그렇게 어려운 말 쓰지 마.

정답_ (a)

STEP 2 Dictation

정답_ 4. Think nothing of it

    5. Don't be so hard on yourself

    6. Forget it

STEP 3 Actual Test

1.

W: Hello. Please, leave a message after the beep.

M: ___________________________________

(a) This is Ricardo. Could you give me a buzz?
(b) I have another call. I'd better run.
(c) Hold it down.
(d) There's no signal.

해석_ W: 안녕하세요. '삐' 소리 후 메시지를 남겨 주세요.

　　 M: ___________________________________

　　 (a) 저는 리카르도예요. 전화주시겠어요?

　　 (b) 다른 전화가 왔어요. 끊어야겠어요.

　　 (c) 조용히 해요.

　　 (d) 신호음이 안 터져요.

해설_ 자동 응답기에서 나오는 말이므로 본인의 이름과 용건을 말하는

　　 (a)가 이어져야 자연스럽다. (b)의 I'd better run.은 전화 영어

　　 에서 '(전화를) 끊어야겠다' 는 의미로 쓰인다.

어휘_ beep '삐' 하는 소리　give ... a buzz ~에게 전화하다

　　 hold it down 조용히 하다

정답_ (a)

2.

M: I can't hear because of the background sound.

W: ___________________________________

(a) Let me call you back later.
(b) Don't make crank calls.
(c) Tell him to call me back.
(d) Buzz off!

해석_ M: 주위가 시끄러워서 잘 안 들려.

　　 W: ___________________________________

　　 (a) 나중에 다시 전화할게.

　　 (b) 장난 전화 걸지 마.

　　 (c) 나한테 전화하라고 그에게 전해 줘.

　　 (d) 전화 끊어!

해설_ 주변이 시끄러워서 잘 안 들린다고 했으므로 나중에 다시 전화

　　 하겠다는 (a)가 적절하다.

어휘_ crank call 장난 전화　buzz off 전화를 끊다

3.

W: Which one is better, doing the paint job or changing the whole bumper?

M: ___________________________________

(a) I think doing the paint job is better.
(b) Don't blow your horn.
(c) My car tipped over.
(d) Can I take my car in?

해석_ W: 도색하는 게 나을까요, 아님 범퍼를 바꾸는 게 나을까요?

　　 M: ___________________________________

　　 (a) 도색하는 게 나을 것 같아요.

　　 (b) 경적을 울리지 마세요.

　　 (c) 제 차가 전복됐어요.

　　 (d) 제 차를 맡겨도 될까요?

해설_ 도색과 범퍼 교환 중 어느 것이 더 나은지 묻고 있으므로 이에 관

　　 한 의견이 담긴 선택지를 고르면 된다.

어휘_ do the paint job 도색하다　blow one's horn 경적을

　　 울리다　tip over 전복되다　take in (정비소에) 차를 맡기다

정답_ (a)

4.

M: Would you like to come to a movie preview?

W: ___________________________________

(a) I'd love to but I can't.
(b) I watched a drive-in movie.
(c) I really enjoyed that movie.
(d) I watched the movie last week.

해석_ M: 영화 시사회에 올래?

　　 W: ___________________________________

　　 (a) 그러고 싶지만 갈 수 없어.

　　 (b) 난 자동차 극장에서 영화를 봤어.

　　 (c) 그 영화 정말 재밌게 봤어.

　　 (d) 지난주에 그 영화 봤어.

해설_ 영화 시사회에 초대하고 있으므로 갈 수 있는지 여부에 대해 언

　　 급한 선택지를 고르면 된다.

어휘_ movie preview 영화 시사회　drive-in movie 자동차

　　 전용 영화

정답_ (a)

5.

W: Would you please choose a photo size?

M: _______________________________________

(a) I'll have the default size.
(b) This camera has auto-focus.
(c) It is a fuzzy image.
(d) Can you tape-record me?

해석_ W: 사진 크기를 골라 주실래요?

　　　 M: _______________________________

　　　 (a) 기본 크기로 할게요.

　　　 (b) 이 카메라는 자동초점 기능이 있습니다.

　　　 (c) 이미지가 흐릿해요.

　　　 (d) 비디오 카메라로 나 찍어줄 수 있니?

해설_ 사진관에서 이루어지는 대화 내용이다. 사진사가 사진 크기를
　　　 고르라고 했으므로 이에 답한 선택지를 고르면 된다.

어휘_ default size 기본 크기　auto-focus 자동초점 기능
　　　 fuzzy 흐릿한

정답_ (a)

Chapter 3 의문사 의문문 유형 익히기

STEP 1 Pretest Clinic

7.

해석_ W: 이번 주말여행 계획에 무슨 문제 있어?

　　　 M: _______________________________

　　　 (a) 시차 적응 안 되겠다.

　　　 (b) 문제는 내 차를 수리해야 된다는 거지.

　　　 (c) 비행기 멀미를 좀 했어.

　　　 (d) 비행기가 연착됐어.

정답_ (b)

8.

해석_ M: 차를 어디에 대야 하지?

　　　 W: _______________________________

　　　 (a) 난 이 스웨터를 원해.

　　　 (b) 차를 뒤로 빼주시겠어요?

　　　 (c) 저쪽에 주차하면 좋을 거야.

　　　 (d) 무단 횡단하면 안 돼.

정답_ (c)

9.

해석_ M: 새로 사귄 친구 크리스티나랑 잘 지내고 있니?
　　　　개 좀 지루하다며.

　　　 W: _______________________________

　　　 (a) 응, 그녀는 재치 있고 유머가 있어.

　　　 (b) 음, 얘기하는 게 좀 재미없어.

　　　 (c) 아니, 정반대야. 그녀는 매우 따분해.

　　　 (d) 천만에. 사장하고 난 사이가 아주 좋아.

정답_ (b)

STEP 2 Dictation

정답_ 7. The catch is that

　　　 8. It will be good if you park over there

　　　 9. she's not the most stimulating
　　　　 conversationalist

STEP 3 Actual Test

1.

M: How many credits did you sign up for this semester?

W: ______________________________________

(a) My credit is bad.
(b) You're rubbing salt in my wounds.
(c) You are just saying that, right?
(d) Not many. Just 12 this time.

해석_ M: 이번 학기에 몇 학점 신청했어?

W: ______________________________________

(a) 난 신용이 나빠.
(b) 아픈 곳을 찌르는구나.
(c) 너 그냥 말로만 그러는 거지, 그렇지?
(d) 많이 안 했어. 이번엔 12학점만 신청했어.

해설_ credit은 여기서 '학점'을 말한다. 따라서 몇 학점을 수강 신청했
는지 묻고 있으므로 이에 답하는 선택지를 고르면 된다. (a)는
credit의 의미를 이용한 함정.

어휘_ sign up 수강 신청하다 rub salt in one's wounds 아
픈 곳을 찌르다

정답_ (d)

2.

W: Why not jump-start it?

M: ______________________________________

(a) You are excused this time.
(b) A tire blew out.
(c) My car was wrecked.
(d) I tried. Any tips?

해석_ W: 차를 밀어서 시동 걸어보는 건 어때?

M: ______________________________________

(a) 이번만 용서할게.
(b) 타이어가 펑크 났어.
(c) 차가 망가졌어.
(d) 해봤어. 다른 방법 없어?

해설_ 차를 밀어서 시동을 걸어보라는 여자의 제안에 이미 그렇게 해
봤다고 응답한 (d)가 가장 적절하다.

어휘_ jump-start (차를) 밀어서 시동 걸다 blow out 타이어가
펑크 나다 wrecked 파손된 tip (유익한) 조언, 묘책

정답_ (d)

3.

M: How come you stood me up yesterday?

W: ______________________________________

(a) Suit yourself.
(b) We must have missed each other.
(c) You gave me the cold shoulder.
(d) I'm in hot water with her.

해석_ M: 어제 왜 나를 바람맞혔니?

W: ______________________________________

(a) 네 맘대로 해.
(b) 길이 서로 엇갈린 모양이다.
(c) 너 나한테 쌀쌀맞게 대했어.
(d) 그녀와 사이가 안 좋아.

해설_ 여자에게 바람맞힌 이유를 묻고 있으므로 이에 관해 언급한 (b)
가 정답이다.

어휘_ stand ... up ~를 바람맞히다 suit oneself 자기 마음대
로 하다 give ... the cold shoulder ~에게 차갑게 대하
다 be in hot water with ~와 사이가 좋지 않다

정답_ (b)

4.

W: What if he is a gold digger?

M: ______________________________________

(a) You are a worry wart. Take him at his word.
(b) Once in a blue moon.
(c) She speaks with a forked tongue.
(d) Fix me up with a pretty woman.

해석_ W: 그가 사기꾼이면 어쩌지?

M: ______________________________________

(a) 걱정도 팔자야. 그 사람 말을 믿어.
(b) 가뭄에 콩 나듯 해.
(c) 그녀는 거짓말을 해.
(d) 예쁜 여자 한 명 소개시켜 줘.

해설_ 사기꾼이면 어쩌냐고 걱정하는 여자를 안심시키는 (a)가 이어져
야 적절하다. worry wart는 '사소한 걱정이 많은 사람'을 뜻하
는 표현으로, 즉 '걱정도 팔자다'라는 의미다.

어휘_ gold digger 사기꾼 take one at one's word ~의 말
을 믿다 once in a blue moon 가뭄에 콩 나듯 speak

with a forked tongue 거짓말하다 fix ... up with
~를 소개시켜 주다

정답_ (a)

5.

M: How would you like to share a cab to the
airport?

W: _______________________________

(a) She owns 5,000 shares in the company.
(b) Let's take a cab.
(c) Why not? But I have to stop by the office on
the way.
(d) You are skating on thin ice.

해석_ M: 공항까지 함께 택시 타고 가는 게 어때요?

W: _______________________________

(a) 그녀는 그 회사 주식 5,000주를 가지고 있어요.
(b) 택시 탑시다.
(c) 그거 좋죠. 근데 가는 길에 사무실에 들러야 해요.
(d) 당신은 위험에 처해 있어요.

해설_ 공항까지 함께 택시 타고 가는 게 어떻겠냐는 남자의 제안에 대
해 답하는 선택지를 고르면 된다. (a)는 share의 의미를 이용한
함정이므로 주의하자.

어휘_ share a cab 함께 택시 타다 share 주식 stop by 들르
다 skate on thin ice 위험에 처해 있다

정답_ (c)

6.

W: What do you say we play some tennis to let
off steam?

M: _______________________________

(a) It's nothing to get steamed up.
(b) Don't pick on me.
(c) I'll foot the bill.
(d) That's what I was going to suggest.

해석_ W: 스트레스 풀기 위해 테니스 좀 치는 거 어때?

M: _______________________________

(a) 그건 화낼 일이 아니야.
(b) 날 괴롭히지 마.
(c) 내가 낼게.
(d) 그게 내가 제안하려고 했던 거야.

해설_ 테니스 치러 가는 것에 대해 의견을 묻고 있으므로 이에 동의하
는 (d)가 적절한 응답이다.

어휘_ let off steam 스트레스를 풀다, 화를 가라앉히다 get
steamed up 화를 내다 pick on 괴롭히다, 못살게 굴다
foot the bill 계산을 치르다

정답_ (d)

7.

M: Which country do you want to transfer
money to?

W: _______________________________

(a) The ATM ate my card.
(b) Why don't you enter your pin number?
(c) Please, update my account book.
(d) From Korea to Argentina.

해석_ M: 어느 나라로 송금하길 원하세요?

W: _______________________________

(a) 현금 인출기가 내 카드를 먹었어요.
(b) 비밀번호를 누르세요.
(c) 통장 정리 좀 해주세요.
(d) 한국에서 아르헨티나로요.

해설_ 송금할 나라를 묻고 있으므로 나라 이름이 언급된 선택지를 고
르면 된다.

어휘_ ATM(= automatic teller machine) 현금 인출기 pin
number 비밀번호 update one's account book 통장
정리를 하다

정답_ (d)

8.

W: How did the T-bone steak turn out?

M: _______________________________

(a) This proposal was very well done.
(b) Ah, this red wine really hit the spot.
(c) It was quite succulent.
(d) Sounds good. I agree with that.

해석_ W: T-bone 스테이크 맛이 어떠셨습니까?

M: _______________________________

(a) 이 제안서 아주 훌륭했어요.
(b) 아, 이 레드와인 정말 딱이에요.
(c) 육즙이 아주 풍부했어요.

(d) 좋은 생각인데요. 그것에 동의합니다.

해설_ 남자에게 스테이크 맛이 어땠는지 묻고 있으므로 이에 관해 언급한 선택지를 고르면 된다.

어휘_ turn out 판명되다 hit the spot 더할 나위 없다
succulent 즙이 많은

정답_ (c)

STEP 1 Pretest Clinic

10.

해석_ W: 지난주 싸운 후부터 제인과 나 사이가 냉랭해졌어.

M: ______________________________

(a) 이봐, 당신 나와의 관계가 아슬아슬해.

(b) 최근 이상하게 날씨가 추웠어.

(c) 제인이 재미있는 이야기로 어색한 분위기를 깼어.

(d) 그녀와 마음을 터놓고 얘기해 봐.

정답_ (d)

11.

해석_ M: 한 그릇 더 드세요.

W: ______________________________

(a) 마실 것 좀 줄게요.

(b) 그를 그렇게 비난하는 건 옳지 않아.

(c) 아니, 됐어요. 충분히 먹었어요.

(d) 당신 도움은 필요없어요.

정답_ (c)

12.

해석_ M: 오늘 밤 통금시간 지나서 집에 와도 돼요? 친구 생일이에요.

W: ______________________________

(a) 난 10시까지 돌아와야 해.

(b) 음, 그 경우엔 전화해. 데리러 갈게.

(c) 말이야 쉽지.

(d) 친구 좋다는 게 뭐니?

정답_ (b)

STEP 2 Dictation

정답_ 10. You should try to have a heart to heart
talk

11. No, thanks. I've had enough

12. in that case, you need to call me

STEP 3 Actual Test

1.

M: Can you make it to the baby shower this Sunday?

W: ______________________________

(a) She deserved to be punished for doing that.
(b) There is going to be a party the day after tomorrow.
(c) Sorry but I can't make it. I'm tied up that day.
(d) It's my turn to express my gratitude.

해석_ M: 이번주 일요일 베이비 샤워에 올 수 있어?

W: ______________________________

(a) 그녀는 그렇게 한 것에 대해 벌 받을 만했어.
(b) 모레 파티가 있을 거야.
(c) 미안하지만 못 가. 그날 바쁘거든.
(d) 내가 고마움을 전할 차례야.

해설_ 일요일에 있을 베이비 샤워에 오라고 초대하고 있으므로 갈 수 있는지 여부에 관해 언급한 선택지를 고르면 된다. Baby shower는 임신 7~8개월 된 예비 엄마와 곧 태어날 아기를 위한 축하 파티로, 이때 초대받은 사람들은 아기를 위한 선물을 준비해 간다.

어휘_ deserve ~할 만하다 be tied up 꼼짝 못하다, 바쁘다 express one's gratitude 감사의 마음을 표하다

정답_ (c)

2.

W: How about some beachcombing, John?
M: ______________________________

(a) Sure. Sounds exciting.
(b) I've got a beachball.
(c) I went to the beach last summer.
(d) Come to Byun-San beach. It's really good for swimming.

해석_ W: 존, 해변에서 조개 줍기 할래?

M: ______________________________

(a) 물론. 재밌겠다.
(b) 비치볼을 가지고 있어.
(c) 지난 여름에 해변에 갔었어.
(d) 변산 해수욕장에 오세요. 수영하기 정말 좋아요.

해설_ 해변에서 조개 줍기를 하자고 제안하고 있으므로 이에 동의를 하는 (a)가 정답이다. beachcomb은 해변을 돌아다니며 빗질하듯(comb) 물건을 줍는 것으로, 보통 예쁜 조개나 소라고둥을 찾는 것을 말한다.

어휘_ go to the beach 해변에 가다

정답_ (a)

3.

M: Would you give up everything to go to China with me?

W: ______________________________

(a) A piece of cake!
(b) At the drop of a hat.
(c) We are in the same boat.
(d) Just a stone's throw away.

해석_ M: 모든 걸 포기하고 저와 함께 중국에 가 주시겠어요?

W: ______________________________

(a) 누워서 떡 먹기죠!
(b) 기꺼이요.
(c) 우리는 같은 처지예요.
(d) 엎어지면 코 닿을 거리죠.

해설_ 함께 중국에 가자는 부탁에 기꺼이 응한 (b)가 정답이다. 각 선택지에 나온 관용 표현들을 잘 익혀 두자.

어휘_ a piece of cake 누워서 떡 먹기 at the drop of a hat 기꺼이, 즉시 in the same boat 같은 처지에 놓인 just a stone's throw away 엎어지면 코 닿을 거리

정답_ (b)

4.

W: Would you tell me a little more about this double-door refrigerator?

M: ______________________________

(a) You're telling me.
(b) Think nothing of it.
(c) That's not my area. I'll get someone.
(d) There are lots of refrigerator with doors.

해석_ W: 이 양문 냉장고에 대해 좀 더 말씀해 주실 수 있나요?

M: ______________________________

(a) 정말 그래요.
(b) 별거 아니에요.

(c) 그건 제 담당 분야가 아닙니다. 다른 사람을 불러 올게요.

(d) 문이 여러 개 달린 냉장고가 많이 있어요.

해설_ 냉장고에 대해 좀 더 설명해 달라고 부탁하고 있으므로 그것을 설명해 줄 수 있는 사람을 불러 오겠다고 응답한 (c)가 정답이다.

어휘_ double-door refrigerator 양문 냉장고

정답_ (c)

5.

W: Why don't you get married and settle down?
M: _______________________________________

(a) You must not leave the matter unsettled.
(b) I am going to Susan's wedding.
(c) I don't wanna give up my career. Leave me alone.
(d) The children settled down when we turned on the TV.

해석_ W: 결혼해서 자리 잡지 그래?
  M: _______________________________

(a) 그 문제를 미해결 상태로 둬선 안 돼요.
(b) 전 수잔의 결혼식에 갈 거예요.
(c) 제 일을 포기하고 싶지 않아요. 저 좀 내버려 두세요.
(d) 우리가 TV를 켜자 아이들이 조용해졌어요.

해설_ 결혼해서 안정을 찾으라는 권유에 대해 부정적인 의사를 표현하고 있는 (c)가 정답이다.

어휘_ settle down (결혼해서) 자리 잡다, 정착하다, 조용해지다
  unsettled 미해결의

정답_ (c)

Chapter 5 주제별 유형 익히기: 대인관계 Ⅱ

STEP 1 Pretest Clinic

13.

해석_ W: 무슨 일 있어?
  M: _________________________________

(a) 아무 일 없어. 그냥 일이 밀려서 그래.
(b) 흥분하지 마.
(c) 골칫거리라는 얘기는 아니야.
(d) 참 잘됐다.

정답_ (a)

14.

해석_ W: 나 갈 때까지 갔어. 더는 일 못하겠다.
  M: _________________________________

(a) 네가 비밀을 말해 버렸어.
(b) 행운은 용감한 사람에게만 오는 거야.
(c) 말도 안 돼. 넌 손가락 하나 까딱하지도 않았잖아.
(d) 넌 목발이 필요해.

정답_ (c)

15.

해석_ M: 난 음악을 그다지 좋아하지 않아요.
  W: _________________________________

(a) 음악가세요?
(b) 전 음치예요.
(c) 그는 록을 좋아하지만 그녀는 재즈를 좋아해요.
(d) 사람마다 취향이 다르죠.

정답_ (d)

STEP 2 Dictation

정답_ 13. I'm just backlogged with work

14. You didn't even lift a finger

15. I'm not big into music

1.

M: What's wrong with the connection?
W: _______________________________

(a) My battery was dead.
(b) I'll transfer your call.
(c) Where would you like it to be connected?
(d) I think we've got a crossed line.

해석_ M: 전화 상태가 왜 이렇죠?
   W: _______________________________

   (a) 배터리가 나갔어요.
   (b) 연결해 드리겠습니다.
   (c) 어디로 연결해 드릴까요?
   (d) 전화가 혼선된 것 같습니다.
해설_ 전화 연결 상태가 이상하다고 말하고 있으므로 이에 대한 원인
   을 언급한 (d)가 정답이다.
어휘_ crossed line (전화의) 혼선
정답_ (d)

2.

W: Could you put me through to personnel, please?
M: _______________________________

(a) I'm losing you.
(b) The line is not clear.
(c) I'll connect you.
(d) Can you hear me any better now?

해석_ W: 인사과로 연결해 주시겠습니까?
   M: _______________________________

   (a) 소리가 잘 안 들려요.
   (b) 전화 연결 상태가 좋지 않네요.
   (c) 연결해 드릴게요.
   (d) 이제 좀 잘 들립니까?
해설_ 여자가 전화 연결을 원하고 있으므로 이에 응하는 (c)가 정답이
   다. (a)는 전화가 잘 안 들릴 경우에, (b)는 전화 연결 상태가 좋
   지 않을 때 쓸 수 있는 표현이다.
어휘_ put ... through ~를 연결시키다 personnel 인사과
정답_ (c)

3.

M: I didn't know you had a knack for taking photos.
W: _______________________________

(a) Not really. I've never tried it.
(b) I am really into it.
(c) Whatever you like.
(d) I have no particular hobbies.

해석_ M: 네가 사진 찍는 데 솜씨가 있는지 몰랐어.
   W: _______________________________

   (a) 꼭 그렇진 않아. 그걸 해본 적이 한 번도 없어.
   (b) 사진 찍는 거에 푹 빠져 있거든.
   (c) 너 좋을대로 해.
   (d) 특별한 취미가 없어.
해설_ 사진 찍는 데 솜씨가 있는지 몰랐다고 말했으므로 사진 찍기에
   푹 빠져 있다는 (b)가 적절하다.
어휘_ knack 기교, 솜씨
정답_ (b)

4.

W: Have you been coughing up any phlegm?
M: _______________________________

(a) I had a urine test.
(b) I have a bad cold.
(c) No, but a lot of phlegm has been coming up.
(d) Yes, every time I cough.

해석_ W: 가래가 나온 적이 있습니까?
   M: _______________________________

   (a) 소변 검사를 했어요.
   (b) 지독한 감기에 걸렸어요.
   (c) 아뇨, 하지만 가래가 많이 나오고 있어요.
   (d) 네, 기침할 때마다요.
해설_ 가래가 나온 적이 있는지 묻고 있으므로 이에 답한 (d)가 정답이
   다.
어휘_ cough up phlegm 가래가 나오다 urine test 소변 검사
정답_ (d)

5.

M: Do you think it suits me better?

W: ______________________________

(a) No, she is going to sue for damages.
(b) Yes, it is perfect for you.
(c) I agree with you.
(d) I need a new outfit for my trip.

해석_ M: 그게 저한테 더 잘 어울린다고 생각하세요?

W: ______________________________

(a) 아니오, 그녀는 손해배상 소송을 제기할 거예요.

(b) 네, 당신에게 완벽하게 어울려요.

(c) 동감이에요.

(d) 여행 갈 때 입을 새 옷 한 벌이 필요해요.

해설_ 옷이 잘 어울리는지 의견을 묻고 있으므로 이에 답한 (b)가 정답이다.

어휘_ sue for damages 손해배상 소송을 제기하다   outfit 의상 한 벌

정답_ (b)

6.

W: Did you know that he is considering running for office for the Mulberry county?

M: ______________________________

(a) Yes, he has lived here for a while.
(b) I haven't seen him for a long time.
(c) No, but I think he is qualified for that.
(d) He has run his own business for years.

해석_ W: 그가 멀버리 카운티를 위해 출마를 고려하고 있다는 사실을 알고 있었어요?

M: ______________________________

(a) 네, 그는 한동안 여기 살았어요.

(b) 전 오랫동안 그를 못 봤어요.

(c) 아니오, 하지만 그가 출마할 자격이 있다고 생각해요.

(d) 그는 수년간 자기 사업을 운영했어요.

해설_ 출마를 고려 중이라는 사실을 알고 있었는지 여부에 대해 묻고 있으므로 Yes/No로 응답한 (a)와 (c) 중 하나가 정답인데, (a)는 질문 내용과 상관이 없으므로 정답은 (c)가 된다.

어휘_ run for office 출마하다   for a while 한동안, 잠시

정답_ (c)

Chapter 6 주제별 유형 익히기: 사회관계

STEP 1 Pretest Clinic

16.

해석_ W: 그가 왜 해고됐지?

M: ______________________________

(a) 무슨 일이 있었는지 정확히는 모르지만, 그는 아주 게을렀어.

(b) 그건 나중에 해.

(c) 그는 장작을 패야 했어.

(d) 도움이 됐다니 너무 기쁘다.

정답_ (a)

17.

해석_ M: 그것들이 최저가에 판매되고 있어.

W: ______________________________

(a) 그들은 욕심이 너무 많아.

(b) 이 방바닥은 불편해.

(c) 그 얘기 꺼내지도 마.

(d) 가서 좀 사자.

정답_ (d)

18.

해석_ W: 오늘 점심은 제가 살게요.

M: ______________________________

(a) 보통 계산서의 10% 를 팁으로 줍니다.

(b) 각자 냅시다.

(c) 이 지역에서 가장 고급 레스토랑이에요.

(d) 전 단 것을 좋아해요.

정답_ (b)

STEP 2 Dictation

정답_ 16. Why did he get axed

17. selling at rockbottom prices

18. I'll buy the lunch today

STEP 3 Actual Test

1.

M: Please remove the contents of your bag and walk through the metal detecter.

W: _______________________________________

(a) I packed this luggage myself.
(b) The metal detecter isn't working.
(c) Okay. Just a moment please.
(d) We need to run your baggage through the X-ray scanner.

해석_ M: 가방 안의 내용물을 꺼내시고 금속 탐지기를 통과해 주십시오.

W: _______________________________

(a) 제가 이 짐을 꾸렸어요.
(b) 금속 탐지기가 고장 났어요.
(c) 알겠어요. 잠시만 기다려 주세요.
(d) 당신의 짐을 엑스레이 검사기로 살펴봐야 합니다.

해설_ 공항 검색대에서 접할 수 있는 대화 내용으로, 검색요원이 소지품을 꺼내고 금속 탐지기를 통과해 달라고 요청하고 있으므로 이에 응하는 선택지를 고르면 된다.

어휘_ walk through ~을 통과하다 metal detecter 금속 탐지기 pack (짐을) 꾸리다 X-ray scanner 엑스레이 검색대

정답_ (c)

2.

W: I feel like throwing up.

M: _______________________________________

(a) Do you need an air sickness bag?
(b) You make me ill.
(c) Put your hands up.
(d) No wonder you got sick.

해석_ W: 토할 것 같아.

M: _______________________________

(a) 비행기 멀미용 봉투가 필요하니?
(b) 넌 날 기분 나쁘게 해.
(c) 양손을 위로 올려.
(d) 네가 병난 것도 무리가 아니지.

해설_ 토할 것 같다고 했으므로 멀미용 봉투가 필요한지 묻는 (a)가 가장 자연스럽다.

어휘_ throw up 토하다 air sickness bag 비행기 멀미용 봉투 no wonder ... ~하는 것이 당연하다

정답_ (a)

3.

M: Could you get me a continental breakfast?

W: _______________________________________

(a) I'd like to order a ham sandwich and a cup of coffee.
(b) I don't like American breakfasts.
(c) I want to skip breakfast.
(d) Yes. Is that all?

해석_ M: 유럽식 아침 식사를 갖다주실래요?

W: _______________________________

(a) 햄 샌드위치와 커피 한 잔 주세요.
(b) 난 미국식 아침 식사를 좋아하지 않아요.
(c) 아침을 거르고 싶어요.
(d) 네. 더 주문하실 거 없으세요?

해설_ 아침 식사를 주문하고 있으므로 이에 응하는 종업원의 말이 이어져야 자연스럽다. 따라서 정답은 (d).

어휘_ continental breakfast 유럽식 아침 식사(커피나 홍차, 그리고 빵 종류로 구성된 간단한 식사) American breakfast 미국식 아침 식사(계란요리, 햄, 베이컨, 과일 등을 곁들인 식사) skip (식사 등을) 거르다

정답_ (d)

4.

W: Are you sure you are able to find a job?

M: _______________________________________

(a) Honestly speaking, chances are looking pretty slim.
(b) The customer is always right.
(c) I have done well until now.
(d) I'm sure nobody wants to work there.

해석_ W: 너 일자리 구할 수 있는 게 확실해?

M: _______________________________

(a) 솔직히 말하면, 가능성이 아주 희박해 보여.
(b) 손님은 왕이야.
(c) 이제까지 일을 잘해 왔어.
(d) 아무도 거기서 일하고 싶어 하지 않는 게 분명해.

해설_ Are you sure...?는 sure 이하의 내용이 믿기지 않거나 놀라울 때 정말인지 확인하는 표현이다. 여기서는 일자리를 구할 수 있는 게 확실한지 묻고 있으므로 이에 관해 언급한 선택지를 고르면 된다.

어휘_ slim (가망 등이) 아주 적은 The customer is always right. 손님은 왕이다.

정답_ (a)

5.

M: We can't find the right person to replace Sam.

W: ________________________________

(a) That job suits you.
(b) He's a morning person.
(c) Keep on trying. We need someone as soon as possible.
(d) I need to replace the vase I broke.

해설_ M: 샘을 대신할 적합한 사람을 찾을 수가 없어.

　　 W: ________________________________

　　 (a) 그 일은 네게 적합해.
　　 (b) 그는 아침형 인간이야.
　　 (c) 계속 애써 줘. 우린 되도록 빨리 다른 사람이 필요해.
　　 (d) 내가 깨뜨린 꽃병을 바꿔야 해.

해설_ 대신 일할 사람을 찾을 수 없다고 했으므로, 이어질 응답으로는 계속 애써 달라고 부탁하는 (c)가 적절하다.

어휘_ replace 대신하다, 제자리에 놓다, 바꾸다 morning person 아침형 인간

정답_ (c)

6.

W: Is there anything I can do to make up for this test?

M: ________________________________

(a) He does not allow to make up exams.
(b) You are just paying lip service to me.
(c) I can't pinpoint it.
(d) You can write a paper.

해설_ W: 이 시험을 보충할 방법이 없을까요?

　　 M: ________________________________

　　 (a) 그는 재시험 치르는 걸 허용하지 않아요.

(b) 입에 발린 소리만 하는군요.
(c) 뭐라 딱 꼬집어 말할 수가 없네요.
(d) 리포트를 쓰면 돼요.

해설_ 시험을 보충할 방법을 묻고 있으므로 (d)가 적절한 응답이다.

어휘_ make up for ~을 보상[보충]하다 make up (시험을) 다시 치르다 pay lip service 입에 발린 소리를 하다 pinpoint 정확하게 지적하다

정답_ (d)

7.

M: No one backed me up on my proposal at the meeting.

W: ________________________________

(a) Back off with the accusations.
(b) There's some problems in your proposal.
(c) I've got a back up plan.
(d) How do I get my chair to go back up?

해설_ M: 회의 때 아무도 내 제안에 대해 지지해 주지 않았어요.

　　 W: ________________________________

　　 (a) 비난하는 걸 그만둬요.
　　 (b) 당신 제안에 몇 가지 문제점이 있어서 그래요.
　　 (c) 대비책이 있어요.
　　 (d) 의자를 어떻게 다시 바로 세우나요?

해설_ 자신의 제안을 아무도 지지해 주지 않았다는 불평에 그 이유를 언급하고 있는 (b)가 정답이다. (d)는 기내에서 승객이 의자 올리는 버튼을 못 찾았을 경우 승무원에게 의자를 어떻게 하면 원래대로 세울 수 있는지 물을 때 사용할 수 있는 표현이다.

어휘_ back up 지지하다, 후진하다 back off 뒤로 물러서다 accusation 비난, 고발 back up plan 대비책

정답_ (b)

8.

W: Professor George, can I sit in on your Ecology class lecture?

M: ________________________________

(a) Sure, thanks for coming by.
(b) Yes, it's been a pleasure talking to you.
(c) Why not? Everyone is welcome to my lectures.
(d) Well, it's up to you.

해석_ W: 조지 교수님, 제가 교수님의 생태학 수업 강의를 청강해도
　　　되나요?

　　　M: _______________________________

　　　(a) 물론이죠, 들러 주셔서 감사합니다.

　　　(b) 네, 얘기 즐거웠습니다.

　　　(c) 물론이지. 내 강의는 누구나 들을 수 있네.

　　　(d) 음, 그건 당신한테 달렸어요.

해설_ 청강을 해도 되는지 허락을 구하고 있으므로 이에 응하는 (c)가
　　　정답이다.

어휘_ sit in on a class 청강을 하다　ecology 생태학　come
　　　by 지나는 길에 들르다

정답_ (c)

9.

M: I'm just browsing.

W: _______________________________

(a) You can browse all kind of models.

(b) It's out of my price range.

(c) I'll go check if we have some in stock.

(d) Well, take your time and call me if you need
　　any help.

해석_ M: 그냥 둘러보는 거예요.

　　　W: _______________________________

　　　(a) 모든 종류의 모델을 살펴보실 수 있습니다.

　　　(b) 너무 비싸서 못 사겠어요.

　　　(c) 재고가 있는지 가서 확인해 볼게요.

　　　(d) 음, 천천히 보시다가 도움이 필요하시면 절 부르세요.

해설_ I'm just browsing.은 I'm just looking.과 마찬가지 표현으로
　　　'그냥 구경 중이다'라는 뜻이다. 따라서 이어질 응답으로는 구
　　　경하다가 도움이 필요하면 부르라는 (d)가 적절하다.

어휘_ out of one's price range 너무 비싸 못 사다, 가격이 예산
　　　을 넘어서다

정답_ (d)

Chapter 7 주제별 유형 익히기:
공공관계

STEP 1 Pretest Clinic

19.

해석_ W: 아담, 왜 다리를 절뚝거리고 있니?

　　　M: _______________________________

　　　(a) 그는 중태야.

　　　(b) 그녀는 과로로 지쳤어.

　　　(c) 발이 저려.

　　　(d) 너 몸 상태가 안 좋아 보여.

정답_ (c)

20.

해석_ M: 일찍 출발해서 교통혼잡을 피해야 할 것 같아.

　　　W: _______________________________

　　　(a) 그럼, 여기서 우회하세요.

　　　(b) 그들은 도로를 다시 포장했어.

　　　(c) 걱정 마. 이 차는 연비가 아주 좋아.

　　　(d) 네 말에 전적으로 동의해.

정답_ (d)

21.

해석_ W: 머리를 어떻게 해드릴까요?

　　　M: _______________________________

　　　(a) 그녀는 머리끝이 갈라졌어요.

　　　(b) 앞머리하는 게 어때?

　　　(c) 층을 내주세요.

　　　(d) 기운 내.

정답_ (c)

STEP 2 Dictation

정답_ 19. My leg is asleep

　　　20. we should get a head start to beat
　　　　　traffic

　　　21. How would you like your hair done

1.

W: There was a car accident at the junction.

M: _______________________________

(a) Oh, no. We should be careful.
(b) The cars are in a rush.
(c) The police are chasing a sports car.
(d) I guess the traffic lights aren't working.

해석_ W: 교차로에서 교통사고가 있었어.

　　　 M: _______________________________

　　　 (a) 저런. 우리도 조심해야 해.
　　　 (b) 차들이 빠르게 달리고 있어.
　　　 (c) 경찰들이 스포츠카 한 대를 뒤쫓고 있어.
　　　 (d) 교통신호가 고장 난 것 같아.

해석_ 교차로에서의 사고 소식을 들었으므로 우리도 조심해야 한다는
　　　 (a)가 가장 적절하다.

어휘_ junction 교차로　in a rush 서둘러, 분주히　chase
　　　 뒤쫓다

정답_ (a)

2.

M: This is a dead end.

W: _______________________________

(a) Keep going straight.
(b) This is the passing lane.
(c) This lane is only for buses.
(d) Then, hang a U-turn.

해석_ M: 여긴 막다른 길이야.

　　　 W: _______________________________

　　　 (a) 쭉 가.
　　　 (b) 이건 추월 차선이야.
　　　 (c) 이 차선은 버스 전용 차선이야.
　　　 (d) 그럼 유턴해.

해석_ 길이 막혀 있다고 말했으므로 다시 돌아서 가자는 (d)가 적절하
　　　 다.

어휘_ dead end 막다른 길　passing lane 추월 차선　hang a
　　　 U-turn 유턴하다

정답_ (d)

3.

W: Excuse me. Can you direct me to the nearest real estate agent, please?

M: _______________________________

(a) Actually, I moonlight as a real estate agent.
(b) Yes. Bear right and go straight until you come across a fork.
(c) I have to go house-hunting.
(d) That's a direct flight.

해석_ W: 실례합니다. 가장 가까운 부동산으로 가는 길을 알려주시겠
　　　 어요?

　　　 M: _______________________________

　　　 (a) 실은, 부업으로 부동산 중개업을 해요.
　　　 (b) 네. 오른쪽으로 돌아서 두 갈래 길이 나올 때까지 쭉 가세요.
　　　 (c) 집 구하러 가야 해요.
　　　 (d) 그건 직항편이에요.

해석_ 길을 묻고 있으므로 가는 방법을 알려주는 선택지를 고르면 된
　　　 다.

어휘_ real estate agent 부동산 중개업　moonlight 부업하다
　　　 bear right 우측으로 돌다 (= turn right)　fork 두 갈래 길
　　　 go house-hunting 집 구하러 가다　direct flight 직항편

정답_ (b)

4.

M: I have a bad sense of direction.

W: _______________________________

(a) Stop bragging about yourself.
(b) No one could make sense of it.
(c) Don't worry. We've got GPS.
(d) Aren't you an assistant director?

해석_ M: 난 길눈이 어두워.

　　　 W: _______________________________

　　　 (a) 허풍 떨지 마.
　　　 (b) 아무도 그걸 이해할 수 없었어.
　　　 (c) 걱정 마. 우리에겐 네비게이션이 있잖아.
　　　 (d) 넌 조감독이지 않아?

해석_ 길눈이 어둡다고 했으므로 이에 관한 해결책이나 조언이 담긴
　　　 선택지를 고르면 된다.

어휘_ brag about ~에 대해 허풍을 떨다　make sense 이해하
　　　 다　GPS (= Global Positioning System) 네비게이션

assistant director 조감독

정답_ (c)

5.

W: I think I might have thrown a disc.

M: _______________________________

(a) When did you last see it?
(b) Ok, but we should take a X-ray to confirm it.
(c) It throbs with pain.
(d) It's not so severe that I can't put up with it.

해석_ W: 제 생각엔 디스크에 걸린 게 아닌가 싶은데요.

M: _______________________________

(a) 그걸 마지막으로 봤던 게 언제죠?
(b) 알겠어요, 하지만 확인을 위해 엑스레이를 찍어야 합니다.
(c) 쑤시듯 아파요.
(d) 참을 수 없을 정도로 아주 심하진 않아요.

해설_ 병원에서 이루어지는 대화다. 환자가 디스크인 것 같다고 말했으므로 디스크가 맞는지 확인차 엑스레이를 찍어야 한다는 (b)가 적절하다.

어휘_ throw a disc 디스크에 걸리다 take a X-ray 엑스레이 촬영을 하다 *cf.* run a CT scan CT 촬영을 하다 throb 욱신욱신 쑤시다 put up with ~을 참다

정답_ (b)

6.

M: I'd like to do a biopsy on that tumor on your arm, Sara.

W: _______________________________

(a) Is it malignant?
(b) Can you put your clothes back on?
(c) Shall I take it down to the lab?
(d) Shall we schedule an appointment?

해석_ M: 사라, 당신 팔에 있는 종양에 대해 조직 검사를 해야겠어요.

W: _______________________________

(a) 악성인가요?
(b) 옷을 다시 입어 주시겠어요?
(c) 그걸 실험실로 가져갈까요?
(d) 약속 시간을 잡을까요?

해설_ 조직 검사를 해야겠다는 의사의 말에 걱정이 됐을 것이므로 악성인지 묻는 (a)가 적절하다.

어휘_ biopsy 조직 검사 tumor 종양 malignant 악성의 lab 실험실 schedule an appointment 약속 시간을 잡다

정답_ (a)

7.

W: What do you think of her new hairdo?

M: _______________________________

(a) I'll remove your rollers in 20 minutes.
(b) It fits her well.
(c) Your hair needs softening first.
(d) Sure. Please take your hairpin out.

해석_ W: 그녀의 새로운 헤어스타일 어때요?

M: _______________________________

(a) 20분 후에 롤을 제거해 드리겠습니다.
(b) 그녀와 잘 어울려요.
(c) 먼저 연화를 해드리겠습니다.
(d) 네. 머리핀을 빼주세요.

해설_ 그녀의 새로운 헤어스타일이 어떤지 묻고 있으므로 이에 관한 의견이 담긴 선택지를 고르면 된다.

어휘_ hairdo 헤어스타일 remove 제거하다 softening 연화 take out 빼다

정답_ (b)

8.

M: I am anxious about the results of her medical tests.

W: _______________________________

(a) Don't worry. She got a clean bill of health.
(b) You have to wear a cast for a month.
(c) Fine, but it still itches a little bit.
(d) I think so.

해석_ M: 그녀의 건강 검진 결과가 걱정돼요.

W: _______________________________

(a) 걱정 마세요. 그녀는 건강에 아무 이상 없어요.
(b) 당신은 한 달간 깁스를 해야 해요.
(c) 좋아요, 하지만 아직 좀 가려워요.
(d) 전 그렇게 생각해요.

Part 2

Chapter 8 주제별 유형 익히기 : 대인관계 I

STEP 1 Pretest Clinic

1.

해석_ W: 다음주 파티에 새 봄 드레스를 입을까 해.

M: 기다리는 게 좋을 거야. 아직 날씨가 많이 추워.

W: 패션을 위해서라면 참을 수 있어.

M: ___________________________

(a) 나한테 화풀이하지 마.

(b) 그 드레스는 너한테 정말 잘 어울려.

(c) 많이 아프니?

(d) 결정은 네가 해. 하지만 감기 걸릴지도 몰라.

정답_ (d)

2.

해석_ M: 제인이 밥을 잘 안 먹는 것 같네요. 음식 가지고 그저 장난치고 있어요.

W: 네, 식성이 까다롭죠. 애 식습관이 정말 걱정스러워요.

M: 언제 우리 집에 오실래요? 그녀를 위해 맛있는 요리를 해줄 수 있어요.

W: ___________________________

(a) 그녀가 밤늦게 간식을 먹어서 그래요.

(b) 먹는 것을 조심해야 해요.

(c) 이거 맛있네요!

(d) 제안에 감사드려요. 당신은 정말 친절하군요.

정답_ (d)

3.

해석_ M: 너 아니? 넌 내가 아는 가장 멋진 사람 중 하나야.

W: 고마워, 근데 속셈이 뭐야?

M: 없어. 진심으로 하는 말이야.

W: ___________________________

(a) 그렇게 말하다니 무례하구나.

(b) 미안하지만, 널 도와줄 수 없어.

(c) 좋아. 칭찬으로 받아들일게.

(d) 이 점은 믿길 바래.

정답_ (c)

해설_ 어떤 여자의 건강 검진 결과를 걱정하고 있으므로 이에 관해 안심시키는 내용이 이어져야 적절하다. 따라서 정답은 (a)로, '건강을 보증하는 증명서(a clean bill)를 받았다', 즉 '건강에 아무 이상이 없다'는 뜻이 담겨 있다.

어휘_ be anxious about ~에 대해 걱정하다 a clean bill of health 건강 증명서 wear a cast 깁스를 하다 itch 가렵다

정답_ (a)

STEP 2 Dictation

정답_ 1. suffer for the sake of fashion
  It's up to you

2. she's a picky eater
  Come over to my house sometime

3. what's the catch
  take it as a compliment

STEP 3 Actual Test

1.

W: Oh, my! What brings you here?
M: I've got to replace my garage door opener.
  So I'm going to the hardware store.
W: Oh, I see. I heard you opened a new store.
  How's business?
M: ________________________________

(a) So far so good.
(b) Well, it looks like we need an extra hand.
(c) Good luck to you.
(d) Mind your own business.

해석_ W: 어머! 네가 여기 웬일이니?
  M: 차고문 개폐기를 교체해야 해. 그래서 철물점에 가는 길이야.
  W: 아, 그렇구나. 새 가게 열었다면서. 장사는 잘되니?
  M: ________________________________

  (a) 지금까진 좋아.
  (b) 음, 일손이 더 필요한 것 같아.
  (c) 행운을 빌어.
  (d) 네 일이나 신경 써.
해설_ 장사가 잘되는지 묻고 있으므로 이에 관해 언급한 (a)가 적절하다.
어휘_ garage door opener 차고문 개폐기 hardware store 철물점 extra hand 여분의 일손
정답_ (a)

2.

W: What's this? A flower basket?
M: I want to apologize for forgetting our
  wedding anniversary.
W: Never mind. I already forgot.
M: ________________________________

(a) I'm really sorry. I won't forget again.
(b) I'm sorry, I was someplace else.
(c) Drop by drop fills the tub.
(d) Don't kid yourself.

해석_ W: 이게 뭐야? 꽃바구니?
  M: 우리 결혼기념일 잊어버린 거 사과하고 싶어.
  W: 신경 쓰지 마. 이미 잊었어.
  M: ________________________________

  (a) 정말 미안해. 다신 안 잊을게.
  (b) 미안, 다시 한 번 말해 줘.
  (c) 티끌모아 태산이야.
  (d) 어림없는 소리 마.
해설_ 결혼기념일을 잊어버린 것에 대해 남자가 사과를 하는 상황이므로 (a)가 적절하다.
어휘_ Drop by drop fills the tub. 〈속담〉 티끌모아 태산.
  Don't kid yourself. 어림없는 소리 마.
정답_ (a)

3.

W: Let me have a whisky on the rocks.
M: Here's your drink. Can I get you anything
  else?
W: No, but when my friends show up, would
  you show them to this table?
M: ________________________________

(a) Certainly, ma'am. I'll take care of that.
(b) Ok, I'll reserve a table for the party.
(c) You should place your order in advance.
(d) I'll pick up the tab.

해석_ W: 얼음 넣은 위스키 주세요.
  M: 여기 있습니다. 그 밖에 뭐 필요하신 거 있으세요?
  W: 아뇨, 근데 제 친구들이 오면 이 테이블로 안내 좀 해주시겠
  어요?
  M: ________________________________

(a) 물론입니다. 그렇게 해드릴게요.

(b) 좋아요, 파티를 위해 테이블을 예약할게요.

(c) 미리 주문하셔야 해요.

(d) 제가 계산할게요.

해설_ 친구들이 오면 자신이 있는 테이블로 안내해 달라고 부탁하고
있으므로 이에 응하는 선택지를 고르면 된다.

어휘_ on the rocks 얼음을 넣은 show up 나타나다 place
one's order 주문하다 in advance 미리 pick up the
tab 계산하다

정답_ (a)

4.

M: We need to talk. I have an ax to grind with
you.
W: What is it now?
M: You shouldn't have raised your voice to the
boss. That was out of line.
W: _______________________________________

(a) I was showing who's boss.
(b) Actually, I was in an incredible hurry.
(c) Yeah, I suppose you're right.
(d) Would you like to sleep on it, then?

해석_ M: 우리 얘기 좀 해요. 당신한테 따질 게 있어요.

W: 또 왜 그래요?

M: 사장한테 그렇게 언성을 높이지 말았어야 했어요. 그건 도가
지나쳤어요.

W: _______________________

(a) 누가 사장인지 보여 주고 있었어요.

(b) 실은, 굉장히 서둘렀어요.

(c) 네, 당신 말이 맞는 것 같네요.

(d) 그럼 좀 더 생각해 볼래요?

해설_ 사장한테 언성을 높인 건 심했다는 남자의 말에 수긍하는 (c)가
적절하다.

어휘_ have an ax to grind 따질 게 있다, 딴 속셈이 있다 raise
one's voice 언성을 높이다 out of line 도가 지나친
incredible 굉장한, 놀라운 sleep on 곰곰이 생각하다

정답_ (c)

5.

W: Let's throw a party for your promotion.
M: How would you prepare it?
W: What about calling a catering service?

M: _______________________________________

(a) Good idea. You took the words out of my
mouth.
(b) I won't stand in the way. You can prepare
a feast by yourself.
(c) You're such a party pooper!
(d) The catering service was excellent.

해석_ W: 당신 승진 파티 열자.

M: 어떻게 준비할 건데?

W: 출장 연회 서비스 부르는 거 어때?

M: _______________________________

(a) 좋은 생각이야. 내가 먼저 말하려고 했는데.

(b) 말리지 않을게. 당신 혼자 연회를 준비하면 돼.

(c) 당신은 정말 분위기 망치는 데 뭐 있어!

(d) 출장 연회 서비스가 아주 훌륭했어.

해설_ 출장 연회 서비스를 부르는 것에 대한 의견을 묻고 있으므로 이
에 동조하는 (a)가 정답이다. take the words out of one's
mouth는 '남이 하려는 말을 앞질러 말하다'의 뜻으로, 즉 자신
이 먼저 출장 연회 서비스를 부르자고 말하려고 했었다는 의미
가 담겨 있다.

어휘_ throw a party 파티를 열다 catering service 출장 연회
서비스 stand in the way 방해가 되다 feast 축하연, 연
회 party pooper 분위기 깨는 사람

정답_ (a)

6.

M: Are you free this Saturday?
W: Sure. I'm off that day.
M: We're having a homecoming party.
Can you come?
W: _______________________________________

(a) It doesn't ring a bell.
(b) Why not? I'm looking forward to it.
(c) I have already been to the party last week.
(d) I'm afraid I'll be working.

해석_ M: 이번주 토요일에 한가하니?

W: 응. 그날 쉬어.

M: 동창회를 열 예정이야. 올 수 있어?

W: _______________________

(a) 생각 안 나.

(b) 물론이지. 기대하고 있어.

(c) 난 지난주에 이미 그 파티에 다녀왔어.

(d) 유감이지만, 일하고 있을 거야.

해설_ 파티에 초대하고 있으므로 이에 응하는 (b)가 정답이다.

어휘_ homecoming party 동창회 ring a bell 생각나다

정답_ (b)

7.

M: Isn't this Ray's cellphone?

W: Yes, it is. Ray went to the garage to tune up his car.

M: This is Herald. Could you tell him to call me back?

W: _______________________________________

(a) Let me check if he's here.

(b) He left the company for another job.

(c) He went on a business trip to Italy.

(d) Sure. I'll have him call you back.

해설_ M: 레이 휴대폰 아닌가요?

　　W: 네, 맞아요. 레이는 차 엔진 점검하려고 카센터에 갔어요.

　　M: 전 헤럴드예요. 저에게 전화하라고 전해 주시겠어요?

　　W: _______________________________

　　(a) 그가 여기 있는지 확인해 볼게요.

　　(b) 그는 다른 직장에 나가려고 회사를 그만뒀어요.

　　(c) 그는 이탈리아로 출장 갔어요.

　　(d) 네. 당신에게 전화하라고 할게요.

해설_ 전화해 달라고 그에게 전해 줄 것을 부탁하고 있으므로 이에 응하는 (d)가 정답이다.

어휘_ garage (자동차) 정비 공장(= repair shop) tune up (엔진 등을) 점검하다

정답_ (d)

8.

W: It's just not my day today.

M: You seem out of sorts. What's the problem?

W: The brand-new toilet is broken already. Would you mind if I ask you to fix it?

M: _______________________________________

(a) You look upset.

(b) I don't have any medicine.

(c) I'm all thumbs. We'd better call someone.

(d) Sure. I'll buy a new toilet.

해설_ W: 오늘은 정말 되는 일이 없네.

　　M: 언짢아 보이는데. 무슨 일이야?

　　W: 새 변기가 벌써 고장 났어. 좀 고쳐 줄래?

　　M: _______________________________

　　(a) 화나 보인다.

　　(b) 가지고 있는 약이 없어.

　　(c) 나 손재주 없잖아. 다른 사람을 부르는 게 좋겠어.

　　(d) 물론이지. 내가 새 변기 사 줄게.

해설_ 변기를 고쳐 달라고 부탁하고 있으므로 이를 거절하는 (c)가 정답이다. be all thumbs는 '서투르다', '손재주가 전혀 없다'란 뜻으로, 즉 자기는 못 고치니까 다른 사람을 부르는 게 좋겠다는 얘기를 하고 있다.

어휘_ out of sorts 기분이 언짢은 brand-new 새로운, 신품의

정답_ (c)

9.

M: I love this party's atmosphere.

W: I think we need some entertainment, though.

M: Why don't you dance for us?

W: _______________________________________

(a) All right. I'll play the piano.

(b) Sorry. I'm good at dancing.

(c) I can't carry a tune.

(d) Of course, I'd be happy to.

해설_ M: 이 파티 분위기가 너무 맘에 들어.

　　W: 하지만 오락거리가 좀 있어야 할 것 같아.

　　M: 우리를 위해 춤 추는 게 어때?.

　　W: _______________________________

　　(a) 좋아. 내가 피아노 연주를 할게.

　　(b) 미안. 나 춤 잘 춰.

　　(c) 나 음치야.

　　(d) 물론, 기꺼이 출 거야.

해설_ 춤을 춰보라는 권유에 기꺼이 응한 (d)가 정답이다.

어휘_ entertainment 오락(거리) carry a tune (가락을 틀리지 않고) 정확히 노래하다

정답_ (d)

Chapter 9 주제별 유형 익히기: 대인관계 II

STEP 1 Pretest Clinic

4.

해석_ M: 얼마나 넣어 드릴까요?

　　 W: 10달러어치 넣어 주세요.

　　 M: 알겠습니다. 그리고 어떤 종류로 넣어 드릴까요?
　　　　 일반이요, 고급이요?

　　 W: _______________________________

　　 (a) 둘 다 좋아요.

　　 (b) 가득 채워 주세요.

　　 (c) 오일을 점검해 드릴까요?

　　 (d) 무연 보통으로 주세요.

정답_ (d)

5.

해석_ M: 밖을 내다봐! 제발 네가 어디로 가고 있는지 주의해서 보라
　　　　 고!

　　 W: 진정해. 닿을 정도는 아니었다고.

　　 M: 뭐라고? 우리가 그 여자한테 끼어들어서 거의 칠 뻔했잖아.

　　 W: _______________________________

　　 (a) 그녀는 곧 나을 거야.

　　 (b) 그냥 할퀸 자국이야.

　　 (c) 알았어, 속도를 줄일게. 잔소리 좀 그만해.

　　 (d) 썩 재밌었어.

정답_ (c)

6.

해석_ W: 내 컴퓨터에 무슨 문제가 있는 거니?

　　 M: 하드 드라이브가 완전 고장 난 것 같아.

　　 W: 이런. 어떡해야 할까?

　　 M: _______________________________

　　 (a) 네가 무슨 생각하는지 내가 어떻게 알아?

　　 (b) 아직 품질 보증 기간이니?

　　 (c) 네 핸드폰 번호 알려줘.

　　 (d) 나한테 도와 달라고 그만 부탁해.

정답_ (b)

STEP 2 Dictation

정답_ 4. I'd like ten bucks worth
　　　　 Regular unleaded

　　 5. We cut her off
　　　　 I'll ease off the gas

　　 6. there's been a complete hard drive failure
　　　　 Is it still under warranty

STEP 3 Actual Test

1.

M: Thank you for your hospitality.
W: It was my pleasure.
M: Next time, I would invite you to my house.
W: _______________________________

(a) Hang loose.
(b) Don't overstay your welcome.
(c) I'll be looking forward to your invitation.
(d) Get off my back.

해석_ M: 환대에 감사드려요.

　　 W: 별말씀을요.

　　 M: 다음번엔 저희 집으로 초대할게요.

　　 W: _______________________________

　　 (a) 좀 편히 쉬고 있어요.

　　 (b) 너무 오래 머물러 눈총받지 말아요.

　　 (c) 당신의 초대를 기대하고 있을게요.

　　 (d) 이제 날 그만 괴롭혀요.

해설_ 다음엔 자신의 집으로 초대하겠다고 말했으므로 기대하고 있겠
　　　 다는 (c)가 적절하다.

어휘_ hang loose 긴장을 풀다, 쉬다　 overstay one's
　　　 welcome 너무 오래 머물러서 미움받다　 get off one's
　　　 back ~를 그만 괴롭히다

정답_ (c)

2.

W: Please, forgive my rude remarks.
M: I should apologize for my comments, too.
W: It just slipped out of my mouth.
M: _______________________________

(a) Catch you late.
(b) Beat it!
(c) Better late than never.
(d) Same here. I was careless when I said that.

해석_ W: 저의 거친 언사를 용서해 주세요.

　　　 M: 저도 제 언사에 대해 사과드려요.

　　　 W: 그건 입에서 그냥 나오는 대로 한 말이었어요.

　　　 M: _______________________________

　　　 (a) 나중에 보자구요.

　　　 (b) 꺼져!

　　　 (c) 늦더라도 안 하는 것보다 나아요.

　　　 (d) 저도 마찬가지예요. 그렇게 말한 건 제가 부주의한 탓이에요.

해설_ 남자와 여자가 서로 사과하는 상황이므로, 이어질 응답으로 자
　　　 연스러운 건 (d)다. Same here.는 '나도 마찬가지다' 라는 뜻으
　　　 로 상대방의 말에 간단히 동조할 때 쓸 수 있는 표현이다.

어휘_ rude remarks 무례한 언사 slip out of ~에서 미끄러지
　　　 듯 나가다 Catch you late. 나중에 보자. Beat it! 꺼져!

정답_ (d)

3.

M: You got all these dents and scratches on
　 your car.
W: I was rear-ended. Can you give me an
　 estimate?
M: It'll cost you 400 dollars.
W: _______________________________

(a) I got caught speeding yesterday.
(b) What? That's a rip off.
(c) You ran the red light.
(d) He was fined for DUI.

해석_ M: 차가 찌그러지고 긁혔네요.

　　　 W: 뒤에서 박았어요. 견적을 내주시겠어요?

　　　 M: 400달러가 들 겁니다.

　　　 W: _______________________________

　　　 (a) 어제 과속으로 걸렸어요.

　　　 (b) 뭐라고요? 이거 완전 바가지군.

　　　 (c) 당신은 적신호를 무시했어요.

　　　 (d) 그는 음주운전으로 벌금을 물었어요.

해설_ 견적비가 400달러라는 얘기를 들었으므로 이에 대한 반응이 이
　　　 어져야 적절하다. 따라서 너무 비싼 견적비에 놀라는 (b)가 정답
　　　 이다.

어휘_ dent 옴폭 들어간 곳 rear-end (차가) ~에 추돌하다 give
　　　 an estimate 견적을 내다 a rip off 바가지 run the red
　　　 light 적신호를 무시하다 fine ~에게 벌금을 과하다 DUI
　　　 (= driving under the influence of drug or alcohol)
　　　 음주운전

정답_ (b)

4.

W: Have you made any international calls since
　 you've been here?
M: Sure. The rates are pretty reasonable.
W: How can I make a call to Japan?
M: _______________________________

(a) I just called my parents in Iceland.
(b) Just dial 001 before the number.
(c) I'll put you through when she is ready.
(d) Hold on a sec.

해석_ W: 여기 온 후로 국제전화 해봤어?

　　　 M: 물론. 요금이 싸던데.

　　　 W: 일본으로 전화하려면 어떻게 해야 돼?

　　　 M: _______________________________

　　　 (a) 아이슬란드에 계신 부모님께 전화드렸어.

　　　 (b) 전화 번호 앞에 001을 돌리기만 하면 돼.

　　　 (c) 그녀가 준비되면 연결해 드릴게요.

　　　 (d) 잠깐 기다려.

해설_ 일본으로 국제전화 거는 방법을 묻고 있으므로 이에 관해 알려
　　　 주는 선택지를 고르면 된다. (d)의 Hold on a sec.은 Hold on
　　　 a second.가 줄여진 표현으로 '잠시 기다려 주세요' 의 뜻이다.

어휘_ reasonable 비싸지 않은, 적당한

정답_ (b)

5.

M: Asia corporation. How can I help you?

W: This is Jessica Lee. Do you have any job openings?

M: Yes, we do. Why don't you send us your resume?

W: _______________________________________

(a) May I ask what this is regarding?

(b) Sorry. He is on another line.

(c) Can you give me your e-mail address, please?

(d) There's a terrible echo on the line.

해석_ M: 아시아 주식회사입니다. 무엇을 도와 드릴까요?

W: 제시카 리입니다. 일자리가 있나요?

M: 네, 있습니다. 이력서를 보내 주시겠어요?

W: _______________________________

(a) 용건이 뭔지 여쭤봐도 될까요?

(b) 죄송해요. 그는 통화 중입니다.

(c) 이메일 주소 좀 알려주시겠어요?

(d) 전화가 심하게 울리네요.

해설_ 남자가 이력서를 보내 달라고 했으므로 이력서를 제출할 이메일 주소를 묻는 (c)가 이어지는 것이 적절하다.

어휘_ job opening 공석, 빈자리

정답_ (c)

6.

W: Do you do alterations here?

M: Yes, we do. What do you need?

W: It is a little too baggy. Could you take in the sides for me?

M: _______________________________________

(a) No problem. I can have it ready for you the day after tomorrow.

(b) I'll take them up about two centimeters.

(c) Yes, I had a little alteration made.

(d) It didn't fit me at first.

해석_ W: 여기서 수선하나요?

M: 네, 합니다. 뭐 하실려고요?

W: 좀 헐렁해서요. 폭 좀 줄여 주실래요?

M: _______________________________

(a) 그럼요. 모레까지 해놓겠습니다.

(b) 기장을 2cm 정도 줄일게요.

(c) 네, 약간 수선했어요.

(d) 처음엔 안 맞았어요.

해설_ 수선집에서 이루어지고 있는 대화다. 폭을 줄여 달라고 부탁했으므로 이에 응하는 (a)가 정답이다.

어휘_ do alterations 수선하다 baggy 헐렁헐렁한 take in the sides 폭을 줄이다 take up 기장을 줄이다

정답_ (a)

STEP 1 Pretest Clinic

7.

해석_ M: 어제가 졸업식이었지, 그렇지 않니?

W: 응. 선생님이랑 우리 반 친구들 모두 졸업식에서 울었어.

M: 뭣 땜에? 졸업식은 즐거운 행사잖아.

W: _______________________________

(a) 모두가 지난 1년 동안 정말 친하게 지냈거든.

(b) 가게에서 우연히 선생님을 만났어.

(c) 그 행사는 2월 28일에 있었어.

(d) 우리가 부른 노래에 선생님이 감동받으셨어.

정답_ (a)

8.

해석_ M: 실례합니다, 손님. 무엇을 도와 드릴까요?

W: 스테이크 주문을 웰던에서 미디엄으로 바꾸고 싶은데요.

M: 죄송합니다. 이미 요리가 다 됐습니다.

W: _______________________________

(a) 아 그래요, 할 수 없죠. 괜찮아요.

(b) 며칠 전에 미디엄 스테이크를 먹었어요.

(c) 괜찮아요. 난 치킨 스프로 할게요.

(d) 웰던 스테이크는 너무 질겨요.

정답_ (a)

9.

해석_ M: 그거 멋있게 생긴 시계네요.

W: 이게 요즘 가장 잘 팔리는 상품이에요.

M: 하지만 좀 비싸네요.

W: _______________________________

(a) 제가 졌어요. 그걸로 주세요.

(b) 돈이 꽤 들었어요.

(c) 그걸로 사신 걸 후회하지 않으실 거예요. 약속드려요.

(d) 돈을 어디에 썼는지 파악해 두세요.

정답_ (c)

STEP 2 Dictation

정답_ 7. had really bonded over the year

8. I'd like to change my steak order
Your dishes have already been made

9. This is quite a hot sale item these days
You won't regret purchasing it

STEP 3 Actual Test

1.

W: Can I interest you in this model? This is our newest release.

M: That's impressive. May I try them on?

W: Sure. Maybe they'll look good on you.

M: _______________________________

(a) Enough is enough.

(b) You have beautiful eyes.

(c) Ok. I'll take them.

(d) That's a clumsy excuse.

해석_ W: 이 모델을 보시겠습니까? 이건 저희 최신품입니다.

M: 인상적인데요. 한번 써 봐도 될까요?

W: 물론이죠. 아마 잘 어울리실 겁니다.

M: _______________________________

(a) 이 정도면 충분해요.

(b) 당신은 아름다운 눈을 가졌어요.

(c) 좋아요. 이걸로 살게요.

(d) 그건 구차한 변명이에요.

해설_ 상점에서 물건을 고르는 상황으로, 대화의 흐름상 점원이 추천해 준 것을 사겠다는 (c)가 적절하다.

어휘_ interest 관심을 갖게 하다 release 발표물 a clumsy excuse 구차한 변명

정답_ (c)

2.

M: The Korean economy is getting worse.

W: That's right. Everyone is feeling the crunch.

M: How's your business going?

W: ____

(a) Well, I'm hurting pretty bad.
(b) I hate this dog-eat-dog world.
(c) He is a pain in the neck.
(d) It takes two to tango.

해석_ M: 한국 경제가 나빠지고 있어요.
　　　W: 맞아요. 모두가 경제적인 어려움을 느끼고 있죠.
　　　M: 당신 사업은 어떠세요?
　　　W: __________________________________
　　　(a) 음, 타격이 심해요.
　　　(b) 이 치열한 세상이 싫어요.
　　　(c) 그는 골칫덩어리에요.
　　　(d) 손뼉도 마주쳐야 소리가 나죠.
해설_ 불경기에 사업은 어떻게 돼가고 있는지 묻고 있으므로 이에 답
　　　하는 (a)가 정답이다.
어휘_ get worse 악화되다, 나빠지다　dog-eat-dog world
　　　치열한 세상　pain in the neck 골칫덩어리　It takes
　　　two to tango. 손뼉도 마주쳐야 소리가 난다.
정답_ (a)

3.
W: What a gorgeous day! I feel like ditching
　　class and going to the beach.
M: Hmm, I can't. I have a class this afternoon.
W: Come on, let's go.
M: ____

(a) I am on the teacher's bad side.
(b) He often cuts class.
(c) His lecture was a waste of time.
(d) No, it's my turn to make a presentation
　　today.

해석_ W: 날씨 정말 좋다! 수업 땡땡이 치고 해변에 가고 싶다.
　　　M: 흠, 난 못 가. 오후에 수업이 있어.
　　　W: 그러지 말고 가자.
　　　M: __________________________________
　　　(a) 선생님한테 찍혔어.
　　　(b) 걘 자주 수업을 빠져.
　　　(c) 그의 강의는 시간 낭비였어.
　　　(d) 안돼, 오늘은 내가 발표할 차례야.

해설_ 수업을 빼먹고 해변에 가자고 조르고 있으므로 이를 받아들이거
　　　나 거절하는 응답 표현이 이어져야 한다.
어휘_ gorgeous 멋진, 굉장한, 훌륭한　ditch/cut (수업을) 빼먹다
　　　on one's bad side ～의 눈 밖에 난
정답_ (d)

4.
M: I'm thinking of starting a small business.
　　Any suggestions?
W: I hear gift shops are popular these days.
M: Hmm... I was thinking of something more in
　　the line of a coffee shop like Starbucks.
W: ____

(a) That won't work. Everywhere you look,
　　there are coffee shops.
(b) I'll let you in on a secret.
(c) That's pretty weak.
(d) He is a real catch.

해석_ M: 소규모 사업을 시작해 볼까 생각 중이야. 뭐 좋은 생각 없어?
　　　W: 요즘 팬시 가게가 뜬다고 하네.
　　　M: 흠… 난 스타벅스 같은 커피점 사업을 생각하고 있었어.
　　　W: __________________________________
　　　(a) 잘 안 될 거야. 고개만 돌리면 보이는 게 커피점이잖아.
　　　(b) 내가 비밀 하나 알려줄게.
　　　(c) 그건 순 억지야.
　　　(d) 그는 완전 킹카야.
해설_ 커피점 사업을 생각하고 있는 남자에게 조언을 해주는 (a)가 적
　　　절하다.
어휘_ gift shop 팬시 가게　let ... in on a secret ～에게 비밀을
　　　누설하다　weak 설득력이 없는　real catch 킹카, 퀸카
정답_ (a)

5.
W: I have a final exam tomorrow, but I'm too
　　exhausted to study.
M: Go ahead and put your feet up for a while.
　　A powernap will do you wonders.
W: Do me a favor and wake me up in about 30
　　minutes, OK?
M: ____

(a) You must be on cloud nine.

(b) No worries. I'll keep my eye on the clock.

(c) It immediately caught my eyes.

(d) I'll wake up in 30 minutes.

해석_ W: 기말고사가 내일인데, 너무 피곤해서 공부를 못 하겠어.

M: 가서 잠깐이라도 좀 자. 그러면 힘이 날 거야.

W: 괜찮다면, 30분 후에 나 좀 깨워 줄래?

M: ___________________________________

(a) 너 정말 행복하겠다.

(b) 걱정 마. 시계 잘 보고 있을게.

(c) 그건 즉시 내 눈을 사로잡았어.

(d) 30분 후에 일어날게.

해설_ 남자에게 30분 후에 깨워 줄 것을 부탁하고 있으므로 이에 응하는 (b)가 정답이다.

어휘_ put one's feet up 누워서 쉬다 power nap 원기회복, 낮잠 do wonders 놀라운 일을 하다 on cloud nine 더할 나위 없이 행복한 keep one's eye on ~에서 눈을 떼지 않다 catch one's eyes ~의 이목을 사로잡다, ~의 관심을 끌다

정답_ (b)

6.

M: Did you hear the news about our summer vacation?

W: No, not yet. Is there big news?

M: Yes, it's going to be a paid vacation and we'll have an additional $1,000 bonus of each.

W: ___________________________________

(a) Well, that might be worth looking into.

(b) Nice. That's really the icing on the cake.

(c) Oh, I highly recommend it.

(d) No way. There's not a grain of truth to that.

해석_ M: 여름 휴가 소식 들었어요?

W: 아뇨, 아직. 빅뉴스라도 있나요?

M: 네, 유급휴가에다 1,000달러씩 보너스도 준데요.

W: ___________________________________

(a) 글쎄요, 조사해 볼 만하겠네요.

(b) 잘됐네요. 정말 금상첨화예요.

(c) 아, 강력히 추천해요.

(d) 말도 안 돼요. 그건 사실무근이에요.

해설_ 유급휴가에 보너스까지 받게 될 거라는 소식을 들었으므로 기쁨이 담긴 응답 표현이 이어져야 자연스럽다.

어휘_ paid vacation 유급휴가 the icing on the cake 금상첨화 a grain of truth 일말의 진실

정답_ (b)

7.

W: I like to see clothes firsthand and try them on before purchasing.

M: Why is that?

W: Shopping on the internet bores me.

M: ___________________________________

(a) What a salesman! You talked me into it.

(b) You are dressed to the nines.

(c) Me, too. I can't trust the stuff on the internet.

(d) You nailed it!

해석_ W: 난 옷을 직접 보고, 사기 전에 그 옷을 입어 보는 걸 좋아해.

M: 그건 왜?

W: 인터넷 쇼핑은 재미가 없어.

M: ___________________________________

(a) 장사 수완이 좋으시군요! 당신이 날 설득시켰어요.

(b) 멋있게 차려입었구나.

(c) 나도 그래. 인터넷에서 파는 물건은 못 믿겠어.

(d) 해냈구나!

해설_ 인터넷 쇼핑은 재미 없다는 여자에 말에 동조하는 (c)가 정답이다. (d)는 상대가 어떤 어려운 일이나 원하던 바를 이뤄냈을 때 '잘했어!', '해냈구나!' 하고 축하 또는 격려해 주는 표현으로, You got it!이라고도 말할 수 있다.

어휘_ talk into 설득해서 ~하게 하다 be dressed to the nines 멋지게 차려입다

정답_ (c)

8.

M: May I help you?

W: My face has broken out again. Can you recommend some good cosmetics?

M: This is good for rugged skin.

W: ___________________________________

(a) You had better not pop the pimple.

(b) You have hives on your neck.

(c) I have bad athlete's feet.

(d) Alright. How much is it?

해석_ M: 무엇을 도와 드릴까요?

W: 얼굴에 또 여드름이 났어요. 좋은 화장품 좀 추천해 주시겠어요?

M: 트러블성 피부엔 이게 좋습니다.

W: _______________________________

(a) 여드름을 짜지 않는 게 좋아.

(b) 너 목에 두드러기 났어.

(c) 심한 무좀에 걸렸어.

(d) 좋아요. 얼마죠?

해설_ 점원이 트러블성 피부에 좋은 제품을 제시했으므로 (d)가 적절한 응답이다.

어휘_ break out (여드름 따위가) 나다 cosmetics 화장품 pop the pimple 여드름을 짜다 hives 두드러기 have athlete's foot 무좀에 걸리다

정답_ (d)

9.

W: Excuse me, waiter. I have a complaint about this steak.
M: What's the matter, ma'am?
W: This meat is too tough.
M: _______________________________

(a) My friends are too fussy about what they eat.
(b) I'm sorry, ma'am. Shall I change it for you?
(c) Don't waste the leftover meat.
(d) Eating quickly is bad for your health.

해석_ W: 웨이터, 여기요. 이 스테이크에 불만이 한 가지 있어요.

M: 무슨 일이신가요, 손님?

W: 고기가 너무 질겨요.

M: _______________________________

(a) 제 친구들은 먹는 것에 너무 까다로워요.

(b) 죄송합니다, 손님. 바꿔 드릴까요?

(c) 남은 고기를 버리지 마세요.

(d) 빨리 먹는 건 건강에 나빠요.

해설_ 고기가 너무 질기다고 불평하고 있으므로 이에 대한 사과의 말이 이어져야 자연스럽다.

어휘_ tough 질긴 fussy 까다로운 leftover 나머지의, 남은

정답_ (b)

10.

M: I'd like to make a toast to Jeffrey and the team.
W: I'll drink to that!
M: This team will be the talk of the town after next week's game.
W: _______________________________

(a) She doesn't drink.
(b) He is so proud of you.
(c) She was the toast of Seoul.
(d) You're telling me.

해석_ M: 제프리와 그 팀을 위해 건배하자.

W: 두말하면 잔소리지!

M: 이 팀은 다음주 시합이 끝난 후 장안의 화제가 될 거야.

W: _______________________________

(a) 그녀는 술을 안 마셔.

(b) 그는 널 너무 자랑스러워해.

(c) 그녀는 서울에서 이름난 미인이었어.

(d) 누가 아니래.

해설_ 남자와 여자 모두 제프리와 그 팀에 대해 긍정적인 평가를 내리고 있으므로 남자의 의견에 동의하는 (d)가 정답이다.

어휘_ make a toast 건배하다 I'll drink to that! 두말하면 잔소리지! the talk of the town 장안의 화제 toast 화제의 인물, 인기인, 이름난 미인

정답_ (d)

STEP 1 Pretest Clinic

10.

해석_ M: 신 선생님과 3시에 작은 수술이 예약돼 있는데 과를 못 찾겠어요.

W: 엘리베이터 타고 2층으로 가세요. 안과 바로 지나서 오른쪽에 있을 거예요.

M: 여기서 수속을 밟아야 하나요, 아님 작은 수술 접수대에서 다시 해야 하나요?

W: _______________________________

(a) 글쎄요, 갖고 계신 보험의 종류에 따라 다르죠.

(b) 가능하다면 이 선생님을 뵙고 싶어요.

(c) 그쪽에서 처리하시면 됩니다.

(d) 할 수 있는 최선을 다할게요.

정답_ (c)

11.

해석_ W: 너 머리가 어떻게 된 거야?

M: 이게 요즘 유행하는 헤어스타일이야.

W: 요즘 패션은 광대처럼 보이는 거니?

M: _______________________________

(a) 서커스에 참여하고 있어.

(b) 가서 머리 염색 다시 하고 와.

(c) 그런 좋지 않은 말은 하지 마.

(d) 샴푸를 하면 컬이 빨리 풀릴 거야.

정답_ (c)

12.

해석_ M: 딸꾹질이 안 멈춰.

W: 숨을 참을 수 있을 때까지 참아 봐.

M: 그렇게 했는데 소용 없었어.

W: _______________________________

(a) 그럼 물을 조금씩 마셔 봐. 괜찮아질 거야.

(b) 재밌겠다.

(c) 발목이 부었어.

(d) 복통이 가라앉고 있어.

정답_ (a)

STEP 2 Dictation

정답_ 10. I have an appointment
just past the optometry department
You can take care of it over there

11. This is the hip hairstyle these days
That's not a nice thing to say

12. I can't stop hiccupping
try sipping some water

STEP 3 Actual Test

1.

M: This is the police department. How can I help you?

W: Hello, officer. I need to make a complaint.

M: About what?

W: _______________________________

(a) Can you take care of it?

(b) I'd like to turn myself in.

(c) It's late and my neighbors are throwing a very loud party.

(d) You're always complaining.

해석_ M: 경찰서입니다. 어떻게 도와 드릴까요?

W: 안녕하세요, 경관님. 항의할 것이 있어서요.

M: 뭐에 대해서요?

W: _______________________________

(a) 처리해 주실 수 있나요?

(b) 자수하고 싶습니다.

(c) 늦었는데 이웃 사람들이 아주 시끄럽게 파티를 하고 있어요.

(d) 당신은 항상 불평만 하는군요.

해설_ 무엇에 대한 항의인지 묻고 있으므로 그 내용을 언급한 선택지를 고르면 된다.

어휘_ police department 경찰서 make a complaint 항의하다, 불평하다 turn oneself in 자수하다

정답_ (c)

2.

W: Did you fill out your entry form?

M: Yes, here it is.

W: How long are you going to stay in the U.K.?

M: _______________________________________

(a) At the immigration office.

(b) About 2 weeks.

(c) I'm here for sightseeing.

(d) Nothing to declare.

해석_ W: 입국 신고서를 작성하셨나요?

M: 네, 여기 있어요.

W: 영국에서 얼마나 오래 머무르실 건가요?

M: _______________________________

(a) 출입국 관리사무소에서요.

(b) 2주 정도요.

(c) 관광차 왔어요.

(d) 신고할 것이 없습니다.

해설_ 얼마나 머무를 건지 묻고 있으므로 기간이 언급된 선택지를 고르면 된다.

어휘_ entry form 입국 신고서(↔ departure form 출국 신고서) immigration office 출입국 관리사무소 sightseeing 관광 declare 신고하다

정답_ (b)

3.

M: Shoot! We'll be late for work.

W: Don't worry. We'll make it on time.

M: Look, traffic is bumper to bumper. How can we make it?

W: _______________________________________

(a) I know a shortcut to the office.

(b) I am in good hands.

(c) I just bought this car.

(d) Do as I've said.

해석_ M: 젠장! 회사에 늦겠는걸.

W: 걱정 마. 제시간에 도착할 거야.

M: 이것 봐, 차가 꽉 밀렸잖아. 어떻게 제시간에 도착할 수 있어?

W: _______________________________

(a) 사무실로 가는 지름길을 알고 있어.

(b) 난 안심하고 있어.

(c) 방금 이 차를 샀어.

(d) 내가 말한 대로 해.

해설_ 남자가 회사에 늦을까 봐 불안해하고 있으므로 사무실로 가는 지름길을 알고 있다며 안심시키는 (a)가 적절하다.

어휘_ shoot 젠장, 이런 make it 제시간에 도착하다 bumper to bumper 차가 꽉 밀린, 교통 체증이 심한 shortcut 지름길 in good hands 전문가의 보살핌을 받고 있는, 안심할 수 있는

정답_ (a)

4.

W: Where did you lose your bag?

M: I think I lost it at the park.

W: What does it look like?

M: _______________________________________

(a) She resembles her father.

(b) You don't look like your mom.

(c) You like the park.

(d) It is a travel bag with blue stripes.

해석_ W: 가방을 어디서 잃어버리셨어요?

M: 공원에서 잃어버린 것 같아요.

W: 어떻게 생겼나요?

M: _______________________________

(a) 그녀는 그녀의 아버지를 닮았어요.

(b) 당신은 당신 엄마를 안 닮았어요.

(c) 당신은 공원을 좋아하는군요.

(d) 파란색 줄무늬가 있는 여행가방이에요.

해설_ 가방이 어떻게 생겼는지를 묻고 있으므로 이에 관한 설명이 담긴 선택지를 고르면 된다.

어휘_ stripe 줄무늬

정답_ (d)

5.

M: Could you tell me where I can get my bike fixed?

W: Sure. There's a store near the Chinese medical clinic.

M: How long does it take to go there?

W: _______________________________________

(a) I ran a stop sign.

(b) I don't know exactly, but it's just a stone's throw from here.

(c) Go straight and turn right at the second intersection.

(d) I have a long way to go.

해석_ M: 어디서 자전거를 고칠 수 있는지 알려주시겠어요?

W: 물론이죠. 한의원 근처에 가게가 있어요.

M: 거기 가는 데 얼마나 걸려요?

W: _______________________

(a) 정지 신호를 무시하고 달렸어요.

(b) 정확히는 모르지만, 여기서 아주 가까워요.

(c) 쭉 가서 두 번째 교차로에서 오른쪽으로 도세요.

(d) 할 일이 태산 같아요.

해설_ 얼마나 걸리는지 묻고 있으므로 시간을 언급하거나 거리 관련 표현이 담긴 선택지를 고르면 된다.

어휘_ Chinese medical clinic 한의원 run a stop sign 정지 신호를 무시하고 달리다 intersection 교차로 have a long way to go 갈 길이 멀다, 할 일이 많이 남아 있다

정답_ (b)

6.

W: He was hit by a car on his way home an hour ago and he hasn't regained consciousness.

M: How are his vital signs?

W: Everything seems to be OK. But he's lost a lot of blood from the impact.

M: _______________________

(a) I forgot my card at home.

(b) I don't know whether he would need a blood transfusion.

(c) You might have contracted H.I.V.

(d) The test isn't 100% accurate.

해석_ W: 그는 1시간 전에 집에 가던 중 교통사고를 당했는데 의식이 돌아오지 않았어요.

M: 그의 활력징후는 어때요?

W: 다 괜찮아 보여요. 하지만 충돌로 인해 피를 많이 흘렸어요.

M: _______________________

(a) 카드를 깜박 집에 두고 왔어요.

(b) 수혈이 필요할지도 모르겠네요.

(c) 당신은 에이즈 바이러스에 감염됐을지도 몰라요.

(d) 검사가 100% 정확하진 않아요.

해설_ 사고를 당한 사람이 피를 많이 흘렸다고 했으므로 (b)가 적절하다.

어휘_ regain consciousness 의식을 되찾다 vital signs 활력징후 (맥박, 혈압, 호흡, 체온을 통틀어 일컫는 말) lose blood 피를 흘리다 contract (병에) 걸리다 H.I.V. 인체 면역 결핍 바이러스, 에이즈 바이러스 accurate 정확한

정답_ (b)

7.

M: Ms. Jane, I have something to tell you.

W: Sure, go ahead.

M: You're probably going to experience a good deal of pain after the operation. So, we are going to keep you under supervision.

W: _______________________

(a) Do you mean I should stay at the hospital?

(b) I'm going to give you a shot to numb the pain.

(c) You should get your eyes examined at least once a year.

(d) Help me out!

해석_ M: 제인 씨, 말씀드릴 게 있는데요.

W: 네, 말씀하세요.

M: 수술 후에 상당한 통증을 느끼실 겁니다. 그래서 당신을 특별 관리할 예정이에요.

W: _______________________

(a) 입원해야 한다는 뜻인가요?

(b) 고통을 완화시켜 줄 주사를 놔 줄게요.

(c) 적어도 1년에 한 번은 시력검사를 해야 해요.

(d) 도와주세요!

해설_ 수술 후 통증으로 인해 특별 관리가 필요하다는 말에 그 의미를 되묻는 (a)가 정답이다.

어휘_ experience pain 통증을 느끼다 a good deal of 많은, 상당한 under supervision 특별 관리하에 give ... a shot ~에게 주사를 놓다 numb (고통을) 완화시키다 help out 도와주다

정답_ (a)

8.

W: Excuse me. I'm looking for some stuff for a baby shower.

M: Sorry, ma'am. Baby supplies are on the fifth floor.

W: Oh, I see. Then, where is the elevator?

M: ______________________________________

(a) It's about a 15 minute walk from here.

(b) My store is right opposite the coffee shop.

(c) Turn right, and go to the exit #7.

(d) Take the green line and then get off at the next station.

해석_ W: 실례합니다. 베이비 샤워에 가져갈 것을 찾고 있는데요.

M: 죄송합니다만, 손님. 아기용품은 5층에 있습니다.

W: 아, 그렇군요. 그럼 엘리베이터는 어느 쪽에 있죠?

M: ______________________________

(a) 여기서 도보로 약 15분 거리입니다.

(b) 저희 가게는 커피점 바로 맞은편에 있어요.

(c) 오른쪽으로 돌아 7번 출구로 가세요.

(d) 녹색 노선을 탄 다음, 다음 역에서 내리세요.

해설_ 엘리베이터의 위치를 묻고 있으므로 이에 답한 (c)가 정답이다.

어휘_ baby supplies 아기용품 right opposite 바로 맞은편에

정답_ (c)

9.

M: Why did you go to the doctor?

W: I was coming down with a cold.

M: Did you get some medicine?

W: ______________________________________

(a) There are some side effects.

(b) No. The doctor said I just need to get some rest.

(c) No. I don't have a cough.

(d) Yes. I take insulin for diabetes.

해석_ M: 병원에 왜 갔어요?

W: 감기 기운이 있어서요.

M: 약 받아 왔어요?

W: ______________________________

(a) 부작용이 좀 있어요.

(b) 아뇨. 의사 선생님이 그냥 좀 쉬라고 했어요.

(c) 아뇨. 기침은 하지 않아요.

(d) 네. 당뇨병 때문에 인슐린을 맞아요.

해설_ 병원에서 약을 받아 왔는지 묻고 있으므로 이에 관해 언급한 선택지를 고르면 된다. 참고로, 여자의 첫 번째 대사에 나오는 것처럼 '~ 기운이 있다'라고 할 땐 현재진행형을 써서 표현한다.

어휘_ come down with (병에) 걸리다 insulin 인슐린
diabetes 당뇨병

정답_ (b)

Part 3

Chapter 12 대화문 주제 파악하기

STEP 1 Pretest Clinic

1.

해석_ W: 3월 판매실적 봤니?

M: 아직 못 봤어. 어떤데?

W: 지난 분기 동안 판매가 늘었어.

M: 그래? 잘됐네. 이유를 아니?

W: 새로운 인재를 기용한 것이 도움이 됐어. 특히, 새 판매 부장이 아주 뛰어나서 판매 팀원들도 그와 함께 일하는 걸 좋아하는 것 같더라.

M: 그게 사실이긴 하지만, 그를 좀 더 지켜봐야 할 것 같아.

W: 질투하니?

M: 천만의 말씀. 난 그냥 그가 정말 얼마나 잘하는지 두고 봐야 한다고 생각할 뿐이야.

Q. 무엇에 관한 대화인가?

(a) 신입사원의 행동

(b) 판매 증가의 이유

(c) 지난번 회의에 관한 브리핑

(d) 직원들을 다루는 방법

정답_ (b)

2.

해석_ M: 안녕하세요. 무엇을 도와 드릴까요?

W: 안녕하세요. 노트북을 고치고 싶은데요.

M: 뭐가 문제죠?

W: 컴퓨터를 켤 때마다 검은 스크린이 갑자기 튀어나와요.

M: 알겠습니다. 하드 디스크에 문제가 있는 것 같네요.

W: 얼마나 심각한데요? 중요한 정보들이 많이 저장돼 있어요. 복구할 수 있나요?

M: 아마도 100% 되진 않겠지만, 최선을 다해 볼게요.

Q. 대화의 주된 내용은 무엇인가?

(a) 인터넷으로 새로운 정보 찾기

(b) 컴퓨터 바이러스 제거하기

(c) 고장 난 컴퓨터 고치기

(d) 하드 디스크 교체하기

정답_ (c)

3.

해석_ M: 네가 좋아하는 거 아무거나 하나 골라. 가격은 걱정하지 말고. 너를 위한 선물이야. 내가 고르는 것보다 이게 낫다고 생각했어.

W: 정말? 결정하기 어렵다.

M: 이 소설은 어때?

W: 그 책은 전에 읽었어. 너 이 아일랜드 소설 읽어 본 적 있니?

M: 응. 첫 부분은 이해하기 힘들었는데, 읽을수록 더 재밌어졌어.

W: 그럼 그걸로 할게. 정말 고마워.

M: 천만에.

Q. 대화의 요점은 무엇인가?

(a) 여자를 위한 선물

(b) 여자가 가장 좋아하는 책

(c) 남자와 여자의 취미

(d) 소설의 감상평

정답_ (a)

STEP 2 Dictation

정답_ 1. Sales increased over the last quarter
Getting some new blood helped
we should wait to see how good he really is

2. I'd like to fix my laptop
a black screen pops up suddenly
I have a lot of important information stored there

3. Choose any one you like
I've read that one before
the more I read the more interesting it got

STEP 3 Actual Test

1.

M: Where are you going now?

W: I'm going downtown to meet my boss.

M: I'm going downtown, too. Do you need a ride?

W: Yes. But, before we go, let's get a snack in the cafeteria.

M: OK. I'll just pack my bag first. You go ahead.

W: I'll order for you. What do you want?

M: Chicken salad is fine. See you soon.

Q. What is the main focus of the conversation?

(a) The man promised to meet his boss in a cafe.

(b) The man and woman are going downtown.

(c) The woman requested to buy a snack.

(d) The woman declined his offer.

해석_ M: 너 지금 어디 가니?

W: 우리 사장님 만나러 시내에 가는 길이야.

M: 나도 시내에 가는 길인데. 차 태워 줄까?

W: 응. 근데 가기 전에 구내식당에서 간단히 뭐 좀 먹자.

M: 좋아. 우선 가방 좀 챙기고. 먼저 가.

W: 네 거 주문해 놓을게. 뭐 먹을래?

M: 치킨 샐러드가 좋아. 곧 보자.

Q. 대화의 주된 요지는 무엇인가?

(a) 남자는 카페에서 그의 사장과 만나기로 약속했다.

(b) 남자와 여자는 시내에 갈 것이다.

(c) 여자는 간식을 사 달라고 부탁했다.

(d) 여자는 그의 제안을 거절했다.

해설_ 두 사람 모두 시내에 가는 길이어서 같이 가는 것에 대한 얘기를 나누고 있으므로 정답은 (b)가 된다.

어휘_ decline 거절하다

정답_ (b)

2.

W: My flight was canceled because of bad weather conditions. How can I get back to Seoul by Friday morning?

M: Isn't there another way to get here?

W: Well, if I take a ship, I will arrive Friday evening.

M: That means you would miss the meeting. It's your turn to do the presentation this time.

W: I have no choice but to wait for a flight. As soon as I find out what's going on, I'll call you.

M: Ok. Please log on to the online messenger at 10 o'clock tomorrow morning, just in case we need to chat.

W: Got it. Good night.

Q. What is the main point of the conversation?

(a) The woman will take a ship for the meeting.

(b) The woman would find another traffic line.

(c) The woman might miss the conference.

(d) The woman will postpone her schedule.

해석_ W: 기상 상태가 나빠서 비행기가 결항됐어. 금요일 아침까지 서울로 어떻게 돌아가지?

M: 여기 올 다른 방법은 없어?

W: 글쎄, 만약 배를 탄다면 금요일 저녁에 도착할 거야.

M: 그건 회의에 참석 못할 거란 얘기잖아. 이번엔 네가 발표할 차례인데.

W: 비행기를 기다릴 수밖에 없어. 상황 봐서 전화할게.

M: 좋아. 혹시 채팅할 필요가 있을지 모르니까 내일 아침 10시에 온라인 메신저 접속해 놔.

W: 알았어. 잘 자.

Q. 대화의 요점은 무엇인가?

(a) 여자는 회의를 위해 배를 탈 것이다.

(b) 여자는 다른 교통편을 찾을 것이다.

(c) 여자는 회의에 참석 못할지도 모른다.

(d) 여자는 그녀의 일정을 연기할 것이다.

해설_ 악천후로 비행기가 결항되어 회의 때까지 도착할 수 없을지도 모른다는 내용이 전개되고 있으므로 정답은 (c)가 된다.

어휘_ have no choice but to ~할 수밖에 없다

정답_ (c)

3.

M: Good morning. How may I help you?

W: Hello. Do you have any group discounts?

M: Sure. Groups of 20 or more receive 10% off.

W: Then, how much is the rate for 30 children and two adults?

M: A child pays $10 and an adult is $15. Your total would be $297. Would this be in cash or credit?

W: Please do a calculation in a lump sum by VISA.

M: OK. Here are your tickets and card. Enjoy your time.

Q. What is the main focus of the conversation?

(a) Making a credit card
(b) Buying tickets at group discount prices
(c) Paying with a Visa card
(d) Lowering the ticket prices

해석_ M: 안녕하세요. 어떻게 도와 드릴까요?

W: 안녕하세요. 단체 할인이 되나요?

M: 물론이죠. 20명 이상이면 10% 할인됩니다.

W: 그럼, 어린이 30명과 어른 2명 요금은 얼마죠?

M: 어린이는 10달러이고 어른은 15달러입니다. 총 297달러가 되겠네요. 현금으로 지불하시겠어요, 아님 카드로 지불하시겠어요?

W: 비자카드로 일시불로 계산해 주세요.

M: 알겠습니다. 티켓하고 카드 여기 있습니다. 즐거운 시간 되세요.

Q. 대화의 주된 내용은 무엇인가?

(a) 신용카드 만들기
(b) 단체 할인가로 티켓 사기
(c) 비자카드로 지불하기
(d) 티켓 가격 깎기

해설_ 매표소에서 이루어지는 대화다. 단체 할인에 대한 질문과 대답이 오가고 있으므로 (b)가 정답임을 알 수 있다.

어휘_ group discount 단체 할인 in a lump sum 일시불로

정답_ (b)

4.

W: I heard you found a new apartment. When are you going to move?

M: This Sunday.

W: If you need any help, I'd be happy to lend a hand.

M: Thanks for saying that, but my relatives will help me. They live nearby.

W: Oh, I see. Then when would you have the housewarming party?

M: Well... I think next Saturday would be good.

How's that for you?

W: It's fine.

Q. What is the main topic of the conversation?

(a) The man's move
(b) The woman's relatives
(c) The man's housewarming party
(d) The woman's new house

해석_ W: 새 아파트를 구했다고 들었어요. 언제 이사 가세요?

M: 이번주 일요일에요.

W: 도움이 필요하시면 기꺼이 도와 드릴게요.

M: 그렇게 말해줘서 고맙습니다만, 친척들이 도와줄 거예요. 근처에 살고 있거든요.

W: 아, 그렇군요. 그럼, 집들이는 언제 할 거예요?

M: 음… 다음주 토요일이 좋을 것 같아요. 어떠세요?

W: 좋아요.

Q. 대화의 주제는 무엇인가?

(a) 남자의 이사
(b) 여자의 친척
(c) 남자의 집들이
(d) 여자의 새집

해설_ 남자가 새 아파트로 이사 가는 것에 관한 대화 내용이므로 정답은 (a)가 된다.

어휘_ lend a hand 돕다 housewarming party 집들이

정답_ (a)

5.

M: Will you join the overseas volunteer program with me?

W: Where would we go?

M: Vietnam. Doesn't that sound great?

W: Well, I don't know. As soon as you told me Vietnam, I got a little nervous.

M: Listen. That's from your mistaken pre-conceptions. I heard from my friend who went there that everybody is nice and friendly, and that she learned a lot of things from them.

W: She did? Um... I need to think some more before I tell you.

M: Ok. I hope you don't miss this golden

opportunity.

Q. What is the main topic of the conversation?

(a) Voluntary service abroad
(b) Charge-free service for the old
(c) Plans to volunteer
(d) Community service near their school

해석_ M: 나랑 해외 자원 봉사 프로그램에 참여할래?
　　 W: 어디로 갈 건데?
　　 M: 베트남. 좋은 생각인 것 같지 않니?
　　 W: 글쎄, 잘 모르겠어. 네가 베트남이라고 말하자마자 좀 긴장됐어.
　　 M: 들어 봐. 그건 네 잘못된 선입견이야. 거기 다녀온 친구한테 들었는데 모든 사람들이 친절하고 호의적이어서 그들에게 많은 것을 배웠대.
　　 W: 그랬대? 음… 생각 좀 더 해보고 말해 줄게.
　　 M: 좋아. 네가 이 절호의 기회를 놓치지 않았으면 좋겠다.

　　 Q. 대화의 주제는 무엇인가?
　　 (a) 해외 자원 봉사
　　 (b) 노인을 위한 무료 봉사
　　 (c) 자원 봉사 계획
　　 (d) 학교 근처의 지역 봉사활동

해설_ 남자가 여자에게 제안한 해외 자원 봉사 프로그램에 관해 대화를 나누고 있으므로 정답은 (a)가 된다.

어휘_ mistaken 잘못된, 오해한 preconception 선입견 golden opportunity 절호의 기회 community service 지역 봉사활동

정답_ (a)

6.

W: Bob, you know what? You are becoming a couch potato. Why don't you go to the gym or play basketball with your friends?
M: It's too chilly outside.
W: What are you eating all that junk food for? I don't want to have to keep nagging you anymore.
M: Mom, let me off just today. I'll stop, starting tomorrow.
W: Are you sure? How can I believe you?
M: Trust me. I'll keep the promise.

W: I'll give you this one last chance.

Q. What is the conversation about?

(a) The man's rudeness
(b) The woman's concern about her son
(c) The man's pledge not to eat junk food
(d) The man's lack of exercise

해석_ W: 밥, 그거 아니? 너 점점 게을러지고 있어. 운동하러 가든지, 아님 친구들이랑 농구하고 노는 게 어떠니?
　　 M: 밖이 너무 추워요.
　　 W: 인스턴트 음식들은 왜 그렇게 많이 먹고 있는 거야? 너한테 계속 잔소리하고 싶지 않다.
　　 M: 엄마, 오늘만 내버려 두세요. 내일부터 안 그럴게요.
　　 W: 정말이야? 널 어떻게 믿니?
　　 M: 절 믿어 주세요. 약속 지킬게요.
　　 W: 마지막으로 이번 한 번만 믿겠어.

　　 Q. 무엇에 관한 대화인가?
　　 (a) 남자의 무례한 태도
　　 (b) 아들에 대한 여자의 걱정
　　 (c) 인스턴트 음식을 먹지 않겠다는 남자의 맹세
　　 (d) 남자의 운동 부족

해설_ 점점 게으름을 피우고 있는 아들의 행동에 대해 걱정하는 내용이므로 (b)가 정답이다.

어휘_ couch potato 게으르고 비활동적인 사람 nag 잔소리하다 let off 면제하다, 놓아주다 rudeness 무례한 태도 pledge 맹세, 서약

정답_ (b)

7.

M: Is work going well these days?
W: Actually, I've decided to quit.
M: What are you talking about? You told me you loved your job.
W: You're right, but I want to go study abroad.
M: Just for the study? What do you want to study?
W: I'd like to go to Spain and study Spanish.
M: I think you're making a rash decision. Why don't you think this more deeply?
W: I'm serious now.

Q. What is the conversation about?

(a) The reason why the woman wants to live in Spain
(b) The man's worries about the woman's decision
(c) The woman's new job
(d) The man's complaint about the woman

해석_ M: 요즘 일은 잘돼 가니?

W: 실은, 나 일 그만두기로 결심했어.

M: 무슨 소리야? 네 일이 너무 좋다고 말했잖아.

W: 맞긴 한데, 유학 가고 싶어.

M: 단지 공부하러? 무슨 공부를 하고 싶은데?

W: 스페인에 가서 스페인어를 공부하고 싶어.

M: 내 생각엔 네가 성급한 결정을 내리고 있는 것 같아. 좀 더 깊이 생각해 보는 게 어때?

W: 나 지금 진지해.

Q. 무엇에 관한 대화인가?

(a) 여자가 스페인에서 살고 싶어 하는 이유
(b) 여자의 결정에 대한 남자의 걱정
(c) 여자의 새 직장
(d) 여자에 대한 남자의 불평

해설_ 일을 그만두고 유학을 가겠다는 여자의 갑작스런 결정에 걱정하면서 좀 더 깊이 생각해 볼 것을 권유하는 내용이므로 정답은 (b)가 된다.

어휘_ rash 성급한

정답_ (b)

8.

W: Hello. This is Amanda from Michell's design group. Is Mr. Smith there?
M: Speaking.
W: I'm calling about your order. I am afraid the black chair that you ordered is out of stock. How about another color?
M: What color do you have? Is there a brown one?
W: Yes, there is. Shall I exchange it for a brown one?
M: Ok. When will I receive it?
W: You will get it in three days. I'm sorry for the inconvenience.

Q. What is the purpose of the conversation?

(a) To confirm the man's order
(b) To advertise new products
(c) To ask for the delivery date
(d) To inform that an ordered item is out of stock

해석_ W: 안녕하세요. 미쉘즈 디자인 그룹의 아만다입니다. 스미스 씨 계십니까?

M: 전데요.

W: 주문하신 것에 대해 말씀드리려고 전화했어요. 죄송합니다만, 주문하신 검정색 의자는 품절됐습니다. 다른 색상은 어떠세요?

M: 어떤 색상이 있죠? 갈색 의자 있나요?

W: 네, 있습니다. 갈색 의자로 바꿔 드릴까요?

M: 좋습니다. 제품을 언제 받게 되나요?

W: 3일 안에 받으실 거예요. 불편을 끼쳐 드려서 죄송합니다.

Q. 대화의 목적은 무엇인가?

(a) 남자의 주문을 확인하기 위해
(b) 새로운 제품을 광고하기 위해
(c) 배송 날짜를 물어보기 위해
(d) 주문한 물건이 품절됐음을 알려주기 위해

해설_ 남자가 주문한 물건이 품절됐음을 알리기 위해 전화를 건 것이므로 (d)가 정답이다.

어휘_ out of stock 품절되어 inconvenience 불편

정답_ (d)

Chapter 13 대화문 내용 파악하기

STEP 1 Pretest Clinic

4.

해석_ W: 대학 생활 어땠니?

M: 음, 많은 교수님과 직원분들이 어려운 순간을 이겨내게 지지
해 주시고 절대 포기하지 않도록 격려해 주셨어.

W: 아주 멋지구나. 룸메이트는 어땠어?

M: 내 룸메이트는 컴퓨터광이었어. 우린 함께 아주 즐거운 시간
을 보냈지.

W: 흥미롭구나. 네가 많은 사람들을 만나고 새로운 것들을 경험
할 기회를 많이 가졌으리라 확신해. 대학 생활에서 틀림없이
많은 것을 배웠을 거야.

M: 대학 시절 굉장한 시간을 가졌다는 것은 의심할 여지가 없지.
그 시간이 사회 생활을 맞이하기 위한 진짜 준비를 하게 해줬
던 것 같아.

Q. 대화에 따르면 남자에 관해 틀린 것은 무엇인가?

(a) 그는 대학에서 굉장한 시간을 보냈다.

(b) 그의 룸메이트는 컴퓨터를 전공했다.

(c) 그는 교직원들에게 도움을 받았다.

(d) 그는 대학 생활을 즐겼다.

정답_ (b)

5.

해석_ M: 헬렌, 요즘 방송일 한다고 들었어. 사실이야?

W: 음, 그런 셈이야. 지역 방송 회사에서 일하기 시작했어.

M: 대단하다. 어떻게 그 일자리를 얻은 거야? 어렵지 않았어?

W: 3학년때 거기서 인턴으로 일했어. 정규직에 첫 발을 내딛었지.

M: 와, 멋지다. 네가 정말 부러워. 비결이 뭐야?

W: 네가 정말 일하고 싶은 분야를 찾아야 해. 난 진짜 일다운 일
을 갖기 전까지 인턴으로 일했고, 그게 실무를 배우는 데 도
움이 됐어.

Q. 대화에 따르면 맞는 것은 무엇인가?

(a) 여자는 4학년 때 인턴이었다.

(b) 여자는 다른 회사에서 인턴으로 일했다.

(c) 경쟁이 치열했다.

(d) 여자는 인턴을 끝낸 후 그 회사에서 일할 기회를 얻었다.

정답_ (d)

6.

해석_ W: 영화 〈크래쉬〉 봤니?

M: 아니. 아직 볼 기회가 없었어.

W: 지금까지 본 최고의 영화들 중 하나였던 것 같아.

M: 그래, 그 영화 음악도 아주 멋지다고 들었어.

W: 그 영화 진짜 봐야 해.

M: 무슨 내용이야?

W: 우리 사회에 영향을 미치는 인종 차별과 고정관념에 관한 거
야.

M: 흥미롭다. 오늘 밤에 봐야지.

Q. 대화에 따르면 맞는 것은 무엇인가?

(a) 남자는 그 영화를 보는 것을 미뤄왔었다.

(b) 남자는 이미 그 영화의 음악을 들었다.

(c) 그 영화는 인종 차별주의와 그와 관련된 문제들에 관한 이야
기다.

(d) 여자는 인종 차별주의자였다.

정답_ (c)

STEP 2 Dictation

정답_ 4. What was college like for you
My roommate was a computer geek
my time there really prepared me to
face the real world

5. I started working at a local broadcasting
company
I got my foot in the door for a full-time
job
it helped me to get a first-hand
experience

6. Haven't had the chance to watch it yet
one of the best movies I have ever seen
racial issues and the stereotypes that
affect our society

STEP 3 Actual Test

1.

M: Kate, can you do an errand for me?

W: No problem, Dad. What is it?

M: After you finish school, go to the bank next to the clothing store, tell Ms. Emily my name and give her this document. She is at window No. 2.

W: That's it?

M: Yes. Here's $10 for your trouble.

W: Thanks. I'm always happy to help you.

Q. What does the man want his daughter to do?

(a) He wants his daughter to buy something.

(b) He wants his daughter to go out together.

(c) He wants his daughter to run an errand.

(d) He wants his daughter to go to school.

해석_ M: 케이트, 심부름 하나 해줄래?

　　　 W: 좋아요, 아빠. 뭔데요?

　　　 M: 학교 끝나고 옷가게 옆에 있는 은행에 가서, 에밀리 씨한테 내 이름을 말하고 이 서류를 전해 주렴. 그녀는 2번 창구에 있어.

　　　 W: 그게 다예요?

　　　 M: 응. 그리고 이건 심부름 값 10달러야.

　　　 W: 고마워요. 아빠를 도와 드려서 늘 행복해요.

　　　 Q. 남자는 그의 딸이 무엇을 하길 원하는가?

　　　 (a) 그는 그의 딸이 뭔가 사오길 원한다.

　　　 (b) 그는 그의 딸이 그와 함께 외출하길 원한다.

　　　 (c) 그는 그의 딸이 심부름해 주길 원한다.

　　　 (d) 그는 그의 딸이 학교에 가길 원한다.

해설_ 은행에 가서 서류를 전해 주라고 부탁하고 있으므로 (c)가 정답임을 알 수 있다.

어휘_ do[run] an errand 심부름하다　window (은행 등의) 창구

정답_ (c)

2.

W: I watched you doing that presentation in Chinese. How come you speak such good Chinese?

M: To tell the truth, my grandfather is Chinese, and I lived in China till I was 10 years old.

W: Wow! Where did you live? I was just in Shanghai last summer vacation. It was different than I expected. Shanghai is quite a thriving city.

M: I lived in Beijing. You're right. Shanghai is thriving because it is a major trade city in China.

W: If you have time, we could go to my home and see the photos I took in China.

M: That's a good idea.

Q. Which is correct according to the conversation?

(a) The woman can speak Chinese.

(b) The man has never lived in China.

(c) The man lived in Beijing as a child.

(d) The woman wants to learn Chinese.

해석_ W: 네가 중국어로 그 발표를 하는 걸 지켜봤어. 어떻게 중국말을 그렇게 잘하니?

　　　 M: 실은, 우리 할아버지가 중국분이셔. 그리고 난 10살 때까지 중국에서 살았어.

　　　 W: 와! 어디 살았다고? 난 작년 여름방학에 상하이에 있었어. 거긴 내가 생각했던 것과 달랐어. 상하이는 꽤 번화한 도시야.

　　　 M: 난 베이징에 살았어. 네 말이 맞아. 상하이는 중국의 주요 무역 도시이기 때문에 번창하고 있어.

　　　 W: 시간 있으면 우리 집에 가서 내가 중국에서 찍은 사진들을 볼 수 있어.

　　　 M: 좋은 생각이야.

　　　 Q. 대화에 따르면 맞는 것은 어느 것인가?

　　　 (a) 여자는 중국어를 말할 수 있다.

　　　 (b) 남자는 중국에서 산 적이 없다.

　　　 (c) 남자는 어릴 때 베이징에서 살았다.

　　　 (d) 여자는 중국어를 배우길 원한다.

해설_ 남자의 첫 번째 대사에 보면, 10살 때까지 중국에서 살았다고 했으므로 (c)가 정답이다.

어휘_ To tell the truth 솔직히 말하면, 실은　thriving 번성하는, 번화한

정답_ (c)

3.

M: This is Hotel Valley. What can I do for you?

W: Hello. I'd like to talk Mr. Evans staying in room 203.

M: Just a moment please. I'm afraid that there isn't that name in our registry.

W: That's impossible. I met him there yesterday. Would you check again?

M: Ok. Please tell me how to spell that name.

W: Oh, no. I'm sorry. I found my mistake. His name is Eden E-D-E-N not Evans.

M: Ok. Here he is. I'll connect you right away.

Q. What was the woman's mistake?

(a) She called the wrong number.

(b) She made a reservation under another name.

(c) She asked for the wrong name of the customer.

(d) She stayed at another hotel.

해석_ M: 밸리 호텔입니다. 무엇을 도와 드릴까요?

W: 안녕하세요. 203호에 묵고 있는 에반스 씨와 통화하고 싶은데요.

M: 잠시만요. 죄송합니다만, 고객 명단에 그런 이름은 없는데요.

W: 그럴 리가 없어요. 어제 거기서 그 사람하고 만났어요. 다시 확인해 주시겠어요?

M: 알겠습니다. 이름 철자가 어떻게 되는지 말씀해 주십시오.

W: 이런. 죄송해요. 제가 실수했네요. 그 사람 이름은 에반스가 아니라 에든이에요. E-D-E-N.

M: 알겠습니다. 여기 있네요. 바로 연결해 드리겠습니다.

Q. 여자의 실수는 무엇이었는가?

(a) 그녀는 잘못된 번호로 전화했다.

(b) 그녀는 다른 이름으로 예약했다.

(c) 그녀는 고객의 이름을 잘못 불렀다.

(d) 그녀는 다른 호텔에 머물렀다.

해설_ 여자의 마지막 대사를 통해, 실수로 통화하고 싶은 사람의 이름을 잘못 말했음을 알 수 있으므로 (c)가 정답이다.

어휘_ registry 등록부 make a reservation 예약하다

정답_ (c)

4.

W: Mike, why were you so late? I called you twice but you didn't pick up.

M: I told you that I would be late today.

W: Sorry, I forgot. Someone called for you. Her name is Susan. Sounds like she has an urgent message for you.

M: Really? Did she mention what it was about?

W: No. She said that when you come home to call her immediately.

M: I should call her now.

W: Wait. There is a memo. She told me to call back to the number I wrote down here.

Q. Which is correct according to the conversation?

(a) The man might not call Susan.

(b) There are many messages for the woman.

(c) The woman didn't say that Susan would call back.

(d) There is a memo for the man.

해석_ W: 마이크, 왜 이렇게 늦었어? 두 번이나 전화했는데 안 받더라.

M: 오늘 늦을 거라고 말했잖아.

W: 미안, 깜빡했다. 전화 왔었어. 수잔이래. 급히 전할 말이 있는 것 같더라.

M: 정말? 무슨 일인지 말했어?

W: 아니. 네가 집에 오면 바로 전화해 달라고 말했어.

M: 지금 전화해야겠다.

W: 잠깐만. 메모해 둔 게 있어. 여기 적어 놓은 번호로 전화해 달래.

Q. 대화에 따르면 맞는 것은 어느 것인가?

(a) 남자는 수잔에게 전화를 걸지 않을지도 모른다.

(b) 여자에게 많은 메시지가 있다.

(c) 여자는 수잔이 다시 전화할 거라는 것을 말하지 않았다.

(d) 남자를 위한 메모가 하나 있다.

해설_ 여자의 마지막 대사에서 메모해 둔 게 있다고 했으므로 (d)가 정답이다.

어휘_ urgent 긴급한

정답_ (d)

5.

M: Excuse me. Can I help you?

W: I'm from DDA firm. I have an appointment with the CEO of this company.

M: Do you have a permit? I'm sorry, but you can't enter the building without it.

W: I didn't know anything about needing a permit. Could you allow me to enter just for today?
M: Ok. May I ask your name?
W: I'm Karen.
M: Follow me. I apologize if you were upset by my behavior. Nowadays I must check everyone thoroughly due to security issues.
W: That's ok.

Q. Which is correct according to the conversation?

(a) The woman forgot her permit.
(b) The woman will not meet the CEO.
(c) The woman arranged to meet the CEO.
(d) The man is working at the personnel department.

해석_ M: 실례합니다. 도와 드릴까요?

W: 저는 DDA 회사에서 왔습니다. 이 회사 사장님과 만나기로 약속이 돼 있어요.

M: 허가증을 가지고 계신가요? 죄송하지만, 허가증 없이는 건물에 들어가실 수 없습니다.

W: 허가증이 필요한지 전혀 몰랐는데요. 오늘만 그냥 들어가게 해 주시겠습니까?

M: 알겠습니다. 성함이 어떻게 되시죠?

W: 카렌입니다.

M: 절 따라오세요. 만약 제 행동이 불쾌하셨다면 사과드립니다. 요즘 보안상의 문제로 모든 사람들을 철저히 확인해야 해서요.

W: 괜찮습니다.

Q. 대화에 따르면 맞는 것은 어느 것인가?

(a) 여자는 허가증을 깜빡했다.
(b) 여자는 사장을 만나지 못할 것이다.
(c) 여자는 사장과 만나기로 약속했다.
(d) 남자는 인사부에서 일하고 있다.

해설_ 여자의 첫 번째 대사에서, 사장과 만나기로 약속이 돼 있다고 말했으므로 (c)가 정답이다.

어휘_ permit 허가증 thoroughly 철저히 personnel department 인사과

정답_ (c)

6.

W: Jack, do you know why Ted looks so depressed?
M: His father was hospitalized a few days ago.
W: Oh. I didn't hear about that. What's wrong with him?
M: I don't know. I'm going to go visit this evening with Jane. Will you come with me?
W: Sure. When will you meet her?
M: We are supposed to meet at 6 in front of the hospital.
W: Then, I'll see you there.

Q. Why are they going to the hospital?

(a) Because their friend's father is in the hospital.
(b) Because their friend has been sick.
(c) Because Jane will come to meet them.
(d) Because the man's father passed away.

해석_ W: 잭, 테드가 왜 우울해 보이는지 아니?

M: 걔네 아버지가 며칠 전에 병원에 입원하셨대.

W: 아. 그런 소식 못 들었는데. 어디가 아프신 거야?

M: 몰라. 오늘 저녁에 제인과 함께 병문안 갈 거야. 너도 같이 갈래?

W: 물론이지. 걔랑 언제 만나기로 했는데?

M: 병원 앞에서 6시에 만나기로 했어.

W: 그럼, 거기서 보자.

Q. 그들은 왜 병원에 가려 하는가?

(a) 그들의 친구 아버지가 병원에 입원해 계시기 때문에
(b) 그들의 친구가 아팠기 때문에
(c) 제인이 그들을 만나러 오기 때문에
(d) 남자의 아버지가 돌아가셨기 때문에

해설_ 병원에 입원해 계신 그들 친구 아버지의 병문안에 관한 내용이 나오므로 정답은 (a)가 된다.

어휘_ hospitalize 병원에 입원시키다 pass away 돌아가시다

정답_ (a)

7.

M: How was your first high school reunion?
W: It was really fun. It's been 5 years since we last met.

M: Wow. Must have been a little awkward.

W: At first it was, but we warmed up after talking about our school days.

M: It must have been fun. I've got a reunion coming up next week that I was hesitant to go to. But after hearing of your experience, I think I should go to the party.

W: I'll bet that you'll have a good time.

Q. Which is correct about the man?

(a) He couldn't go to the reunion party.

(b) He determined to go to the reunion.

(c) He is the woman's best friend.

(d) He sent the invitation to his friends by email.

해석_ M: 첫 고등학교 동창회 어땠어?

W: 정말 재밌었어. 5년 만에 만났지.

M: 와. 좀 어색했겠다.

W: 처음엔 그랬는데 학창시절 얘기를 나누고 나서 친숙해졌어.

M: 재밌었겠다. 다음주에 동창회가 있는데 갈까 망설였어. 근데 네 얘길 듣고 나니 가는 게 좋을 것 같다.

W: 네가 즐거운 시간을 보내게 될 거라고 장담해.

Q. 남자에 관해 맞는 것은 어느 것인가?

(a) 그는 동창회 파티에 가지 못했다.

(b) 그는 동창회에 가기로 결심했다.

(c) 그는 여자의 가장 친한 친구다.

(d) 그는 그의 친구들에게 이메일로 초대장을 보냈다.

해설_ 여자의 얘기를 듣고 동창회에 가야겠다고 했으므로 정답은 (b)가 된다. (c)는 남자와 여자가 서로 친구인 건 맞지만 가장 친한 사이인지는 알 수 없으므로 정답이 될 수 없다.

어휘_ reunion 동창회 warm up 친숙해지다

정답_ (b)

8.

W: When are you leaving for your business trip?

M: I'm leaving tomorrow at dawn, so I'm worried about being able to wake up. I think I should stay up all night.

W: You should go home early today. When do you usually finish work?

M: Around 7 o'clock.

W: You may take off at 4 o'clock today.

M: Thank you. Who will be in charge of my work while I'm in England?

W: Matt will take care of it.

M: Please tell him to check the email.

Q. What is the man going to do tomorrow?

(a) He's going to come to the office.

(b) He's going to meet Matt.

(c) He's going on a vacation.

(d) He's going to go abroad.

해석_ W: 출장 언제 떠나죠?

M: 내일 새벽에 떠나요. 그래서 일어날 수 있을지 걱정돼요. 날 밤 새야 할 것 같아요.

W: 오늘은 집에 일찍 가는 게 좋겠네요. 보통 일이 언제 끝나죠?

M: 7시쯤요.

W: 오늘은 4시에 가도 좋아요.

M: 감사합니다. 제가 영국에 가 있는 동안 누가 제 일을 맡죠?

W: 매트가 맡을 거예요.

M: 그에게 메일 확인하라고 전해 주세요.

Q. 남자는 내일 무엇을 할 것인가?

(a) 그는 회사에 출근할 것이다.

(b) 그는 매트를 만날 것이다.

(c) 그는 휴가를 갈 것이다.

(d) 그는 해외로 갈 것이다.

해설_ 남자의 영국 출장에 관한 대화이므로 (d)가 정답이다.

어휘_ come to the office 출근하다

정답_ (d)

9.

M: Thank you for coming to my house. Would you like something to drink, green tea, apple juice or coffee?

W: I'd like a cup of coffee.

M: Black or milk?

W: Milk, please. Black is not my cup of tea.

M: Here you are.

W: It smells good. Where did you get it?

M: I bought it at the new coffee shop in the mall.

W: I should buy some too. Let's go there

together in a little bit.

Q. Which is correct according to the conversation?

(a) The woman likes drinking black coffee.
(b) The woman came to the man's house-warming party.
(c) The woman will buy coffee.
(d) The woman and man will go shopping.

해석_ M: 우리 집에 와 줘서 고마워. 뭐 마실래, 녹차, 사과 주스, 아님 커피?
W: 커피 마실래.
M: 블랙, 아님 밀크?
W: 밀크로 줘. 블랙은 내 타입이 아니야.
M: 여기 있어.
W: 향이 좋다. 어디서 샀니?
M: 쇼핑몰 안의 새로 생긴 커피점에서 샀어.
W: 나도 좀 사야겠다. 좀 있다가 거기 같이 가자.

Q. 대화에 따르면 맞는 것은 어느 것인가?

(a) 여자는 블랙커피 마시는 것을 좋아한다.
(b) 여자는 남자의 집들이에 왔다.
(c) 여자는 커피를 살 것이다.
(d) 여자와 남자는 쇼핑을 하러 갈 것이다.

해설_ 남자에게 커피를 어디서 샀는지 물으면서 같이 사러 가자고 했으므로 (c)가 정답이다.

어휘_ one's cup of tea ~의 취향(에 맞는 것)

정답_ (c)

10.

W: How about applying for this internship program?

M: Internship? Tell me more about it.

W: Ok. It's a good chance to learn about accounting and working in a company. Plus, If you do well at the internship, there's an opportunity to be hired at the company.

M: Did you apply?

W: I applied to another company. I'm not interested in accounting. But you are majoring in accounting, so it would be a good experience for you.

M: Thanks for thinking of me. I'll give it a shot.

W: You'll do great.

Q. What will most probably happen following the conversation?

(a) The man will submit his resume for the internship.
(b) The woman will apply for an accounting internship.
(c) The man will be hired to the company.
(d) The woman will interview for a job.

해석_ W: 이 인턴십 프로그램에 지원해 보는 게 어때?
M: 인턴십? 좀 더 얘기해 봐.
W: 좋아. 회계와 회사 일을 배울 수 있는 좋은 기회야. 게다가, 인턴 시기에 잘해 내면 그 회사에 고용될 기회를 얻을 수 있어.
M: 넌 지원했니?
W: 난 다른 회사에 지원했어. 회계에 관심이 없거든. 하지만 넌 회계를 전공하고 있으니까 좋은 경험이 될 거야.
M: 생각해 줘서 고마워. 한번 시도해 볼게.
W: 넌 잘할 수 있을 거야.

Q. 대화 후 가장 일어날 것 같은 일은 무엇인가?

(a) 남자는 인턴십을 위해 이력서를 제출할 것이다.
(b) 여자는 회계 인턴십에 지원할 것이다.
(c) 남자는 그 회사에 고용될 것이다.
(d) 여자는 취업 면접을 볼 것이다.

해설_ 여자가 남자에게 인턴십 프로그램의 지원을 제안하는 대화 내용이다. 여자의 얘기를 듣고 시도해 보겠다고 했으므로 (a)가 정답임을 알 수 있다.

어휘_ accounting 회계 give it a shot 한번 시도해 보다

정답_ (a)

Chapter 14 대화문 내용 추론하기

STEP 1 Pretest Clinic

7.

해석_ M: 이번 여름방학에 크루즈 여행가는 거 어때?

W: 그거 아주 좋겠다. 난 카리브해를 항해하고 싶어.

M: 좋아. 하지만 난 좀 더 북쪽 지역으로 생각하고 있었어.

W: 서인도 제도 말이야? 하지만 거긴 이미 갔었잖아.

M: 아니, 서인도 제도 말고. 멀리 북쪽 알래스카 지역으로 갈까 생각하고 있었어.

W: 와! 그럼 연어낚시, 사금 채취하기, 그리고 개 썰매 타기를 할 수 있겠다!

M: 동의하는 걸로 생각할게.

Q. 대화를 통해 추론할 수 있는 것은?

(a) 여자는 연어낚시 하러 가는 걸 무서워한다.

(b) 남자는 이미 카리브해를 다녀왔다.

(c) 그들은 신혼여행 가기를 원한다.

(d) 그들은 알래스카로 여행갈 계획이다.

정답_ (d)

8.

해석_ W: 회의가 아직 시작 안 됐으면 좋겠는데.

M: 네가 주요 발표를 하니까 너 없이 시작하지 않을 거야.

W: 네 말이 맞을 수도 있지만, 늦은 것 말고도 이미 충분히 긴장하고 있어.

M: 그건 네 잘못이 아니야. 고객은 급한 상황이었고 아무도 그걸 해결할 수 없었어.

W: 그것 때문에 준비할 시간이 많이 없었어.

M: 너무 걱정 마. 모든 게 잘될 거야.

Q. 여자에 관해 추론할 수 있는 것은?

(a) 그녀는 회의에서 중요한 역할을 할 것이다.

(b) 그녀는 발표 준비를 하고 있다.

(c) 그녀는 회의를 시작했다.

(d) 그녀는 위급한 상황에 처했다.

정답_ (a)

9.

해석_ M: 계란은 어떻게 먹을래?

W: 늘 먹던 대로, 노른자가 위로 가게 해줘.

M: 오늘은 좀 다르게 먹는 게 어때? 난 후딱 오믈렛을 만들 생각

이었는데.

W: 그 속에 뭘 넣을 건데?

M: 햄, 치즈, 피망, 당근…. 알잖아, 전통 스페인식 오믈렛 말이야.

W: 난 네가 뭔가 다른 요리를 하는 줄 알았는데.

M: 좋아. 그럼, 올리브, 치즈, 양파는 어때?

W: 듣기만 해도 군침 돈다.

Q. 대화를 통해 추론할 수 있는 것은?

(a) 여자는 달걀 반숙을 원한다.

(b) 남자는 아침 식사를 요리하고 있다.

(c) 여자는 그녀의 계란을 삶았다.

(d) 그들은 간식을 좋아하지 않는다.

정답_ (b)

STEP 2 Dictation

정답_ 7. What do you think about taking a cruise

I was thinking of somewhere a bit further north

I'll take that as a yes

8. they would start without you since you're giving the main presentation

I'm already nervous enough without being late

Because of that I had far less time to prepare

9. The same as usual, sunny-side up

I was thinking of whipping up an omelet

My mouth is watering, just hearing about it

STEP 3 Actual Test

1.

W: Do you know where the new conference center is? It opened last month.

M: Yes, I do. It's three blocks away from here.

W: Please tell me exactly. I have to go there to attend the board meeting this afternoon.

M: Sure. Go out the main entrance and turn right. Go straight a couple of blocks down the street and you'll see a sign for our firm. Turn right there.

W: I'm sorry. Could you tell me again?

M: Ok. Then, I'll make a map.

Q. What can be inferred from the conversation?

(a) The man has been to the new conference center.

(b) The woman has a high position in the corporation.

(c) The woman will ultimatly take a taxi.

(d) The man described how to go there again.

해석_ W: 새 회의센터 어딘지 알아? 지난달에 오픈했잖아.

M: 응, 알아. 여기서 세 블록 떨어져 있어.

W: 정확히 알려줘. 오늘 오후에 임원회의 참석하러 거기 가야 해.

M: 그래. 회사 정문으로 나가서 오른쪽으로 돌아. 길 아래로 몇 블록 직진해 가면 우리 회사 간판이 보일 거야. 거기서 오른쪽으로 돌아.

W: 미안. 다시 한 번 말해 줄래?

M: 좋아. 그럼 약도를 그려 줄게.

Q. 대화를 통해 추론할 수 있는 것은?

(a) 남자는 새 회의센터에 갔다 온 적이 있다.

(b) 여자는 회사에서 높은 직책을 맡고 있다.

(c) 여자는 결국 택시를 탈 것이다.

(d) 남자는 그곳에 가는 방법을 다시 설명했다.

해설_ 오후에 임원회의에 참석하러 가야 한다고 했으므로 그녀의 직급이 높을 것임을 짐작할 수 있다. 따라서 정답은 (b). (a)는 남자가 회의센터의 위치를 알고 있다고 해서 그곳에 가봤다고는 단정지을 수 없으므로 정답이 될 수 없다.

어휘_ board 중역(회) main entrance 정문

정답_ (b)

2.

M: Honey, why have you got so much housework piled up?

W: I've had a lot of things to do. Can you buy me some detergent and soap?

M: How much should I get?

W: 1kg of neutral detergent and 3 bars of soap.

M: Ok. Anything else?

W: Get some baby food and don't forget to take the membership card.

Q. What can be inferred from the conversation?

(a) The man and woman have done their housework.

(b) The man will go to the store.

(c) The man will buy kitchen utensils.

(d) The man has helped his wife.

해석_ M: 자기야, 집안일이 왜 이렇게 많이 밀렸어?

W: 할 일이 너무 많았어. 세제랑 비누 좀 사다 줄래?

M: 얼마나 사야 하는데?

W: 중성세제 1kg짜리랑 비누 3개.

M: 좋아. 다른 건 없어?

W: 이유식 좀 사오고, 멤버십 카드 가져가는 거 잊지 마.

Q. 대화를 통해 추론할 수 있는 것은?

(a) 남자와 여자는 그들의 집안일을 끝냈다.

(b) 남자는 가게에 갈 것이다.

(c) 남자는 주방용품을 살 것이다.

(d) 남자는 그의 아내를 도왔다.

해설_ 여자가 세제와 비누, 그리고 이유식을 사다 달라고 했으므로 (b)가 정답임을 알 수 있다.

어휘_ pile up 쌓이다 detergent 세제 baby food 이유식 kitchen utensil 주방용품

정답_ (b)

3.

W: Good morning. Why do you look so bad?

M: I didn't get much sleep last night.

W: Why don't you sleep more? It's a holiday.

M: I'd like to, but I have to be at the University to prepare for my graduation thesis.

W: Then, when will you come back home?

M: I'm not sure but maybe around 8 p.m.

W: Can you come by 7? I was hoping you could look after your brother while I'm out with your father.

M: Ok.

Q. What can be inferred from the conversation?

(a) The woman will take care of her children.
(b) The man has been sick with the flu.
(c) The woman and her son will go out tonight.
(d) The man will stay home with his brother tonight.

해석_ W: 안녕. 왜 그렇게 안 좋아 보이니?

M: 지난밤에 잠을 많이 못잤어요.

W: 좀 더 자지 그래? 휴일이잖아.

M: 저도 그러고 싶은데 졸업 논문 준비하러 학교에 가야 해요.

W: 그럼 집에 언제 올 거니?

M: 확실하진 않은데 아마 저녁 8시쯤요.

W: 7시까지 올 수 있니? 아빠랑 외출해 있는 동안 네 동생을 돌
봐 주길 바라고 있었어.

M: 알겠어요.

Q. 대화를 통해 추론할 수 있는 것은?

(a) 여자는 그녀의 아이들을 돌볼 것이다.

(b) 남자는 독감에 걸렸다.

(c) 여자와 그녀의 아들은 밤에 외출할 것이다.

(d) 남자는 오늘 밤 그의 동생과 함께 집에 있을 것이다.

해설_ 외출해 있는 동안 동생을 돌봐 달라고 부탁했으므로 (d)가 정답
임을 알 수 있다.

어휘_ graduation thesis 논문

정답_ (d)

4.

M: What's wrong with you?
W: I have terrible morning sickness. Isn't there any medicine for that?
M: How long have you had morning sickness?
W: For three days maybe.
M: You shouldn't take any medicine.
W: What if it gets worse?
M: If that's the case, it would be better to stay in the hospital.

Q. What can be inferred about the woman?

(a) She was sick in the morning.

(b) She twisted her ankle while jogging this morning.
(c) She is expecting.
(d) She needs radiation therapy.

해석_ M: 어디가 불편하세요?

W: 입덧이 심해요. 입덧에 먹는 약은 없나요?

M: 얼마 동안 입덧을 하셨나요?

W: 아마 3일 정도요.

M: 어떠한 약도 복용하시면 안 됩니다.

W: 더 심해지면 어쩌죠?

M: 그런 경우엔 입원하시는 게 좋겠어요.

Q. 여자에 관해 추론할 수 있는 것은?

(a) 그녀는 아침에 아팠다.

(b) 그녀는 오늘 아침 조깅하는 동안 발목을 삐었다.

(c) 그녀는 임신 중이다.

(d) 그녀는 방사선 치료가 필요하다.

해설_ 입덧이 심하다고 했으므로 여자가 임신 중임을 알 수 있다.

어휘_ morning sickness 입덧 twist one's ankle 발목을 삐
다 expect 〈진행형으로〉 임신 중이다 radiation therapy
방사선 치료

정답_ (c)

5.

W: Do you know where Jane is? I haven't seen her today.
M: She called in sick this morning.
W: Jimmy, tell me the truth. Is she job hunting?
M: Actually, I think so. She must be thinking the grass is greener at another company.
W: What's her complaint? If she had told me, I would have taken it seriously.
M: I can't figure her out. She is a closed book.

Q. What can be inferred from the conversation?

(a) Jane is sick.
(b) Jane is well-read.
(c) The grass is green.
(d) Jane might quit her job.

(d) They will write a petition to the mayor.

해석_ M: 매년 일어나는 홍수에 넌더리가 나.

W: 우리가 뭔가 해야 해.

M: 알아, 하지만 자연재해를 막기 위해 우리가 할 수 있는 일이 뭘까?

W: 시장에게 탄원서를 보내는 게 어떨까?

M: 신경이나 쓸까?

W: 내년에 선거에 출마하려면 그래야지.

M: 그래, 좋았어.

W: 올해는 이 홍수를 끝내야만 해.

Q. 대화를 통해 추론할 수 있는 것은?

(a) 남자는 완전히 지쳤다.

(b) 여자는 막다른 골목에 다다를 것이다.

(c) 그들은 선거에 출마할 것이다.

(d) 그들은 시장에게 탄원서를 쓸 것이다.

해설_ 매년 일어나는 홍수에 넌더리가 난다며 더 이상의 자연재해를 막을 수 있는 방법에 대해 얘기를 나누고 있는 내용이다. 시장에게 탄원서를 보내자는 여자의 의견에 남자도 찬성의 뜻을 나타냈으므로 (d)가 정답임을 알 수 있다.

어휘_ annual 해마다의 flood 홍수 prevent 막다 natural disaster 자연재해 petition 탄원서 burn out 기진맥진하다 hit a dead end 막다른 길에 다다르다

정답_ (d)

해석_ W: 제인 어딨는지 알아요? 오늘 그녀를 못 봤어요.

M: 오늘 아침에 아파서 못 나온다고 전화했어요.

W: 지미, 사실대로 얘기해요. 그녀가 다른 일자리를 찾고 있나요?

M: 실은, 그런 것 같아요. 그녀는 다른 회사가 더 좋아 보인다고 생각하나 봐요.

W: 그녀의 불만이 뭐예요? 내게 말했다면 진지하게 받아들였을 텐데.

M: 그녀의 마음을 알 수가 없어요. 그녀는 이해하기 어려운 사람이에요.

Q. 대화를 통해 추론할 수 있는 것은?

(a) 제인은 아프다.

(b) 제인은 책을 많이 읽는다.

(c) 잔디가 푸르다.

(d) 제인은 직장을 그만둘지도 모른다.

해설_ 남자의 두 번째 대사를 통해 제인이 새 직장을 구하고 있음을 짐작할 수 있으므로 정답은 (d)가 된다.

어휘_ call in sick 아파서 결근[결석]하겠다고 전화하다 The grass is greener (on the other side). 〈속담〉 남의 떡이 더 커 보인다. figure out 이해하다 closed book 이해하기 어려운 사람 well-read 책을 많이 읽은

정답_ (d)

6.

M: I'm sick and tired of these annual floods.

W: We have to do something about it.

M: I know, but what can we do to prevent a natural disaster?

W: Maybe we should write a petition to the mayor.

M: Do you think he cares?

W: He'd better if he wants to run for office next year.

M: Ok, sounds great.

W: We have to strike an end to these floods this year.

Q. What can be inferred from the conversation?

(a) The man is totally burnt out.

(b) The woman will hit a dead end.

(c) They will run for office.

7.

W: Did you hear the news about Tom and Sarah?

M: What news?

W: Tom asked Sarah to marry him but she turned him down.

M: Really? I thought they were engaged for 3 years.

W: Yes. They were planning to tie the knot next year.

M: But, what changed Sarah's mind?

W: Tom cheated on her while he was in America on business.

M: Really? Thank God Sarah's not marrying that player.

Q. What can be inferred from the conversation?

(a) Tom and Sarah split up.
(b) Tom and Sarah will tie the knot next year.
(c) Tom got up on the wrong side of the bed today.
(d) Tom hangs on Sarah's every word.

8.

M: I still can't believe I'm in Paris. Tell me I'm not dreaming.
W: Okay, you're not. Why don't we find a hotel first?
M: Look at that hotel. Doesn't it look like a hundred-year-old chateau?
W: Wow! That's beautiful. Let's go and check it out.
M: I love the ambiance here. Oh, look at that woman. Isn't her style so avant-garde?
W: Yes. Quite a bunch of fashionable people here.

M: There's a concierge. Let's ask him about this hotel.
W: I wish I could say adieu to my small ugly dorm and stay in this hotel forever.

Q. What can be inferred from the conversation?

(a) They think the hotel is old-fashioned.
(b) They have a hankering to stay at the hotel.
(c) They can stay in the hotel their whole life.
(d) They are checking out.

9.

W: Jeff! I heard you got dumped. Is it true?
M: I don't want to talk about it. Just leave me alone.
W: Come on. Take it like a man. It's not the end of the world. Besides, she wasn't even

your type of girl.
M: I told you. Just drop it!
W: Keep your chin up! Let me hook you up with a pretty one.
M: Are you teasing me? Get out of here!

Q. What can be inferred from the conversation?

(a) The man is pulling her leg.
(b) The woman is hooking the man up with a pretty girl.
(c) The woman is a college drop-out.
(d) The man broke up with his girlfriend.

해석_ W: 제프! 너 차였다면서. 정말이야?

　　 M: 말하고 싶지 않아. 그냥 혼자 내버려 둬.

　　 W: 왜 그래. 남자답게 받아들여. 세상 끝난 것도 아닌데. 게다가 걘 네 스타일도 아니었잖아.

　　 M: 말했지. 그 얘기 그만 좀 해!

　　 W: 기운 내! 내가 예쁜 여자 소개시켜 줄게.

　　 M: 나 놀리니? 여기서 나가!

　　 Q. 대화를 통해 추론할 수 있는 것은?

　　 (a) 남자는 여자를 놀리고 있다.

　　 (b) 여자는 남자에게 예쁜 여자를 소개시켜 줄 것이다.

　　 (c) 여자는 대학 중퇴자다.

　　 (d) 남자는 여자친구와 헤어졌다.

해설_ 여자친구에게 차인 남자를 위로하고 있으므로 (d)가 정답임을 알 수 있다. 여자가 예쁜 여자를 소개시켜 주겠다고는 말했지만 실제 소개시켜 줄지는 알 수 없으므로 (b)는 정답이 될 수 없다.

어휘_ get dumped 차이다 Drop it! 그 얘기 그만둬! keep one's chin up 기운을 내다 hook up with 소개시켜 주다 tease 괴롭히다, 놀리다 pull one's leg ～를 놀리다 drop-out 중퇴자 break up with ～와 헤어지다

정답_ (d)

10.

M: You know what? The science building caught on fire last night.
W: Oh, really? That's terrible!
M: Fortunately, the fire fighters got there before too much damage occured.
W: Do they know what caused the fire?

M: They say it was one of the electrical outlets.
W: You know how old the building is. They should tear it down and build a brand new one.
M: You took the words right out of my mouth.

Q. What can be inferred from the conversation?

(a) They will tear the building down.
(b) They are looking for electrical outlets.
(c) The damage wasn't extensive.
(d) The fire fighters were inept.

해석_ M: 그거 알아? 지난밤에 과학관에 불이 났어.

　　 W: 아, 정말? 그거 참 안됐구나!

　　 M: 다행히도 큰 피해가 나기 전에 소방수들이 왔어.

　　 W: 화재 원인이 뭔지 안데?

　　 M: 전기 콘센트 중 하나였대.

　　 W: 건물이 얼마나 오래됐는지 알잖아. 건물을 허물고 새로 지어야 해.

　　 M: 내 말이 그 말이야.

　　 Q. 대화를 통해 추론할 수 있는 것은?

　　 (a) 그들은 그 건물을 허물 것이다.

　　 (b) 그들은 전기 콘센트를 찾고 있다.

　　 (c) 피해는 크지 않았다.

　　 (d) 소방수들은 서툴렀다.

해설_ 남자의 두 번째 대사에서, 큰 피해가 나기 전에 소방수들이 왔다고 했으므로 (c)가 정답임을 알 수 있다.

어휘_ catch on fire 불이 나다 electrical outlet 전기 콘센트 tear down 허물다 take the words out of one's mouth ～이 말하려고 하는 것을 먼저 말하다 extensive 광범한, 대규모의 inept 서투른

정답_ (c)

Part 4

Chapter 15 담화문 주제 파악하기

STEP 1 Pretest Clinic

1.

해석_ 한 국제 비행사가 어제 시드니에 도착했을 때 체포됐으며, 수백만 달러의 마약 밀수와 돈세탁을 한 후 현금으로 채워진 여행용 가방들을 호주 밖으로 운반한 혐의를 받았습니다. 그는 비행기 조종사로서의 특수 신분을 이용해 수하물 검사를 피해 멜버른과 시드니에서 돈 가방을 가져와 그것들을 베트남으로 돌아가는 비행기들에 실은 것으로 알려졌습니다.

Q. 기사를 가장 잘 요약한 것은 어느 것인가?

(a) 비행사가 마약 밀수로 체포되었다.
(b) 비행기 사고가 시드니에서 일어났다.
(c) 조종사가 승객들의 짐을 훔쳤다.
(d) 비행기는 기상 상태가 나빠 이륙할 수 없었다.

정답_ (a)

2.

해석_ 그릇에 계란 노른자와 우유를 함께 넣고 부드러워질 때까지 휘저으세요. 가루 반죽 한 피를 표면에 밀가루를 약간 뿌린 후 얇아질 때까지 늘려 주세요. 그 얇게 편 반죽피 위에 약 3cm 간격으로 모짜렐라 치즈를 조금씩 놓으세요. 얇게 편 또 한 피의 반죽을 그 위에 덮으세요. 라비올리 같은 모짜렐라 꾸러미들을 만들기 위해 2~3cm의 사각 형태로 자르세요. 가장자리들을 포크로 누르세요. 남아 있는 가루 반죽피와 모짜렐라를 가지고 이 과정을 반복하세요. 뜨거운 기름에 노랗게 익을 때까지 살짝 튀기세요. 종이 타월 위에 놓고 기름이 빠져 나가게 하고, 천일염으로 간을 맞추세요.

Q. 무엇에 관한 글인가?

(a) 요리법
(b) 레스토랑의 주 요리 광고
(c) 가스레인지 사용법
(d) 재료를 저장하는 방법

정답_ (a)

3.

해석_ 한 보고서에 따르면, 대중적인 패스트푸드는 많은 양의 소금이 함유되어 있어 건강에 위험한 것으로 나타났습니다. 소금은 심장마비, 신부전증, 그리고 뇌졸중을 포함하여 고혈압과 심장혈관 질환과 아주 밀접한 연관이 있습니다. 나트륨이 많이 든 음식을 먹는 아이들은 비만, 천식, 그리고 고혈압에 걸릴 위험이 있습니다.

Q. 화자가 이야기하려고 하는 요점은 무엇인가?

(a) 소금은 많은 요리의 가장 중요한 재료다.
(b) 짠 음식은 체중 감소에 도움이 된다.
(c) 짠 음식은 다양한 병의 원인이 된다.
(d) 어린이들은 패스트푸드를 그만 먹어야 한다.

정답_ (c)

STEP 2 Dictation

정답_ 1. carrying suitcases stuffed with cash
in a multimillion-dollar drug-running and money-laundering operation
privileged status as an airline pilot to bypass customs bag checks

2. Combine the egg yolk and milk in a bowl and stir
Roll one sheet of dough out
Top with another sheet of dough
Shallow fry in hot oil until golden

3. contain high levels of salt so they are a health danger
There is a strong link between salt
Children who eat a high sodium diet are at risk of developing obesity, asthma

STEP 3 Actual Test

1.

The biggest enemy of your waistline may be sitting on your desk or waiting for you in front of the vending machine. It's the sweet tea you order at lunch, the soft drink you sip all day, the sports drink you guzzle after a run or that margarita you enjoy when you go out to eat. These are high in caloric value and threaten your health.

Q. What is the main point the speaker is trying to make?

(a) You should drink less refreshing beverages.
(b) You need to drink lots of beverages after exercising.
(c) Drinking alcohol is bad for your health.
(d) You should have low-fat food.

 당신 허리둘레의 가장 큰 적은 당신의 책상 위에 있거나 자판기 앞에서 당신을 기다리고 있을지도 모릅니다. 그것은 점심 때 주문하는 달콤한 티, 온종일 조금씩 마시는 탄산음료, 달리기를 한 후 꿀꺽꿀꺽 마시는 이온 음료나 외식할 때 즐기는 마르가리타입니다. 이것들은 칼로리가 높고 당신의 건강을 위협합니다.

Q. 화자가 이야기하려고 하는 요점은 무엇인가?

(a) 청량음료를 적게 마셔야 한다.
(b) 운동한 후에 음료수를 많이 마셔야 한다.
(c) 술을 마시는 것은 건강에 나쁘다.
(d) 저지방 음식을 먹어야 한다.

해설_ 허리살의 가장 큰 적이 무엇인가에 대해 언급하고 있는 글이다. 달콤한 티, 탄산음료 등이 바로 가장 큰 적이며 건강을 위협한다고 했으므로 정답은 (a)다.

어휘_ waistline 허리의 둘레 sip 조금씩 마시다 guzzle 꿀꺽꿀꺽 마시다 margarita 마르가리타(테킬라 술과 레몬즙의 칵테일) be high in caloric value 칼로리가 높다 refreshing beverage 청량음료 low-fat 저지방의

정답_ (a)

2.

Looking for an inexpensive way to celebrate Valentine's Day? Here are some ideas. Make a Valentine's Day movie date with your sweetie. Prepare some popcorn, a couple of DVDs, and a list of movies you want to watch together. Presenting a gift card or making a photo book is also a good idea.

Q. What is the main point of the talk?

(a) The way to make an event with your friends
(b) The way to make a gift for your lover
(c) The way to spend the holidays with your family
(d) The way to save money on special days

해석_ 발렌타인데이를 축하하기 위한 저렴한 방법을 찾고 계신가요? 여기 몇 가지 아이디어가 있습니다. 당신의 연인과 함께 발렌타인데이를 영화 관람의 날로 만드세요. 팝콘, DVD 2∼3장, 그리고 함께 보고 싶은 영화 목록을 준비하세요. 상품권을 주거나 사진첩을 만드는 것 또한 좋은 아이디어입니다.

Q. 담화의 요점은 무엇인가?

(a) 친구들과 함께 이벤트를 만드는 방법
(b) 연인을 위해 선물을 만드는 방법
(c) 가족과 함께 휴일을 보내는 방법
(d) 특별한 날에 돈을 아끼는 방법

해설_ 글 첫 부분에 발렌타인데이를 축하하기 위한 저렴한 방법 몇 가지가 있다고 말하며 그것에 대한 내용이 이어지고 있으므로 (d)가 정답이다.

어휘_ inexpensive 비싸지 않은

정답_ (d)

3.

If you have health insurance that requires co-insurance or a co-payment, it may be less expensive to pay full price for immunizations at the County Health Department. They're offered on a walk-in basis. The department charges on a sliding-fee scale based on income. For a child's diphtheria-tetanus-pertussis vaccine, that's $21.96. An adult TD booster is $22.18, but most uninsured people must pay more — $42.05.

Q. Which of the following best summarizes the talk?

(a) Health insurance can be disburdened from expensive medical expense.
(b) Health insurance has expanded in many medical areas.
(c) Medical expense will rise dramatically more than last year.
(d) New vaccine program succeeded in clinical tests.

해설_ 만약 공동보험이나 본인 부담액을 필요로 하는 건강보험을 가지고 있다면, 보건소에서 예방 주사 접종 시 드는 전체 비용이 적게

들 수 있다. 예방 주사 접종은 예약 없이 받을 수 있다. 보건소는 소득을 토대로 차등 적용을 해 비용을 청구한다. 어린이를 위한 디프테리아-파상풍-백일해 백신 접종 비용은 21.96달러이다. 어른의 파상풍-디프테리아 예방 접종은 22.18달러이지만, 보험에 들지 않은 대부분의 사람들은 그보다 더 많은 42.05달러를 내야 한다.

Q. 담화를 가장 잘 요약한 것은 어느 것인가?

(a) 건강보험은 값비싼 의료비의 부담을 덜어줄 수 있다.

(b) 건강보험은 많은 의료 부문에서 확대됐다.

(c) 의료비는 작년보다 더 급격히 오를 것이다.

(d) 새로운 백신 프로그램이 임상실험에서 성공했다.

해설_ 글 첫 부분에 건강보험을 가지고 있을 경우 예방 주사를 맞을 때 드는 비용이 줄어들 수 있다고 말하면서 이에 대한 구체적인 설명이 이어지고 있으므로, 정답은 (a)다.

어휘_ health insurance 건강보험 co-insurance 공동보험 co-payment 본인 부담액 immunization 예방 주사 walk-in basis 예약 없이 sliding-fee scale 차등 diphtheria 디프테리아 tetanus 파상풍 pertussis 백일해 booster (면역제의) 두 번째 예방 주사 disburden 부담을 덜어주다 dramatically 급격히 clinical test 임상실험

정답_ (a)

4.

Gorilla numbers have grown in an eastern Congo park that is home to some of the world's last remaining mountain gorillas. A census released by the Congolese Wildlife Authority shows 10 gorillas have been born since August 2007 in Virunga National Park. Park director Curtis Mayes called it "a triumph for conservation."

Q. What is the main idea of the talk?

(a) Gorillas should live in the mountain.

(b) Gorillas are threatened with extinction.

(c) Gorillas in the park have experienced a baby boom.

(d) Gorillas will be moved from Congo park to Virunga National Park.

해석_ 고릴라의 수가 세계에서 마지막 남아 있는 마운틴 고릴라들의 서식지인 콩고 동부지역의 공원에서 증가했다. 콩고 야생동물 기관에 의해 발표된 고릴라 개체수 조사에 따르면, 2007년 8월 이래로 비룽가 국립공원에서 10마리의 고릴라가 태어났다. 공원 관장인 커터스 메이스는 이를 "(고릴라) 보호의 승리"라고 말했다.

Q. 담화의 요지는 무엇인가?

(a) 고릴라는 산에서 살아야 한다.

(b) 고릴라는 멸종 위기에 처해 있다.

(c) 공원에 사는 고릴라는 출생률이 급상승했다.

(d) 고릴라는 콩고 공원에서 비룽가 국립공원으로 옮겨질 것이다.

해설_ 콩고 동부지역의 공원에서 고릴라의 수가 증가했고, 2007년 8월 이래로 비룽가 국립공원에서 10마리의 고릴라가 태어났다는 내용이므로 (c)가 정답이다.

어휘_ mountain gorilla 마운틴 고릴라 census 개체수 조사 Congolese 콩고의 conservation 보호 extinction 멸종

정답_ (c)

5.

The Arctic's sea ice is shrinking at an alarming rate, with scientists fearful of the impact on wildlife, global weather patterns and countries jostling for vast oil, gas and coal resources. The Herald's Environment Editor, Marian Wilkinson, has just returned from a trip to the Arctic on a Canadian icebreaker. She was surprised that the ice was shrinking so fast.

Q. What is the best title for the talk?

(a) Global Warming Warning
(b) The Recognition of Environmental Pollution
(c) The Scarcity of National Resources
(d) Resource Development

해석_ 북극해의 해빙이 놀라운 속도로 줄어들고 있으며, 과학자들은 야생 생물, 전 세계 기후 양상, 그리고 거대한 석유, 가스, 석탄 자원을 차지하려 다투고 있는 국가들에게 미칠 영향에 대해 두려워하고 있다. 헤럴드 환경 기자, 마리안 윌킨슨은 캐나다 쇄빙선을 타고 북극해 여행에서 막 돌아왔다. 그녀는 얼음이 그렇게 빠르게 녹고 있다는 것에 깜짝 놀랐다.

Q. 담화에 가장 적합한 제목은 무엇인가?

(a) 지구 온난화에 대한 경고
(b) 환경오염의 인식
(c) 국가 자원의 부족
(d) 자원 개발

해설_ 북극해의 해빙이 급속도로 줄어들고 있다는 점과, 야생 생물, 전 세계 기후 양상 등에 미칠 영향에 대한 두려움을 나타내고 있으므로 (a)가 적절하다.

어휘_ Arctic 북극의 sea ice 해빙 at an alarming rate 놀라운 속도로 jostle 경합하다 vast 거대한 icebreaker 쇄빙선 scarcity 부족, 결핍

정답_ (a)

6.

Teenagers who spend a lot of time watching TV or playing video games are at higher risk of developing depression as young adults, a study has found. An expert in adolescent mental health with the National Depression Initiative, Beyond Blue, said spending too much time watching TV or using other electronic media could have a cascading effect.

Q. What is the main point of the talk?

(a) Juvenile crime is influenced by violent scenes on TV.
(b) Teenagers's moods are impacted by TV and electronic media.
(c) Young adults feel tired after playing video games.
(d) These days teenagers depend on computers and TV.

해설_ 한 연구에 따르면, TV를 많이 보거나 비디오 게임을 많이 하는 십대들은 젊은 성인들처럼 우울증에 걸릴 위험이 더 높은 것으로 나타났습니다. 국립 우울증 발의 기관인 Beyond Blue의 청소년 정신 건강 전문가는 TV를 보거나 다른 전자 미디어를 사용하는 데 지나치게 많은 시간을 보내는 것은 연쇄 반응을 가져올 수도 있다고 말했다.

Q. 담화의 요점은 무엇인가?

(a) 청소년 범죄는 TV에 나오는 폭력 장면에 의해 영향을 받는다.
(b) 십대들의 감정은 TV와 전자 미디어에 크게 영향받는다.
(c) 젊은 성인들은 비디오 게임을 하고 난 후 피로를 느낀다.
(d) 요즘 십대들은 컴퓨터와 TV에 의존한다.

해설_ TV를 많이 보거나 그 밖의 다른 전자 미디어를 많이 사용할 경우 우울증에 걸릴 위험이 높다고 했으므로 (b)가 정답이다.

어휘_ adolescent 청소년기의 cascade 단계적으로 행하다, 폭포처럼 떨어지다 juvenile 청소년 impact 강한 영향을 주다

정답_ (b)

7.

Miikka made 36 saves, and Michael scored on a power play in the first period of the Calgary Flames' 2-0 victory over the Los Angeles Kings on Thursday night. Rene Bourque added an empty-netter with 36 seconds remaining. The Flames are leading 3-0-0 against Los Angeles this season.

Q. What is the report about?

(a) Calgary Flames gained a victory over Los Angeles Kings on Thursday.
(b) Michael scored a lot on Thursday game.
(c) Los Angeles Kings lost the game at first on Thursday.
(d) Calgary and Los Angeles tied the match on Thursday.

해석_ 목요일 저녁 로스앤젤레스 킹스에 캘거리 플레임스가 2대 0으로 승리한 경기의 전반전에서 미카는 36세이브를 기록했고, 마이클은 파워 플레이를 펼치며 득점을 했다. 르네 부르크는 36초를 남긴 상황에서 추가 득점을 했다. 플레임스는 이번 시즌에서 로스앤젤레스에 3승 0무 0패로 앞서가고 있다.

Q. 무엇에 관한 기사인가?

(a) 목요일에 캘거리 플레임스는 로스앤젤레스 킹스를 이겼다.
(b) 마이클은 목요일 경기에서 득점을 많이 했다.
(c) 로스앤젤레스 킹스는 목요일 경기에서 처음으로 졌다.
(d) 캘거리와 로스앤젤레스는 목요일 경기에서 동점을 이뤘다.

해설_ 목요일 저녁에 열린 경기에서 캘거리 플레임스가 로스앤젤레스 킹스를 2대 0으로 이긴 소식을 전하고 있으므로 정답은 (a)다.

어휘_ save (경기에서) 상대방의 득점을 방해함 tie 동점이 되다

정답_ (a)

8.

Gold is used in electronic equipment because it's dependable in extremes of heat and humidity. In the Hubble Space Telescope, for example, gold was used for contacts and connectors that will long outlive the telescope's usefulness.

Q. What is the talk about?

(a) Introduction of new equipment
(b) A space development plan
(c) Use of an electric machine
(d) Use of gold for electronic equipment

해석_ 금은 전자 장비에 사용되는데, 이는 극심한 열과 습기에 견뎌 낼 수 있기 때문이다. 예를 들어 허블 우주 망원경 속에서 금은 망원경을 아주 오래 쓸 수 있도록 해줄 접촉 장치와 연결기로 사용되었다.

Q. 무엇에 관한 담화인가?

(a) 새로운 장비의 소개
(b) 우주 개발 계획
(c) 전기 기계의 사용
(d) 전자 장비에서 금의 사용

해설_ 금이 전자 장비에 활용된다는 내용을 담고 있으므로 정답은 (d)가 된다.

어휘_ extremes 극단적인 상태 humidity 습기 telescope 망원경 contact 접촉 장치 connector 연결기 outlive 보다 오래 남다[계속하다]

정답_ (d)

9.

As the mentor of knitters, Elizabeth Zimmerman, once said, "Knit on, with confidence and hope, through all crises." Well, those are good words for this somber holiday season, and a little humor is a welcome break from all the doom and gloom. Whatever makes you laugh, find some time this season to smile, giggle and enjoy yourself.

Q. What is the main point of the talk?

(a) Humor is the key to overcome depression.

(b) People need to learn a sense of humor.
(c) If you smile, your fortune will improve.
(d) Nothing is more important than smiling.

해석_ 뜨개질 하는 사람들의 스승인 엘리자베스 짐머맨은 이렇게 말한 적이 있습니다. "모든 위기를 무시하고 자신감과 희망을 가지고 뜨개질을 하세요." 음, 이런 우울한 휴일 시즌을 위해서 좋은 말이입니다. 그리고 작은 유머는 모든 절망적인 상태를 잊게 해줍니다. 여러분이 무엇때문에 웃든지간에 이번 시즌에는 웃고, 낄낄 거리고, 즐기는 시간을 찾으세요.

Q. 담화의 요점은 무엇인가?

(a) 유머는 우울증을 극복하는 수단이다.
(b) 사람들은 유머 감각을 배워야 한다.
(c) 웃으면 운명이 더 좋게 변할 것이다.
(d) 웃는 것보다 더 중요한 것은 없다.

해설_ 작은 유머가 모든 절망적인 상태를 잊게 해주므로 이번 시즌에는 웃고 즐기는 시간을 찾아보라고 제안하는 글이다. 따라서 정답은 (a).

어휘_ mentor 선도자, 좋은 조언자, 스승 knitter 뜨개질하는 사람 somber 우울한, 침울한 welcome 환영받는 break 파괴, 중단, 탈출 doom and gloom 절망적 상태 giggle 낄낄 웃다

정답_ (a)

Chapter 16 담화문 내용 파악하기

4.

해석_ 사우스 섬의 시장은 임금이나 수당이 아닌 임의 경비 지출에서 5% 예산 삭감을 준비해 줄 것을 자치구 부서에 요청했다고 말했습니다. 그는 사우스 섬 구(區)가 6월 30일에 끝나는 이번 회계 연도는 괜찮을 것이라고 말했습니다. 그러나 그는 다음 회계 연도에 대해선 확신하지 않았습니다. 사우스 섬 구는 관광 사업 침체로 타격을 받았습니다. 이 섬에서 보다 짧은 휴가를 보내는 방문객들이 줄어든 것은 세수(稅收)가 감소했음을 의미합니다.

Q. 시장은 왜 예산 삭감을 요청했는가?

(a) 경제적 이윤의 감소 때문에

(b) 시장이 관광 산업에 투자하기로 결정했기 때문에

(c) 부진한 국가 경제 때문에

(d) 가장 큰 회사들 중 하나가 파산했기 때문에

정답_ (a)

5.

해석_ 우리 가족은 어제 뉴스를 봤습니다. 나는 충격을 받았습니다. 17,000마리의 미국 개와 고양이를 병들게 한 오염된 중국산 단백질 분말이 현재 사람들이 먹는 음식에서도 발견되었습니다. 미 농무부는 오염된 애완동물용 사료를 먹인 6,000마리의 돼지와 250만 마리 이상의 영계가 인간 소비 시장에 팔렸다는 것을 인정하고 있습니다. 어떻게 그 유독한 중국산 단백질 분말이 수입될 수 있나요? 정부는 국제 수입 검사를 강화해야 합니다.

Q. 담화의 어조는 어떠한가?

(a) 찬성하는

(b) 지지하는

(c) 중립적인

(d) 비판적인

정답_ (d)

6.

해석_ 하와이 고등학교 체육 협회의 임원진은 월요일에 다가오는 학년에 세 가지 스포츠 시즌 변경을 앞당기는 것을 투표로 결정하였습니다. 2008~2009학년부터 여자 농구는 봄에서 겨울로, 소프트볼은 겨울에서 봄으로, 그리고 남자 배구는 가을에서 봄으로 옮겨질 것입니다.

Q. 담화에 따르면, 내년에 무엇이 바뀔 것인가?

(a) 학교 운동회 시작일

(b) 세 가지 스포츠 시즌

(c) 체육 협회 임원진

(d) 야구팀 멤버들

정답_ (b)

STEP 2 Dictation

정답_ 4. a 5 percent budget cut to be taken from discretionary spending

he's uncertain about the following fiscal year.

has been hit by the tourism slowdown

5. The contaminated Chinese protein powder that has sickened

has now turned up in the human food supply

were sold for human consumption

should reinforce international import inspection

6. to move up the changing of seasons for three sports to the upcoming school year

girls basketball will be moved from spring to winter

STEP 3 Actual Test

1.

Do you have a cat that tends to be on the mischievous side, or one that's sweet and mellow? Enter their photos online in Wichita Paws' "Naughty & Nice" contest for a chance to win one of two $50 gift cards to a local pet store. Go to our web site for entry instructions and sneak a peek at other cat owners' photos. The deadline for entries is 5 p.m. Feb. 18. Finalists in both categories will be featured in

The Eagle on Feb. 21, then registered users can vote online for their favorites.

Q. Which of the following is true according to the advertisement?

(a) The winner receives a gift card to a local pet store.
(b) Anyone with a pet can participate in this contest.
(c) You might get a prize if you make the top 10.
(d) You should send the picture by the end of Feb.

해석_ 장난기 있거나 사랑스럽고 명랑한 고양이를 가지고 계신가요? 고양이의 사진을 Wichita Paws의 "못되거나 멋지거나" 콘테스트 사이트에 올리세요. 지역 애완동물 가게에서 쓸 수 있는 50달러짜리 상품권 2장 중 하나를 얻을 수 있는 기회를 위해서요. 참가 등록 지침 사항을 보시려면 저희 웹사이트를 방문해 주세요. 그리고 다른 고양이 소유주들이 올린 사진들을 살짝 엿보세요. 참가 등록 마감은 2월 18일 오후 5시입니다. 두 부문의 최종 진출 사진들은 2월 21일자 〈이글〉에 특집 기사로 다뤄질 것입니다. 그러고 나면 회원 가입자들은 자신이 가장 좋아하는 사진에 온라인 투표를 할 수 있습니다.

　Q. 광고에 따르면 어느 것이 사실인가?

　(a) 우승자는 지역 애완동물 가게에서 사용할 수 있는 상품권을 받는다.
　(b) 애완동물을 가진 사람은 누구든지 이 콘테스트에 참가할 수 있다.
　(c) 만약 10위 안에 든다면 상을 탈지도 모른다.
　(d) 2월 말까지 사진을 보내야 한다.

해설_ 콘테스트를 통해 지역 애완동물 가게에서 쓸 수 있는 상품권을 얻을 수 있는 기회를 가질 수 있다고 했으므로 정답은 (a)가 된다.

어휘_ mischievous 장난이 심한, 장난기 있는 mellow 즐거운, 명랑한 naughty 못된, 개구쟁이의 entry 참가 등록 sneak a peek 살짝 엿보다 feature 대서특필하다

정답_ (a)

2.

2009 is the first year this sort of air-included travel bargain has become widely available. For many years, cruise liners and cruise brokers have offered amazingly cheap repositioning cruises — some of them costing only $50 a day, including meals. But the repositioning cruise also requires that passengers make at least one expensive crossing of the Atlantic by air.

Q. Which of the following is correct according to the advertisement?

(a) The product includes round-trip air fare.
(b) Passengers can buy the ticket at the special price.
(c) This package item requires an expensive airplane fare.
(d) You won't pay for lunch meals.

해석_ 2009년 처음으로 항공료가 포함된 여행 특가품을 폭넓게 이용할 수 있게 되었습니다. 여러 해 동안, 유람 여객기들과 중개인들은 놀라운 가격 전환을 꾀한 크루즈 상품을 제공했습니다. 그들 중 일부 상품은 식사까지 포함해서 하루 50달러밖에 들지 않습니다. 하지만 가격 전환을 꾀한 그 크루즈 상품은 또한 승객들이 비행기로 대서양을 횡단할 때 적어도 한 번은 비싼 값을 내야 합니다.

　Q. 광고에 따르면 맞는 것은 어느 것인가?

　(a) 그 상품은 왕복 항공료가 포함돼 있다.
　(b) 승객들은 특가로 티켓을 구매할 수 있다.
　(c) 이 패키지 상품은 비싼 항공 운임을 요한다.
　(d) 점심 값은 내지 않을 것이다.

해설_ 항공료가 포함돼 있으며, 대서양을 횡단할 때 적어도 한 번은 비싼 값을 내야 한다고 했으므로 (a)가 정답임을 알 수 있다. 비행 기표가 아닌 여행 특가품에 대한 광고이므로 (b)는 틀리다.

어휘_ amazingly 놀랍게도 reposition 〈제품의〉 이미지[시장 전략 등]의 전환을 꾀하다

정답_ (a)

3.

It has features like Power Brakes, Power Door Locks, Power Windows, Power Mirrors, AM/FM Stereo & CD Player, and 3 Point Seat Belts. You will never worry about being broke from increasing gas prices. This one gets excellent gas mileage. For additional savings, print the ad on our web site and show it to Joann Robinson for an additional $200 Off. This offer is not valid with any other offers. Please call 336-2692 for any questions.

Q. What is being advertised?

(a) A computer
(b) An audio system
(c) A vehicle
(d) A boiler

해석_ 이것의 특징으로는 파워 브레이크, 파워 도어 락, 파워 윈도우, 파워 미러, AM/FM 스테레오 라디오 및 CD 플레이어, 그리고 3단계 안전벨트를 들 수 있습니다. 오르는 기름 값 때문에 파산할 것을 걱정하지 않으셔도 됩니다. 이것은 연비가 아주 우수합니다. 추가 할인을 원하신다면, 200달러 추가 할인을 위해 웹사이트의 광고를 프린트해서 조안 로빈슨에게 보여 주세요. 이 (할인) 제공 서비스는 다른 어떤 제공 서비스와 함께 받으실 수 없습니다. 질문이 있으시면 336-2692로 연락 주세요.

Q. 무엇을 광고하고 있는가?

(a) 컴퓨터
(b) 오디오 시스템
(c) 자동차
(d) 보일러

해설_ Power Brakes(파워 브레이크), Power Door Locks(파워 도어 락), Power Mirrors(파워 미러) 등의 특징으로 보아, 자동차 광고임을 알 수 있다.

어휘_ feature 특징, 특색 break 파산시키다 gas mileage 연비

정답_ (c)

4.

Leslie Edelson loved to sing and play guitar. But her greatest talent was listening. She died in December at age 76. She worked for 25 years as a secretary at Rex Hospital. Music education was her great passion, though, and in the 1960s, she taught music at Temple Beth Oregon. She also volunteered teaching music at Boylan Heights School in the 1970s. Her memorial service was held this month.

Q. What did Leslie Edelson do for 25 years?

(a) She did an assistant job at a hospital.
(b) She did a teaching job at school.
(c) She did a cleaning job at school.
(d) She did a nursing job at a hospital.

해석_ 레슬리 에델슨은 노래 부르며 기타 치는 것을 사랑했습니다. 그러나 그녀의 가장 뛰어난 재능은 청력이었죠. 그녀는 76세의 나이로 12월에 세상을 떠났습니다. 그녀는 25년 동안 렉스 병원에서 비서로 일했습니다. 하지만 음악 교육은 그녀의 가장 큰 열정이었고, 1960년대에 템플 베스 오리건에서 음악을 가르쳤습니다. 그녀는 또한 1970년대에 보일란 하이츠 학교에서 음악을 가르치는 봉사활동을 했습니다. 그녀의 추모식은 이번 달에 치러졌습니다.

Q. 레슬리 에델슨은 25년 동안 무엇을 했는가?

(a) 그녀는 병원에서 비서로 일했다.
(b) 그녀는 학교에서 선생님으로 일했다.
(c) 그녀는 학교에서 청소부로 일했다.
(d) 그녀는 병원에서 간호사로 일했다.

해설_ 렉스 병원에서 비서로 일했다고 했으므로 (a)가 정답이다.

어휘_ memorial service 추모식

정답_ (a)

5.

Is Christmas your favorite time of year? Then you must make a road trip to Santa Claus House in North Pole, just outside of Fairbanks. Itching to escape Alaska but still yearning for that Christmas spirit? These great towns will provide you with an abundance of holiday cheer.

Q. What is the advertisement about?

(a) Going to Santa Claus House
(b) Meeting Santa Claus with your children
(c) Sending a letter to Santa Claus
(d) Travelling in North Pole with your family

해석_ 1년 중 크리스마스가 가장 좋아하는 시기입니까? 그렇다면 당신은 페어뱅크 바로 바깥쪽에 있는 북극의 산타클로스 집으로 자동차 여행을 가야겠군요. 알래스카를 달아나고 싶어 못 견딜 테지만 여전히 크리스마스의 정신을 갈구하고 계십니까? 이 멋진 마

을들에서는 당신에게 아주 풍부한 축하주를 제공해 줄 것입니다.

Q. 무엇에 관한 광고인가?

(a) 산타클로스 집에 가기

(b) 자녀들과 함께 산타클로스 만나기

(c) 산타클로스에게 편지 보내기

(d) 가족과 함께 북극 여행하기

해설_ 크리스마스에 산타클로스 마을로 여행을 오라는 내용의 광고이므로 정답은 (a)다.

어휘_ make a road trip 자동차 여행을 하다 itch to ~하고 싶어 안달이다 yearn 동경하다 an abundance of 많은, 풍부한 holiday cheer (크리스마스·신년 따위에 마시는) 축하주

정답_ (a)

6.

This is, of course, one of the best ways to help Mother Earth. The granddaddy of this idea is using reclaimed wood, which is wood salvaged from other buildings and sites. Old school gym floors make wonderful hardwood flooring for homes, and many old manufacturing plants also have usable wood floors, said Linda Mason Hunter, author of "Creating a Safe and Healthy Home."

Q. According to the talk, what does 'This' mean?

(a) Constructing with wood
(b) Recycling wood
(c) Creating different material
(d) Building a new house

해석_ 이것은 물론 대지를 도와주는 가장 좋은 방법 중 하나입니다. 이 아이디어의 일인자는 다른 건물이나 부지에서 구해 온 재생 나무를 이용하는 것입니다. 오래된 학교 체육관 바닥은 가정에 쓰이는 훌륭하고 단단한 바닥재로 되어 있고, 많은 오래된 제조공장 또한 유용한 나무 바닥재를 깔았다고 《안전하고 건강한 집 만들기》의 저자 린다 메이슨 헌터가 말했습니다.

Q. 담화에 따르면 '이것'의 의미는 무엇인가?

(a) 나무로 짓기

(b) 나무 재활용하기

(c) 다른 재료를 개발하기

(d) 새집 짓기

해설_ 첫 부분에 나온 This의 의미를 파악하는 문제로, 두 번째 문장에 결정적 단서가 나와 있다. 이 아이디어의 일인자가 reclaimed wood(재생 나무)를 이용하고 있다고 했으므로 정답이 (b)임을 알 수 있다.

어휘_ mother earth 대지(大地) granddaddy 대가, 일인자 reclaim (폐물을) 재생하다 salvage (폐품을) 이용하다 hardwood 단단한 나무 flooring 바닥재 manufacturing plant 제조공장

정답_ (b)

7.

"The Timothy Wenk Magic Show" returns to the Public Library for a free performance at 10:30 a.m. Saturday in the children's area. Magician Wenk has done shows in the United States, Europe and Japan. He has performed at the White House five times. The 45-minute program is recommended for children 4 to 10 years old who are accompanied by a parent or caregiver.

Q. Which of the following is true according to the advertisement?

(a) Children under 10 years should go with their guardian.
(b) A magician is planning to perform at the White House.
(c) A show will begin at 10:30 a.m. next Sunday.
(d) You can buy tickets by Internet reservation or a booking office.

해석_ "티모시 웬크 마술쇼"가 토요일 아침 10시 30분 무료 공연을 위해 공공 도서관의 어린이 구역으로 돌아옵니다. 마술사 웬크는 미국, 유럽, 그리고 일본에서의 공연을 마쳤습니다. 그는 백악관에서 5번의 공연을 했습니다. 45분간 진행되는 이 공연은 부모님이나 보호자가 동반된 4살부터 10살까지의 아이들에게 권장됩니다.

Q. 광고에 따르면 어느 것이 사실인가?

(a) 10살 이하의 어린이는 보호자와 함께 가야 한다.

(b) 마술사는 백악관에서 공연할 계획이다.

(c) 공연은 다음주 일요일 아침 10시 30분에 시작할 것이다.

(d) 인터넷 예약이나 매표소에서 티켓을 살 수 있다.

8.

"The Fisherman and His Wife" opens this week with performances at J&E schools. The lively musical is based on the Brothers Grimm tale about a talking fish, with original music by Marti. The performance is part of MAPA's Educational Theatre Tours. Performance slots are still available for J&E schools. For more information, contact Collmer at 244-8760.

Q. What is the advertisement about?

(a) A recital
(b) An opera
(c) An independent film
(d) A musical

9.

Maui Electric is required to pay wind farms as though they were burning oil. The wind farm benefits from tax credits also, and Maui Electric uses less oil. However, there is a more useful energy source. It's nuclear energy. At night it could pump seawater upcountry to storage and let it flow back to generate hydropower or to reduce the soot from the Puunene sugar mill.

Q. According to the talk, what is the more beneficial energy?

(a) Nuclear energy
(b) Tidal energy
(c) Hydropower
(d) Wind power

Chapter 17 담화문 내용 추론하기

STEP 1 Pretest Clinic

7.

해석_ 작년에 다른 어떤 전기 발전 기술보다 더 많은 풍력이 유럽에 설치되었습니다. 평균 20개의 풍력 터빈이 일하는 요일마다 설치되었습니다. 유럽 풍력 협회에서 발표한 통계 자료에 의하면, 작년에 유럽 연합에서 확립한 모든 새로운 전기 발전 용량 중 43%가 풍력이었고, 이는 가스, 석탄, 그리고 원자력 발전을 포함한 모든 다른 기술을 뛰어넘은 것이었습니다.

Q. 담화를 통해 추론할 수 있는 것은?

(a) 풍력은 유럽에서 널리 사용되어지고 있다.
(b) 풍력은 조만간 대체 에너지원이 될 것이다.
(c) 유럽은 다른 나라들도 풍력을 설치하기를 원한다.
(d) 에너지 자원은 미래에 더 부족해질 것이다.

정답_ (a)

8.

해석_ 진흙의 아마존 강에 추락한 비행기의 뒷부분에 타고 있던 네 사람이, 비행기가 다른 24명을 죽음으로 끌어내며 가라앉았을 때 간신히 비상구를 열고 무사히 헤엄쳐 나왔다고 일요일에 경찰당국이 말했습니다. 대부분의 희생자들은 생일 파티를 하러 가기 위해 비행기를 전세 낸 편부모 가정의 회원들이었습니다. 7명의 아이들이 죽었습니다.

Q. 기사를 통해 추론할 수 있는 것은?

(a) 비행기에 탄 사람들은 생일 파티에 참석하지 못했다.
(b) 비행기는 태평양에 추락했다.
(c) 대부분의 사람들은 그 사고에서 살아남았다.
(d) 조종사는 잘못된 노선을 취했다.

정답_ (a)

9.

해석_ 버락 오바마 대통령은 수년간 연방 공무원들이 다른 문제들은 해결이 안 됐는데 오직 건강보험 개혁에 대해서 떠들어 대기만 하고 일 처리를 제대로 못해 왔다고 말합니다. 건강보험에 대한 회담을 시작하면서, 오바마는 치솟는 가격이 "지금 매 30초마다 미국의 파산을 야기한다"고 호소했습니다. 그는 목요일에 클린턴 행정부의 건강보험에 대한 철저한 조사에 반대했던 몇몇 사람들을 포함해 백악관에 초대된 100명 이상의 전문가들과 정책 입안자들에게 연설을 하고 있었습니다.

Q. 기사를 통해 추론할 수 있는 것은?

(a) 오바마는 미국의 불경기를 해결하는 데 어려움을 겪고 있다.
(b) 전문가들은 국내 경제가 가까운 미래에 회복될 것이라고 전망한다.
(c) 대통령은 건강보험 개혁이 잘 이뤄지지 않았다고 생각한다.
(d) 클린턴 행정부는 도처에 많은 적을 갖고 있다.

정답_ (c)

STEP 2 Dictation

정답_ 7. than any other electricity generating technology
20 wind turbines were installed for every working day
exceeding all other technologies including gas, coal and nuclear power

8. managed to open an emergency door and swim to safety
dragging 24 others to their death
members of a single family that had chartered the plane

9. while problems have gone unresolved
causes a bankruptcy in America every 30 seconds
including some who opposed the Clinton administration's health-care overhaul

STEP 3 Actual Test

1.

Businesses are laying off employees by the thousands. Macy's is cutting 7,000 jobs and Microsoft is letting go of 5,000 employees. Smith Kline may eliminate as many as 6,000 jobs, including some in the Triangle. But across North Carolina, the hundreds of thousands of people who work in government jobs have been spared the sort of job cuts that are becoming commonplace in the private sector.

Q. What can be inferred from the report?

(a) Many people will lose their position.
(b) The government is trying to make new jobs.
(c) The companies said that they would hire employees next year.
(d) People want to quit their jobs due to low benefits.

해석_ 기업들은 수천 명의 직원을 해고할 것입니다. 메이시는 7,000개의 일자리를 없앨 것이고 마이크로소프트는 5,000명의 직원을 해고할 것입니다. 스미스 클라인은 3교대 일부를 포함하여 6,000개의 일자리를 없앨지도 모릅니다. 그러나 노스캐롤라이나 전역에 공무원으로 일하는 수십만 명의 사람들은 민영 부문에서는 흔해지고 있는 일자리 나누기를 해오고 있습니다.

Q. 기사를 통해 추론할 수 있는 것은?

(a) 많은 사람들이 그들의 직장을 잃을 것이다.
(b) 정부는 새로운 일자리를 만들기 위해 애쓰고 있다.
(c) 회사들은 내년에 직원을 채용할 것이라고 말했다.
(d) 사람들은 낮은 복지혜택 때문에 그들의 직장을 그만두길 원한다.

해설_ 기업들이 수천 명의 직원을 해고할 예정이라고 했으므로 (a)가 정답임을 알 수 있다.

어휘_ lay off 임시 해고하다 let go of 해고하다 eliminate 제거하다 commonplace 평범한 private sector 민영 부문, 사기업

정답_ (a)

2.

A soap opera is an ongoing, episodic work of fiction, usually broadcast on television or radio. Programs described as soap operas have existed as an entertainment long enough for audiences to recognize them simply by the term soap. The name soap opera stems from the original dramatic serials broadcast on radio. These early radio serials were broadcast in weekday daytime slots when mostly housewives would be available to listen; thus the shows were aimed at and consumed by a predominantly female audience.

Q. What can be inferred from the talk?

(a) The term soap opera has been generally applied to any romantic serial.
(b) Evening soap operas sometimes differ from the general format.
(c) Soap opera is popular mostly among housewives.
(d) The term soap opera derived from original drama serials on TV.

해석_ 연속극은 대개 텔레비전이나 라디오에서 방송되는, 계속 이어지는 에피소드풍의 픽션이다. 연속극으로 묘사되는 프로그램들은 청취자들이 단순히 "비누(soap)"라는 용어만으로도 인식할 수 있을 정도로 아주 오랫동안 오락물로서 존재해 왔다. soap opera라는 이름은 라디오의 원조 드라마 시리즈물 방송에서 생겨났다. 이들 초기 라디오 시리즈물은 대부분의 주부들이 들을 수 있는 평일 낮 시간대에 방송되었다. 따라서 연속극은 주로 여성 청취자들을 거냥했으며, 그들에 의해 소비되었다.

Q. 담화를 통해 추론할 수 있는 것은?

(a) "연속극"이라는 용어는 일반적으로 로맨틱 시리즈물에 적용되었다.
(b) 저녁 연속극은 때때로 일반 구성과 다르다.
(c) 연속극은 주로 주부들 사이에서 인기가 있다.
(d) "연속극"이라는 용어는 텔레비전의 원조 드라마 시리즈물에서 생겨났다.

해설_ (a)와 (b)는 글을 통해 알 수 없으며, (d)는 라디오의 원조 드라마 시리즈물에서 비롯된 것이므로 맞지 않다. 따라서 마지막 부분을 통해 추론 가능한 (c)가 정답이다.

어휘_ soap opera 연속극 ongoing 진행 중인, 계속되는 episodic 에피소드풍의 stem from ~에서 생기다 slot (텔레비전·라디오 등의) 시간대 predominantly 주로, 대개

정답_ (c)

3.

After the cold front moves through on Friday, the weekend will start out chilly Saturday morning. The weather pattern will shift to a dry and mild one from Sunday through Tuesday. Highs will climb to near 60 degrees on the plains on Monday. In the mountains, Sunday and Monday will be dry, mild and pleasant. More snow may arrive in the high country by next Tuesday and continue into Wednesday.

Q. Which of the following can be inferred from the forecast?

(a) It is difficult for people to drive in the high mountains because of snow.
(b) The cold weather starts on Friday morning.
(c) It will be windy and chilly on Sunday in the mountains.
(d) The mountain's temperature will be in the 60s.

해석_ 금요일 한랭전선이 지나간 후, 주말에는 토요일 아침부터 추워질 것입니다. 날씨는 일요일부터 화요일까지 건조하고 포근한 양상으로 바뀔 것입니다. 월요일 평지에는 최고 기온이 60도 가까이 오르겠습니다. 산악지역은 일요일과 월요일에 건조하고 포근하며 쾌적할 것입니다. 다음주 화요일까지 고지대에 더 많은 눈이 내리면서 수요일까지 이어질 가능성이 있습니다.

Q. 일기 예보를 통해 추론할 수 있는 것은?

(a) 고지대에 사는 사람들은 눈 때문에 차를 운전하기 힘들 것이다.
(b) 추운 날씨는 금요일 아침에 시작된다.
(c) 산악지역은 일요일 바람이 불고 추울 것이다.
(d) 산악지역의 기온은 60도가 될 것이다.

해설_ 고지대에는 많은 눈이 내릴 것이라고 했으므로 그곳에 사는 사람들은 차를 운전하고 다니기가 쉽지 않을 것이다. 따라서 정답이 (a)임을 알 수 있다.

어휘_ cold front 한랭전선 chilly 차가운, 쌀쌀한 shift 바뀌다 mild 온화한, 따뜻한, 포근한 climb 오르다 plain 평원, 평지

정답_ (a)

4.

United States Steel Corp., a major supplier of material to automakers, announced it was curbing production in the face of slumping demand for cars. "We are in an automotive depression, as shell-shocked consumers, fearful for their jobs, the value of their homes and stock market assets, are wary of making

the sizable investment in purchasing new vehicles," S&P Equity Research analyst Levy wrote in a research note after sales data was released Tuesday.

Q. What can be inferred from the report?

(a) There will be a big discount on cars in America.
(b) It's likely that demand for cars will increase.
(c) Weak consumer spending reduced the demand for cars.
(d) There is increasing demand for fuel-efficient cars.

해석_ 자동차업자들의 주 원자재 납품업체인 미국 철강 사는 승용차의 수요 급감에 직면하여 철강 생산을 줄이고 있다고 발표했습니다. S&P 증권 연구소 분석가 레비는 화요일 판매 수치가 발표된 후 조사 보고서에 "우리는 자신들의 일자리와 주택 가격 및 주식 시장 자산에 대해 두려워하며 심한 충격을 받은 소비자들이 새 자동차 구입에 있어서 상당한 돈을 투자하는 데 조심스러워함에 따라 자동차 불황에 처해 있다"고 썼다.

Q. 기사를 통해 추론할 수 있는 것은?

(a) 미국에서는 대규모 자동차 세일이 있을 예정이다.
(b) 자동차 수요가 증가할 것으로 보인다.
(c) 취약한 소비지출이 자동차 수요를 감소시켰다.
(d) 연비가 좋은 자동차들에 대한 수요가 증가하고 있다.

해설_ 소비자들이 새 차 구입을 위한 지출을 꺼려해 자동차 불황에 처해 있다는 내용이므로 (c)가 정답임을 알 수 있다.

어휘_ automaker 자동차 제조업자 curb 억제하다 slump 갑자기 쇠퇴하다 automotive 자동차의 shell-shocked 심한 충격을 받은 wary of ~을 조심하는 sizable 상당한 크기의, 꽤 많은

정답_ (c)

5.

Here are just a few ways to determine whether your child safety seat is safe. The book will tell you if the safety seat has all of its parts and will also tell you how to use it correctly. You will also want to check for possible damage, such as cracks in the plastic, frayed straps, stiff buckles or harness adjusters.

Q. What can be inferred from the advertisement?

(a) The book mentions safety rules.
(b) The book helps you protect your child from an accident.
(c) The book tells you how to use a seat belt.
(d) The book introduces various seat belts in the world.

해석_ 여기 여러분 자녀의 안전 좌석이 안전한지 여부에 관해 결정할 수 있는 몇 가지 방법이 있습니다. 이 책은 여러분에게 안전 좌석이 그것에 필요한 모든 부품을 구비하고 있는지에 대해, 그리고 정확하게 사용하는 방법에 대해서도 알려줄 것입니다. 여러분은 또한 플라스틱 부분의 갈라진 금, 해진 벨트, 빡빡한 버클이나 안전벨트 조정 장치와 같은 일어날 수 있는 손상에 대해서 점검하기를 원할 것입니다.

Q. 광고를 통해 추론할 수 있는 것은?

(a) 이 책은 안전규칙에 대해 언급한다.
(b) 이 책은 자녀를 사고로부터 보호하는 데 도움을 준다.
(c) 이 책은 안전벨트 사용법을 알려준다.
(d) 이 책은 세계의 다양한 안전벨트를 소개한다.

해설_ 아이의 안전 좌석에 필요한 모든 부품들이 구비돼 있는지와 정확한 사용법 등에 대해 알려줄 것이라고 했으므로 (b)가 정답임을 알 수 있다.

어휘_ crack 갈라진 금 fray 해어지다 strap 가죽끈 stiff 술술 움직이지 않는, 빡빡한 harness 안전벨트 adjuster 조정 장치

정답_ (b)

6.

Hello, Mr. Tim. This is Sally. Now that I am a teacher, I often wonder if I make a difference in my students' lives. But when I do, I think back to your class and am reminded that, yes, the children do walk away with lifelong gifts. Thank you for all you did for me. Give me a call as soon as you get this message. Hope to hear from you soon.

Q. What can be inferred from the message?

(a) Sally is looking forward to meeting Mr. Tim.
(b) Mr. Tim used to give his students books.
(c) Sally will call Mr. Tim back later.
(d) Sally is trying to be a good teacher.

해석_ 안녕하세요, 팀 선생님. 저 샐리예요. 제가 교사가 되고 보니, 제가 아이들의 인생에 영향을 줄지 자주 의문을 품습니다. 하지만 그럴 때마다 선생님의 수업을 돌이켜 보고, 네, 아이들이 일생의 선물을 가지고 떠나는 모습을 상기합니다. 선생님께서 제게 해 주신 모든 것에 감사드립니다. 이 메시지 확인하시는 대로 전화 주세요. 그럼 연락 기다리고 있겠습니다.

Q. 메시지를 통해 추론할 수 있는 것은?

(a) 샐리는 팀 선생님을 만나기를 기대하고 있다.
(b) 팀 선생님은 학생들에게 책을 주곤 했다.
(c) 샐리는 팀 선생님에게 나중에 다시 전화할 것이다.
(d) 샐리는 좋은 교사가 되고자 노력하고 있다.

해설_ 자신이 가르치는 아이들에게 영향을 주는지에 대해 자주 고민한다는 내용으로 보아 (d)가 정답임을 알 수 있다.

어휘_ make a difference 영향이 있다 think back to ~을 돌이켜 보다 walk away 떠나다 lifelong 일생의

정답_ (d)

7.

A urine test was never part of any of my annual checkups. But protein in the urine is one of the earliest signs of kidney disease. That simple test might have prevented me from losing both kidneys. Nearly 100,000 men, women and children are now on the waiting list for a lifesaving organ transplant. With early detection kidney disease can be prevented. So please get screened often.

Q. What can be inferred about the speaker?

(a) The speaker would highly recommend a lifesaving organ transplant.
(b) The speaker was not satisfied with his health checking results.
(c) The speaker got a kidney transplant.
(c) The speaker is working for The National Kidney Foundation.

해석_ 매년 받는 건강 검진에 소변 검사가 포함된 적이 한 번도 없었습니다. 하지만 단백뇨는 신장 질환의 초기 증상 중 하나입니다. 그

간단한 검사만 받았어도 제가 양쪽 신장을 모두 잃게 되지는 않았을 거예요. 거의 십만 명의 남성, 여성, 그리고 아이들이 현재 생명 유지에 필요한 장기 이식 대기자 명단에 올라 있습니다. 일찍 발견하기만 하면 신장 질환은 예방될 수 있어요. 그러니 자주 검사 받아 보세요.

Q. 화자에 대해 추론할 수 있는 것은?

(a) 화자는 생명 유지에 필요한 장기 이식을 적극 추천한다.

(b) 화자는 그의 건강 검진 결과에 만족하지 않았다.

(c) 화자는 신장 이식을 받았다.

(d) 화자는 미국 신장 재단에서 일하고 있다.

해설_ 양쪽 신장을 잃었다고 했으므로 신장이식 수술을 받았음을 알 수 있다. 따라서 정답은 (c).

어휘_ urine test 소변 검사　checkup 건강 검진　kidney 신장　lifesaving 구명의　detection 발견, 탐지

정답_ (c)

Final Test

Part 1

1.

W: Nice to meet you. I moved next door of you yesterday.

M: ___________________________________

(a) Great. Welcome to the neighborhood.

(b) Hello. You live in another city?

(c) My mother visited your house last weekend.

(d) I'm new here. Where is downtown?

해석_ W: 만나서 반갑습니다. 어제 당신 옆집으로 이사 왔어요.

M: ___________________________________

(a) 잘됐네요. 이사 오신 걸 환영합니다.

(b) 안녕하세요. 당신은 다른 도시에 사시죠?

(c) 저희 엄마가 지난 주말에 당신 집을 방문했어요.

(d) 여기가 처음이라서요. 시내가 어디에 있죠?

해설_ 남자의 옆집으로 새로 이사 온 여자가 인사를 건네고 있다. 따라서 환영한다는 (a)가 이어지는 것이 적절하다.

어휘_ move 이사하다

정답_ (a)

2.

M: I don't think we need to waste time waiting for him.

W: ___________________________________

(a) Not really. Let's take a taxi.

(b) I don't think you should throw away those shoes.

(c) He has been waiting for us about 30 minutes.

(d) But he told me that he would no doubt come.

해석_ M: 우리가 그 사람을 기다리는 데 시간 낭비할 필요가 없다고 생각해.

W: ___________________________________

(a) 꼭 그렇진 않아. 택시를 타자.

(b) 네가 그 신발을 버리지 않는 게 좋을 것 같아.

(c) 그는 약 30분 동안 우리를 기다리고 있어.

(d) 하지만 그가 틀림없이 올 거라고 말했어.

해설_ 더 이상 시간 낭비하며 기다릴 필요가 없다는 남자의 말에 이어
질 응답으로, 그가 꼭 올 거라고 했다며 반대 의사의 뜻을 담은
(d)가 적절하다.

어휘_ throw away 버리다   no doubt 의심할 바 없이

정답_ (d)

3.

W: How did you sleep last night?
M: ____

(a) I have a hangover.
(b) Sleep tight.
(c) Not well, I've had insomnia these days.
(d) Classical music was peaceful to listen to.

해석_ W: 어젯밤에 잘 잤어요?

　　 M: ____

　　 (a) 숙취가 남아 있어요.

　　 (b) 푹 자도록 해요.

　　 (c) 별로요, 요즘 불면증이 있어서요.

　　 (d) 클래식 음악을 들으면 마음이 평온했어요.

해설_ 어젯밤에 잘 잤는지 묻고 있으므로 불면증 때문에 제대로 못 잤
다는 (c)가 적절하다.

어휘_ hangover 숙취   sleep tight 푹 자다   insomnia 불면증

정답_ (c)

4.

M: I'm sorry that I didn't attend your wedding.
W: ____

(a) Never mind. I didn't go there, either.
(b) Don't worry. The meeting was postponed a
    week.
(c) That's ok. You were on a business trip at the
    time.
(d) Don't apologize to me. It was our fault.

해석_ M: 네 결혼식에 참석 못해서 미안해.

　　 W: ____

　　 (a) 신경 쓰지 마. 나도 거기 안 갔어.

　　 (b) 걱정하지 마. 회의는 일주일 연기됐어.

　　 (c) 괜찮아. 너 그때 출장 중이었잖아.

　　 (d) 나한테 사과하지 마. 그건 우리 잘못이었어.

해설_ 결혼식에 가지 못한 것에 대해 사과하고 있으므로 괜찮다고 응
답한 (c)가 적절하다.

어휘_ attend 참석하다   postpone 연기하다

정답_ (c)

5.

M: How can I make a call to the New York
   branch?
W: ____

(a) Just press 3 and dial the number.
(b) Let me ask for the New York branch.
(c) The easiest way is going on foot.
(d) Their lines are always busy.

해석_ M: 뉴욕 지사에 어떻게 전화를 걸 수 있나요?

　　 W: ____

　　 (a) 3번을 누르시고 전화번호를 누르세요.

　　 (b) 뉴욕 지사에 물어볼게요.

　　 (c) 가장 쉬운 방법은 걸어가는 거예요.

　　 (d) 그들은 항상 통화 중이에요.

해설_ 뉴욕 지사로 전화 거는 방법을 묻고 있으므로 이에 대한 설명이
담긴 선택지를 고르면 된다.

어휘_ make a call 전화하다   branch 지사, 지점

정답_ (a)

6.

W: Would you like to add some salt?
M: ____

(a) No, thank you. I'm full already.
(b) No. There's already enough.
(c) Ok. It's a bit salty.
(d) I want to redo my order.

해석_ W: 소금을 좀 더 넣으시겠어요?

　　 M: ____

　　 (a) 아니, 됐어요. 이미 배불러요.

　　 (b) 아뇨. 이미 충분히 들어 있어요.

　　 (c) 좋아요. 약간 짜요.

　　 (d) 주문을 다시 하고 싶어요.

해설_ 소금을 더 넣길 원하는지 묻고 있으므로 (b)가 정답이다. (a)는
뭔가를 더 먹겠냐는 질문을 받았을 때 사양하는 응답 표현으로
적절하다.

정답_ (b)

7.

M: I heard that the museum will be closed for a month.

W: _______________________________

(a) Oh, no! I haven't seen the 15th century Oriental painting exhibit yet.
(b) Right. My apartment will be remodeled, too.
(c) When are you going to the museum?
(d) Really? I'd love to go to the museum.

해석_ M: 박물관이 한 달간 폐관될 거래.

　　W: _______________________________

　　(a) 이런! 15세기 동양화 전시품을 아직 못 봤는데.

　　(b) 맞아. 우리 아파트도 리모델링할 거야.

　　(c) 박물관에 언제 갈 거야?

　　(d) 정말? 박물관에 가고 싶다.

해설_ 박물관이 한 달간 문을 닫을 거라는 말에 이어질 응답으로, 아직 15세기 동양화 전시품을 보지 못했다며 안타까움을 표현한 (a)가 적절하다.

어휘_ Oriental painting 동양화 exhibit 전시품 remodel 개조하다

정답_ (a)

8.

M: Sarah, how long will you stay in London?
W: _______________________________

(a) I will not go visit to London.
(b) It took around 3 days.
(c) It's four days a month.
(d) I haven't decided yet.

해석_ M: 사라, 런던에 얼마나 오래 머무를 거니?

　　W: _______________________________

　　(a) 런던에 가지 않을 거야.

　　(b) 3일 정도 걸렸어.

　　(c) 한 달에 4일이야.

　　(d) 아직 결정 못했어.

해설_ 얼마나 오래 머무를 건지 묻고 있으므로 아직 결정 못했다는 (d)가 정답이다.

정답_ (d)

9.

W: We have a new team member joining us this season.

M: _______________________________

(a) I hope our team has better results this year.
(b) I saw you practicing with your teammates.
(c) Maybe our manager will decide it.
(d) I want you to be in the same team as me.

해석_ W: 이번 시즌에 우리와 합류할 새 팀원이 있어.

　　M: _______________________________

　　(a) 올해 우리 팀의 성적이 나아졌으면 좋겠다.

　　(b) 네가 팀원들과 연습하는 걸 봤어.

　　(c) 아마도 우리 감독님이 그걸 결정하실 거야.

　　(d) 네가 나랑 같은 팀에 있길 원해.

해설_ 새로운 팀원이 합류할 거라는 말을 들었으므로 그로 인해 팀 성적이 향상됐으면 좋겠다는 내용의 (a)가 이어지는 것이 적절하다.

어휘_ results 성적

정답_ (a)

10.

M: Don't lose anymore weight. You've lost enough already.

W: _______________________________

(a) I have been going to the gym.
(b) My father said the same thing.
(c) I think she needs to diet.
(d) You're right. I should go on a diet.

해석_ M: 더 이상 살 빼지 마. 이미 충분히 뺐어.

　　W: _______________________________

　　(a) 체육관에 다니고 있어.

　　(b) 우리 아빠도 같은 말씀을 하셨어.

　　(c) 그녀는 식이요법을 해야 할 것 같아.

　　(d) 네 말이 맞아. 다이어트를 시작해야겠어.

해설_ 더 이상 살을 뺄 필요가 없다는 남자의 말에 어울리는 응답은 아빠도 똑같은 말을 했다는 (b)밖에 없다. You're right. 부분만 듣고 (d)를 정답으로 혼동하지 않도록 유의하자.

어휘_ go on a diet 다이어트를 시작하다
정답_ (b)

11.

W: Is everything alright? What do you think of today's dishes?

M: ___________________________________

(a) They were all good except for the dessert.
(b) Could you please clear the table?
(c) This coffee tastes strong.
(d) It's ok, but I dislike mutton.

해석_ W: 뭐 문제 없으신가요? 오늘 음식은 어떠셨어요?

　　 M: ___________________________________

　　 (a) 디저트 빼고는 다 좋았어요.
　　 (b) 테이블 좀 치워 주시겠어요?
　　 (c) 이 커피는 맛이 강해.
　　 (d) 괜찮지만, 전 양고기를 싫어해요.

해설_ 음식 맛이 어땠는지 묻고 있으므로 이에 관해 언급한 선택지를
　　 고르면 된다.

어휘_ except for ~를 제외하고　mutton 양고기

정답_ (a)

12.

M: Jenny, when will you wake up tomorrow morning?

W: ___________________________________

(a) Tomorrow is the beginning of school.
(b) Right. It's a holiday.
(c) I always have breakfast at 8:00.
(d) I should get up at 7 o'clock.

해석_ M: 제니, 내일 아침에 몇 시에 일어날 거니?

　　 W: ___________________________________

　　 (a) 내일은 개학이에요.
　　 (b) 맞아요. 휴일이에요.
　　 (c) 전 항상 8시에 아침을 먹어요.
　　 (d) 7시에 일어나야 해요.

해설_ 몇 시에 일어날 건지 묻고 있으므로 이에 응답한 (d)가 정답이다.

어휘_ wake up 잠깨다, 일어나다

정답_ (d)

13.

W: What brings you here?

M: ___________________________________

(a) My brother and I are going to a concert.
(b) I came here by train.
(c) I'm about to bring out some chocolate cream pie.
(d) I have an appointment with Mr. Lee.

해석_ W: 무슨 일로 오셨습니까?

　　 M: ___________________________________

　　 (a) 남동생과 난 콘서트에 갈 거야.
　　 (b) 여기에 기차로 왔어요.
　　 (c) 막 초콜릿 크림 파이를 가져오려는 참이야.
　　 (d) 이 선생님과 약속이 돼 있는데요.

해설_ 찾아온 용건을 묻고 있으므로 이에 관한 내용이 담긴 선택지를
　　 고르면 된다.

어휘_ bring out 가져오다

정답_ (d)

14.

W: What's the matter with your wife? She doesn't look well.

M: ___________________________________

(a) She is coming next week.
(b) She can't divulge that.
(c) She has a little morning sickness.
(d) Well, I'll get back to you on that tomorrow.

해석_ W: 부인께 무슨 일이 있나요? 안 좋아 보이네요.

　　 M: ___________________________________

　　 (a) 그녀는 다음주에 와요.
　　 (b) 그녀는 그걸 밝힐 수 없어요.
　　 (c) 입덧을 좀 해요.
　　 (d) 글쎄요, 그거에 대해선 내일 연락드릴게요.

해설_ 몸이 안 좋아 보인다고 했으므로 그 이유에 대해 언급한 (c)가 적
　　 절하다.

어휘_ look well 건강해 보이다　divulge 누설하다, 폭로하다

정답_ (c)

15.

M: Even if your work doesn't win this contest, don't ever give up.

W: _______________________________________

(a) I won't, but it would be quite a disappointment.
(b) I know you entered the contest last year.
(c) Yes. The competition was fierce.
(d) I know, but I lost my job.

해석_ M: 네 작품이 이번 대회에서 우승하지 못하더라도 절대 포기하지 마.

　　 W: _______________________________________

　　 (a) 포기 안 해. 하지만 무지 실망스러울 거야.
　　 (b) 작년에 네가 그 대회에 참가했다는 거 알아.
　　 (c) 그래. 경쟁이 치열했어.
　　 (d) 알아, 하지만 난 일자리를 잃었어.

해설_ 포기하지 말라는 격려의 말에 이어질 응답으로 (a)가 가장 적절하다.

어휘_ enter (경기 등에) 참가하다　competition 경쟁, 경기　fierce 치열한

정답_ (a)

Part 2

16.

M: Good evening. Did you bring your invitation?
W: I don't have it. Do I need it to enter?
M: I'm sorry, but this event is "invitation only."
W: _______________________________________

(a) Dear me! Is there any other way?
(b) No. How can I get to the party?
(c) Could you send me the invitation letter?
(d) No thanks. I have another reference.

해석_ M: 안녕하세요. 초대장 가지고 오셨습니까?

　　 W: 초대장 없는데요. 들어가려면 그게 필요한가요?

　　 M: 죄송합니다만, 이 행사는 초대 받으신 분만 참여하실 수 있습니다.

　　 W: _______________________________________

　　 (a) 이런! 다른 방법이 없나요?
　　 (b) 아뇨. 어떻게 파티에 갈 수 있죠?
　　 (c) 초대장을 보내 주시겠어요?
　　 (d) 아니, 괜찮아요. 다른 신원 증명서를 가지고 있어요.

해설_ 초대장이 있어야만 들어갈 수 있다는 말을 들었으므로 이에 곤혹스러워하는 (a)가 적절하다. Dear me!는 어떤 일에 대해 곤혹스러움이나 놀람 등을 표현할 때 쓰는 감탄사다.

어휘_ reference 신원 증명서, 추천서

정답_ (a)

17.

M: Come here, Kate. Why don't you smile when you are serving customers?
W: Sorry. But the women over there are being so picky.
M: It's your job. You can do it well, can't you?
W: _______________________________________

(a) Do you know how to serve these main dishes?
(b) Yes. I need to practice making a speech.
(c) No. I'll never take care of them.
(d) Yes. I'll try to do better next time.

해석_ M: 이리 와 봐요, 케이트. 손님들에게 서빙할 때 좀 웃는 게 어때요?

　　 W: 죄송해요. 하지만 저기 있는 여자들이 너무 까다롭게 굴어요.

　　 M: 그게 당신 일이잖아요. 잘할 수 있죠?

　　 W: _______________________________________

　　 (a) 이 주 요리들을 어떻게 내놓는지 아세요?
　　 (b) 네. 저는 연설 연습을 해야 해요.
　　 (c) 아뇨. 저는 그들을 절대 돌보지 않을 거예요.
　　 (d) 네. 다음엔 더 잘하도록 노력해 볼게요.

해설_ 음식점 주인이 여종업원에게 웃는 낯으로 손님을 대하라고 지적하고 있는 상황이다. 따라서 다음엔 더 잘해 보겠다는 (d)가 이어지는 것이 적절하다.

어휘_ picky 까다로운　make a speech 연설하다

정답_ (d)

18.

M: Good job! I was impressed with your dancing.
W: I was so nervous. Where were your seats?
M: I sat in the front row. These flowers are for you.
W: _______________________________________

(a) Thank you. You didn't have to do that.
(b) They go nice with your outfit.
(c) Thanks a lot. Isn't the ticket expensive?
(d) I saw you during the middle of the performance.

해석_ M: 잘했어! 네 춤이 인상적이었어.
W: 나 무지 긴장했었어. 어디 앉았었니?
M: 맨 앞줄에 앉았어. 이 꽃은 너를 위한 거야.
W: ______________________________
(a) 고마워. 굳이 그러지 않아도 되는데.
(b) 그것들이 네 옷과 잘 어울려.
(c) 정말 고마워. 그 티켓 비싸지 않아?
(d) 공연 중간에 널 봤어.

해설_ 남자에게 꽃다발을 받았으므로 이에 고마움을 전하는 (a)가 이어져야 적절하다. (c) 역시 고맙다는 응답으로 시작하지만, 이어지는 문장이 대화 내용과 전혀 상관 없는 내용이므로 주의하자.
어휘_ row 좌석 줄
정답_ (a)

19.

M: Jenny, how much longer do I have to wait for you? I'll give you one more minute.
W: Sorry! I'm almost ready. Dad, which one is better, the red coat or the black jacket?
M: They both look fine.
W: ______________________________

(a) Why are you putting on that suit?
(b) Ok. I'll take a black one. How much is it?
(c) Please just pick one.
(d) I don't like the red coat.

해석_ M: 제니, 얼마나 더 기다려야 되니? 1분 더 줄게.
W: 죄송해요! 준비 거의 다 됐어요. 아빠, 빨간 코트랑 검정 재킷 중 어떤 게 나아요?
M: 둘 다 좋아 보여.
W: ______________________________
(a) 왜 그 정장을 입었어요?
(b) 좋아요. 검정 걸로 할게요. 얼마죠?
(c) 하나만 골라 주세요.
(d) 빨간 코트는 맘에 안 들어요.

해설_ 둘 다 좋아 보인다고 했으므로 하나만 골라 달라고 부탁하는 (c)

가 가장 적절하다.
어휘_ pick 고르다
정답_ (c)

20.

W: Did you get any messages for me? Mr. Lin told me he called this morning.
M: I have one. Is he from J&U company?
W: Right. What did he say?
M: ______________________________

(a) He said he would call back after lunch time.
(b) Well. The connection was lost for a moment.
(c) He quit his work last year.
(d) I have no idea where my cellular phone is.

해석_ W: 메시지 받은 거 있어요? 린 씨가 오늘 아침에 전화한다고 했어요.
M: 하나 있어요. J&U 회사 사람인가요?
W: 맞아요. 그가 뭐라고 했어요?
M: ______________________________
(a) 점심시간 후에 다시 전화하겠다고 했어요.
(b) 음. 잠시 연결이 끊겼어요.
(c) 그는 작년에 일을 그만뒀어요.
(d) 내 휴대폰이 어디 있는지 모르겠어요.

해설_ 메시지 내용을 묻고 있으므로 이에 관해 언급한 (a)가 정답이다.
어휘_ connection 연결
정답_ (a)

21.

M: This novel is quite popular these days. Have you read it?
W: No, I haven't. Ah! Did you read the book that Jane recommended?
M: Sure. But it didn't move me and I couldn't understand the author's intention.
W: ______________________________

(a) Jane said that it has an unhappy ending.
(b) Right. I was touched by it too, but I didn't like the background.
(c) I don't think so. It was recommended reading.
(d) You told me we should book our tickets.

해석_ M: 이 소설이 요즘 꽤 인기더라. 읽어 봤니?

　　 W: 아니, 안 읽었어. 아! 너 제인이 추천해 준 책 읽었어?

　　 M: 물론. 하지만 감동적이지도 않고 작가의 의도도 이해할 수 없었어.

　　 W: _______________________________

　　 (a) 제인이 그러는데, 불행한 결말로 끝난대.

　　 (b) 맞아. 나도 감동받긴 했는데, 배경이 맘에 안 들었어.

　　 (c) 난 그렇게 생각지 않아. 추천 도서였거든.

　　 (d) 네가 나한테 우리 티켓을 예약해야 한다고 말했잖아.

해설_ (a), (d)는 문맥상 적합하지 않고 (b)는 남자가 감동받지 않았다는 데에 동의하면서 이어지는 내용이 반대되므로 적절하지 않다.

어휘_ move 감동시키다　 intention 의도

정답_ (c)

22.

M: Excuse me. Is this the right way to go to the Thirteenth Avenue?

W: No. It's the way to Fifteenth Avenue.

M: Then, how can I drive there?

W: _______________________________

(a) Go straight and turn left at the second intersection.

(b) Sure. You can go there by subway.

(c) I'm not sure, but it takes 10 minutes to get there.

(d) I got a driver's license last Monday.

해석_ M: 실례합니다. 이 길이 13번가로 가는 길 맞나요?

　　 W: 아뇨. 15번가로 가는 길이에요.

　　 M: 그럼 거기까지 차로 어떻게 갈 수 있나요?

　　 W: _______________________________

　　 (a) 직진하셔서 두 번째 교차로에서 좌회전하세요.

　　 (b) 물론이죠. 지하철로 거기에 갈 수 있어요.

　　 (c) 확실진 않지만, 거기 가는 데 10분 걸려요.

　　 (d) 지난 월요일에 운전면허증을 땄어요.

해설_ 차로 어떻게 운전해 갈 수 있는지 묻고 있으므로 가는 방법을 알려주는 (a)가 정답이다.

어휘_ driver's license 운전면허증

정답_ (a)

23.

M: I heard you are doing two part-time jobs as a waiter and a baby sitter.

W: Right. I'm working pretty hard.

M: Why are you overworking yourself?

W: _______________________________

(a) I will watch your work until you're finished.

(b) Because I like going shopping.

(c) It's hard to find a part-time job these days.

(d) I'm saving money for travelling.

해석_ M: 네가 웨이터와 베이비시터로 두 가지 아르바이트를 한다고 들었어.

　　 W: 맞아. 아주 열심히 일하고 있지.

　　 M: 왜 그렇게 무리하는 거니?

　　 W: _______________________________

　　 (a) 네 일이 끝날 때까지 지켜볼 거야.

　　 (b) 쇼핑가는 걸 좋아하기 때문이야.

　　 (c) 요즘엔 알바 구하기가 힘들어.

　　 (d) 여행 가려고 돈을 모으고 있어.

해설_ 무리하게 일하는 이유를 묻고 있으므로 이에 관한 내용이 담긴 선택지를 고르면 된다.

어휘_ overwork oneself 과로하다

정답_ (d)

24.

M: Is your neighbor Chinese?

W: Yes, he is. His name is Mr. Wang and he is a tycoon.

M: I didn't know that. But how come he drives that old BMW?

W: _______________________________

(a) I guess it's the Chinese way of living.

(b) He got caught in traffic.

(c) I guess driving a four wheeler is more fun.

(d) The car runs very well.

해석_ M: 너네 이웃 사람 중국인이야?

　　 W: 응, 맞아. 왕 씨라고 하는데 재계 거물이야.

　　 M: 그걸 몰랐네. 근데 왜 그렇게 낡은 BMW를 몰고 다니지?

　　 W: _______________________________

(a) 그게 중국 생활방식인 것 같아.

(b) 그는 교통 체증에 걸렸어.

(c) 4륜 구동 차량을 운전하는 게 더 재밌는 것 같아.

(d) 그 차는 아주 잘 달려.

해설_ 재계 거물이면서도 낡은 차를 몰고 다니는 이유를 묻고 있으므로 이에 관해 언급한 (a)가 정답이다.

어휘_ tycoon 재계 거물 get caught in traffic 교통 체증에 걸리다 four wheeler 4륜 구동 차량

정답_ (a)

25.

M: I'd like to have my wisdom teeth pulled. I can't eat well because of them.

W: Ok. First, you should sign an operative permit.

M: Where do I sign?

W: _________________________________

(a) You should write this from the top.

(b) You can sign at the bottom.

(c) I signed the contract yesterday.

(d) These are celebrities' signatures.

해석_ M: 사랑니를 빼고 싶은데요. 그것들 땜에 음식을 잘 못 먹겠어요.

　　　W: 좋아요. 먼저 수술 동의서에 사인을 해주셔야 합니다.

　　　M: 어디에 사인하죠?

　　　W: _________________________________

　　　(a) 맨 위에서부터 이걸 쓰셔야 해요.

　　　(b) 맨 아래에 사인하시면 됩니다.

　　　(c) 어제 계약서에 사인했습니다.

　　　(d) 이것들은 유명인사의 사인입니다.

해설_ 수술 동의서의 어느 쪽에 사인을 해야 하는지 묻고 있으므로 사인 위치를 가르쳐 주는 (b)가 정답이다.

어휘_ wisdom tooth 사랑니 operative permit 수술 동의서 celebrity 유명인사

정답_ (b)

26.

W: Honey, would you stop pressuring John to be a lawyer?

M: He should follow in my foot steps. Wouldn't that be nice?

W: But there's a saying, "Different strokes for different folks." We can't force him to follow our ways.

M: _________________________________

(a) Well, I think so.

(b) Forget about it.

(c) That's the way.

(d) All right. If you insist.

해석_ W: 여보, 존한테 변호사가 돼야 한다고 강요하지 말아요.

　　　M: 걘 내 뒤를 이어야 해. 그럼 좋지 않겠어?

　　　W: 하지만 '사람마다 제각각이다' 라는 말도 있잖아요. 우리 방식을 따르라고 강요할 순 없어요.

　　　M: _________________________________

　　　(a) 음, 그런 것 같아.

　　　(b) 잊어버려.

　　　(c) 그게 방법이군.

　　　(d) 알았어. 당신이 정 그렇다면.

해설_ 사람마다 제각각이니 부모의 방식을 따르라고 강요할 수 없다며 남편을 설득하고 있으므로 (d)가 적절하다.

어휘_ follow in one's foot steps ~의 선례를 따르다 Different strokes for different folks. 사람마다 제각각이다.

정답_ (d)

27.

M: These boxes look heavy. Can I help you?

W: Thank you. But are you free now?

M: Don't worry. Where do I put the boxes?

W: _________________________________

(a) The elevator will be repaired by 2 o'clock.

(b) These boxes are too massive.

(c) Thanks for advising me.

(d) Please put them down in front of the door.

해석_ M: 이 상자들 무거워 보인다. 도와줄까?

　　　W: 고마워. 근데 너 지금 한가해?

　　　M: 걱정 마. 상자들 어디에 놓을까?

　　　W: _________________________________

　　　(a) 엘리베이터는 2시까지 고쳐질 거야.

　　　(b) 이 상자들 너무 무겁다.

　　　(c) 충고해 줘서 고마워.

　　　(d) 문 앞에 내려놔 줘.

해설_ 어디에 두어야 하는지를 묻고 있으므로 놓을 장소가 언급된 (d)
가 정답이다.

어휘_ massive 무거운, 부피가 큰 put down 아래로 내려 놓다

정답_ (d)

28.

M: You see the guy over there?
W: You mean the guy in blue?
M: No, the guy with the black hat. Is he a
　 regular?
W: ______________________________________

(a) No, I didn't go with him.
(b) Yes, he is. What's his name again? I've gone
　　 blank.
(c) Yes, he's cleaning the floor.
(d) No, he's not married. He's single.

해석_ M: 저기 있는 남자 보여?
　　 W: 파란 옷 입은 남자 말이니?
　　 M: 아니, 검정 모자 쓴 남자. 저 사람 우리 단골이야?
　　 W: ______________________________

　　 (a) 아니, 그와 함께 가지 않았어.
　　 (b) 응, 맞아. 이름이 뭐라고 했지? 전혀 기억이 안 나.
　　 (c) 응, 그는 바닥 청소를 하고 있어.
　　 (d) 아니, 그 사람 결혼 안 했어. 미혼이야.

해설_ 검정 모자를 쓴 남자가 자기네 단골인지 묻고 있으므로 이에 답
　　 한 (b)가 정답이다. 뒷부분에 나온 I've gone blank.는 갑자기
　　 머릿속이 백지처럼 하얘지면서 아무것도 생각나지 않는 경우에
　　 쓸 수 있는 표현이다.

어휘_ regular 단골손님 go blank 머릿속이 하얘지다

정답_ (b)

29.

M: Where is your husband?
W: He's working now.
M: It's midnight! You mean he's working all
　 night?
W: ______________________________________

(a) Yes, I used to do it a lot at my old job.
(b) No, but I've always wanted to learn.
(c) Actually, he is on graveyard shift.
(d) No, he is too busy to help.

해석_ M: 네 남편 어딨니?
　　 W: 지금 근무 중이야.
　　 M: 자정이야! 밤새 일한단 말이야?
　　 W: ______________________________

　　 (a) 응, 내 예전 직장에서 많이 하곤 했어.
　　 (b) 아니, 하지만 항상 배우고 싶었어.
　　 (c) 실은, 그 사람 야간 근무조야.
　　 (d) 아니, 그는 너무 바빠서 도와줄 수 없어.

해설_ 자정인데 밤새 일하냐며 놀라 묻는 남자에게 야간 근무조라고
　　 말해 주는 (c)가 적절하다.

어휘_ graveyard shift 야간 근무조

정답_ (c)

30.

M: What is your opinion? Is an early education
　 helpful for kids?
W: For me, I don't think so. It only stresses
　 them out.
M: It really does. There is a proper time to
　 acquire knowledge.
W: ______________________________________

(a) Where there's a will there's a way.
(b) Here goes nothing.
(c) It's like reaching for the stars.
(d) Slow and steady wins the race.

해석_ M: 네 의견은 어때? 조기 교육이 아이들에게 도움이 되니?
　　 W: 내 경우에, 난 그렇게 생각지 않아. 아이들을 스트레스로 지
　　　 치게 만들 뿐이야.
　　 M: 정말 그래. 지식을 습득하는 데 적당한 때가 있잖아.
　　 W: ______________________________

　　 (a) 뜻이 있는 곳에 길이 있지.
　　 (b) 밑져야 본전이지.
　　 (c) 그건 하늘의 별 따기야.
　　 (d) 천천히, 그리고 꾸준히 가면 결국 이기는 거야.

해설_ 조기 교육에 대해 부정적인 견해를 보이고 있으므로 (d)가 가장
　　 자연스러운 응답이다. 각 선택지에 나온 관용 표현들을 잘 기억
　　 해 두자.

어휘_ early education 조기 교육 acquire 배우다, 습득하다

정답_ (d)

Part 3

31.

M: Let me introduce myself first. I have my own company related to the Internet.

W: Wow, that's awesome. How did you build and start up your own firm? How did you raise the capital for it?

M: That's a good question. My business plan won first place and $5,000 in a competition when I was senior in college.

W: When did you start your career?

M: My career started before I even graduated. I encourage you to take classes specific to the area that you are actually interested in.

W: That really makes me think about my career and life after graduation. Thanks for your advice.

Q. What is true about the man according to the conversation?

(a) He had to raise money to invest in a new firm.
(b) He started his career after he graduated.
(c) He was a computer geek during his college life.
(d) He won a prize in college.

해석_ M: 먼저 제 소개부터 할게요. 전 인터넷과 관련된 회사를 경영하고 있습니다.

　　 W: 와, 멋지네요. 어떻게 회사를 세우고 시작했나요? 자본은 어떻게 마련하셨어요?

　　 M: 그거 좋은 질문이네요. 대학 4학년 때 제 사업 계획이 대회에서 1등상과 5,000달러를 따냈어요.

　　 W: 언제 일을 시작하셨어요?

　　 M: 졸업 전부터 일을 시작했어요. 당신이 진짜 관심 있는 특정 분야의 수업들을 들을 것을 권해 드립니다.

　　 W: 졸업 후의 제 직업과 삶에 대해서 생각하게 만드네요. 조언 감사합니다.

　　 Q. 대화에 따르면 남자에 관해 사실인 것은 무엇인가?

　　 (a) 그는 새로운 회사에 투자하기 위해 돈을 모아야만 했다.
　　 (b) 그는 졸업 후에 일을 시작했다.
　　 (c) 그는 대학시절 동안 컴퓨터광이었다.
　　 (d) 그는 대학교 때 상을 탔다.

해설_ 대학 4학년 때 대회에서 1등을 했다고 했으므로 (d)가 정답이다.

어휘_ related to ~와 관계가 있다　awesome 아주 멋진　specific 특정한

정답_ (d)

32.

M: What was your role in the film?

W: I played a pianist named Suzzi. She was a brilliant musician whose career was ruined because of a car accident.

M: Sounds interesting. I'd like to hear more. Is it based on a true story?

W: Yes. It was an honor to be in the movie for me. It will move your heart for sure.

M: What would you do if you were in that situation in your life?

W: Suzzi is so brave and independent in the film. It wouldn't be easy for me to keep hope as well as her but I would try to do my best.

Q. Which is correct about the woman?

(a) She is sort of a coward in real life.
(b) She wouldn't be able to overcome the problem.
(c) She had the role of Suzzi in the movie.
(d) She is going to see the movie.

해석_ M: 그 영화에서 네 역이 뭐였어?

　　 W: 수지라는 이름의 피아니스트 역을 맡았어. 그녀는 훌륭한 음악가였지만 교통사고로 피아니스트로서의 생애가 끝났지.

　　 M: 흥미롭게 들리는데. 좀 더 듣고 싶다. 실화를 바탕으로 한 거야?

　　 W: 응. 나로서는 그 영화에 참여할 수 있어서 영광이었어. 네 마음을 뭉클하게 만들어 줄 거라고 확신해.

　　 M: 네가 살면서 그런 상황에 놓인다면 어떻게 할 거니?

　　 W: 영화 속에서 수지는 아주 용감하고 독립적이야. 그녀처럼 희망을 간직한다는 게 쉽진 않겠지만 최선을 다할 거야.

　　 Q. 여자에 관해 맞는 것은 어느 것인가?

　　 (a) 그녀는 실제 삶에서 겁쟁이인 편이다.
　　 (b) 그녀는 그 문제를 극복할 수 없었다.
　　 (c) 그녀는 영화에서 수지 역을 맡았다.

(d) 그녀는 영화를 보러 갈 것이다.

해설_ 여자의 첫 번째 대사에, 수지라는 피아니스트 역을 맡았다는 얘기가 나오므로 정답은 (c)가 된다.

어휘_ brilliant 훌륭한   ruin 파멸시키다   coward 겁쟁이

정답_ (c)

33.

M: Lydia, I thought you had a date with John today. Why are you still here?

W: I was supposed to go see John in the afternoon but I'm having a bad hair day. So I asked to meet him tomorrow.

M: Oh man, Lydia. You look great! There's nothing wrong with your hair.

W: I was so anxious to see him but I didn't want to make a bad impression.

M: Haven't you seen him before? I thought you've already met.

W: My friend Lisa introduced him to me once but this is the real first date for us.

Q. What is true about the woman according to the conversation?

(a) She has known John for a long time.
(b) She canceled their date because health problems.
(c) She hasn't seen John before.
(d) She wants to meet John the day after the original date.

해석_ M: 리디아, 오늘 네가 존이랑 데이트 있는 줄 알았는데. 왜 아직 여기 있는 거야?

W: 오후에 존을 만나러 가기로 했었는데 오늘 머리가 엉망이야. 그래서 내일 만나자고 했어.

M: 이런, 리디아. 너 멋져 보여! 네 머리 전혀 이상하지 않아.

W: 그가 너무 보고 싶었지만 나쁜 인상을 주고 싶지 않았어.

M: 전에 그를 본 적이 없어? 난 두 사람이 이미 만난 줄 알았는데.

W: 내 친구 리사가 한 번 소개시켜 줬는데, 우리 둘이 하는 데이트는 이번이 처음이야.

Q. 대화에 따르면 여자에 관해 사실인 것은 무엇인가?

(a) 그녀는 존을 오랫동안 알고 있다.
(b) 그녀는 건강상의 문제로 데이트를 취소했다.

(c) 그녀는 전에 존을 본 적이 없다.
(d) 그녀는 원래 약속한 날짜 다음날에 존을 만나고 싶어 한다.

해설_ 머리 모양이 엉망이라 데이트를 내일로 미뤘으므로 (b)는 틀리다. 또 친구 리사의 소개로 한 번 본 적이 있지만 둘만의 데이트는 처음이라고 했으므로 (a), (c) 역시 맞지 않다. 따라서 정답은 (d).

어휘_ bad hair day 아무리 해도 머리 모양이 마음같이 나오지 않는 날   Oh, man. 이런

정답_ (d)

34.

M: What classes are you taking this semester?

W: I haven't decided yet. I want to study Sociology and Chemistry.

M: I think Chemistry was much more demanding for me. I took it last semester and it wasn't that easy. If you like measuring things and calculating math formulas, you might find it interesting.

W: That sounds good, but I want to start easy and work my way up.

M: In that case, I think it would be better for you to take Chemistry 101. That's for beginners.

W: Ok. Then I will take that. Hope that it is still available.

Q. Which is correct according to the conversation?

(a) The woman is not going to take Sociology.
(b) The woman likes mathematics.
(c) There are some spaces left in the class.
(d) The man is majoring in Chemistry.

해석_ M: 이번 학기에 어떤 과목 들을 거야?

W: 아직 결정 못했어. 사회학이랑 화학을 공부하고 싶어.

M: 내겐 화학이 훨씬 어려웠던 것 같아. 지난 학기에 들었는데 그렇게 쉽지 않았어. 네가 사물을 측정하고 수학 공식 계산하는 걸 좋아한다면, 재밌게 느낄지도 몰라.

W: 좋을 것 같긴 한데, 난 쉬운 것부터 단계적으로 듣고 싶어.

M: 그럼, 101 화학 수업을 듣는 게 나을 것 같다. 입문자들을 위한 거거든.

W: 좋아. 그럼 그거 들을래. 자리가 아직 남아 있으면 좋겠다.

Q. 대화에 따르면 맞는 것은 어느 것인가?

(a) 여자는 사회학을 듣지 않을 것이다.

(b) 여자는 수학을 좋아한다.

(c) 그 수업에는 자리가 몇 개 남아 있다.

(d) 남자는 화학을 전공하고 있다.

해설_ 측정하고 공식 계산하는 걸 좋아하면 화학 수업을 들으려는 남자의 말에 따르고 있으므로 (b)가 정답임을 알 수 있다.

어휘_ sociology 사회학 chemistry 화학 demanding 큰 노력을 요하는, 힘든 math formula 수학 공식 work up 서서히 나아가다 mathematics 수학 major 전공하다

정답_ (b)

35.

M: Hi, Kelly, You have a dog. I didn't know that. Where did you get it?

W: She was a stray. I found her abandoned in the street.

M: That was so nice of you. Did you go to see a veterinarian? You should have her examined.

W: Of course, I did. Fortunately, she's fine. By the way, I call her Stacy. Actually, we are on a walk right now.

M: I'm so glad to hear that you have a new companion.

W: Thanks. See you later.

Q. Which is correct according to the conversation?

(a) The woman met her friend Stacy in the street.

(b) The woman came back from the doctor's office.

(c) The woman is raising an abandoned dog.

(d) The dog's leg was broken when the woman found it.

해석_ M: 안녕, 켈리, 너 개 있구나. 그걸 몰랐었네. 어디서 난 거야?

W: 길 잃은 개였어. 길에 버려진 걸 발견했지.

M: 너 참 착하다. 동물병원에는 가 봤니? 그 개 검사해 봐야 해.

W: 당연히 갔었지. 다행히도 아무 이상 없어. 그건 그렇고, 난 이 개를 스테이시라고 불러. 실은, 우리 지금 산책 중이야.

M: 네게 새 친구가 생겨서 너무 기쁘다.

W: 고마워. 나중에 또 보자.

Q. 대화에 따르면 맞는 것은 어느 것인가?

(a) 여자는 길에서 그녀의 친구 스테이시를 만났다.

(b) 여자는 병원에서 돌아왔다.

(c) 여자는 버려진 개를 기르고 있다.

(d) 여자가 개를 발견했을 때 그 개의 한 쪽 다리가 부러져 있었다.

해설_ 길에 버려진 걸 발견했다고 했으므로 정답은 (c)가 된다.

어휘_ veterinarian 수의사 on a walk 산책 중에 companion 친구

정답_ (c)

36.

W: Greg. Can you fix the toilet?

M: Where is the plumber's phone number?

W: Come on, you can handle it.

M: Oh, please. You know that I'm all thumbs.

W: I'm sick and tired of doing all of the chores around here!

M: Okay, I'll help out next time. Take it easy. Why don't we catch a flick?

W: You're impossible!

Q. Which is correct according to the conversation?

(a) The woman is upset at the man.

(b) The woman isn't feeling very well.

(c) The man will fix the toilet.

(d) The man is watching a movie.

해석_ W: 그렉. 변기 좀 고쳐 줄래요?

M: 배관공 전화번호가 어디 있더라?

W: 그러지 말고 해 봐요. 당신은 할 수 있어요.

M: 좀 봐줘. 나 손재주 없는 거 당신도 알잖아.

W: 모든 집안일에 진저리가 나요!

M: 알았어, 다음번에 도와줄게. 진정해. 영화 보러 갈래?

W: 당신은 구제불능이야!

Q. 대화에 따르면 맞는 것은 어느 것인가?

(a) 여자는 남자에게 화가 나 있다.

(b) 여자는 몸 상태가 별로 안 좋다.

(c) 남자는 변기를 고칠 것이다.

(d) 남자는 영화를 보고 있다.

37.

M: Where did my report go? That's so weird.

W: Calm down. Where was the last place you saw it? I think you should retrace your steps.

M: I did that. I rushed back to school and walked down to the cafeteria, up to the library, and then checked my bag again.

W: Why didn't you go to the gym? If memory serves me right, you went swimming this morning.

M: Oh, I'm not myself today. I left it there.

W: It happens.

Q. Which is correct according to the conversation?

(a) The man dropped his report on his way home.
(b) The man will go to the gym for swimming.
(c) The man will go to school to find his report.
(d) The man forgot his report at the gym.

38.

M: Excuse me. I want to send these as two packages.

W: They're quite heavy. What's in the boxes?

M: Teacups.

W: They may be broken. We recommend that you use special wrapping when you pack fragile things.

M: Ok. I'll do that. How much will that cost?

W: It's $7 per package, but special wrapping add $3 each.

Q. How much is the total cost of package?

(a) $10
(b) $20
(c) $30
(d) $40

정답_ (b)

39.

M: Jenny, what are you doing after work?

W: Nothing special. Why do you ask?

M: I'd like to watch a movie. Will you go with me?

W: Of course, I'm always up for a movie. What do you want to watch?

M: Look. This is today's theatre schedule.

W: Do you know what this movie is?

M: It's an action film. I read a review of it in a magazine. It doesn't sound bad.

W: I'd love to see it.

Q. Which is correct about the woman?

(a) She has another appointment.
(b) Her hobby is watching TV.
(c) She will go to the theater.
(d) She doesn't like action movies.

해석_ M: 제니, 오늘 일 끝나고 뭐 해?

W: 별거 없는데. 왜 묻니?

M: 영화 보고 싶어서. 같이 갈래?

W: 물론, 영화 보는 거라면 언제든 환영이지. 어떤 거 보고 싶은데?

M: 봐. 이게 오늘 영화 시간표야.

W: 이 영화가 뭔지 아니?

M: 액션 영화야. 잡지에서 영화평을 읽었어. 나쁘지 않더라.

W: 이 영화 보고 싶다.

Q. 여자에 관해 맞는 것은 어느 것인가?

(a) 그녀는 다른 약속이 있다.

(b) 그녀의 취미는 TV를 보는 것이다.

(c) 그녀는 영화를 보러 갈 것이다.

(d) 그녀는 액션 영화를 좋아하지 않는다.

해설_ 같이 영화 보러 가자는 남자의 제안을 흔쾌히 받아들였으므로 (c)가 정답이다.

어휘_ be up for 기꺼이 ~할 준비가 되어

정답_ (c)

40.

M: Congratulations on your daughter winning the piano contest.

W: Thank you. I was surprised that she has such a good ear for music.

M: Good for you. If she practice continuously, she will become a great pianist.

W: I hope she will. How about your son?

M: He is good at swimming. But he lacks tenacity.

W: Don't worry. Nobody knows the future.

M: You're right. We can just do our best to bring them up well.

Q. Which is correct according to the conversation?

(a) The man's son won the competition.
(b) The woman's daughter has a talent for playing the piano.
(c) The woman wants the man's son to get along with her daughter.
(d) The man congratulated the woman on her victory.

해석_ M: 따님이 피아노 콩쿠르에서 우승한 거 축하드려요.

W: 감사합니다. 저도 딸아이가 음악에 그렇게 소질이 있다는 데 놀랐어요.

M: 잘됐네요. 그 애가 계속 피아노를 연습한다면 훌륭한 피아니스트가 될 거예요.

W: 저도 그렇게 되길 바래요. 댁의 아드님은 어때요?

M: 걔는 수영을 잘해요. 근데 끈기가 부족하죠.

W: 걱정 마세요. 앞날은 아무도 모르는 거예요.

M: 맞아요. 우리는 아이들을 잘 키우기 위해 최선을 다하기만 하면 돼요.

Q. 대화에 따르면 맞는 것은 어느 것인가?

(a) 남자의 아들은 대회에서 우승했다.

(b) 여자의 딸은 피아노에 재능이 있다.

(c) 여자는 남자의 아들과 그녀의 딸이 잘 지내길 원한다.

(d) 남자는 여자의 승리를 축하했다.

해설_ 여자의 딸이 피아노 콩쿠르에서 우승했다고 했으므로 정답은 (b)가 된다.

어휘_ have a good ear for ~에 소질이 있다, ~에 조예가 깊다

tenacity 끈기

41.

M: Sujin, what's that you're drawing with your computer?

W: It's a snow scene of the Tae Gwan Ryung sheep pasture.

M: Oh, you've been there. How was it?

W: It was beautiful. I was also able to feed the sheep.

M: That sounds fun. I really want to do that. By the way, you have a talent for drawing.

W: Well, it's just fun. My computer is recording my drawing. So after I finish it, I can see the entire course of my drawing from sketching to painting.

M: Wow, that's fascinating. I'd like to see you draw.

Q. What will the woman probably do next after she finishes the drawing?

(a) Take the man to the sheep pasture
(b) Teach painting to the man
(c) See her drawing again
(d) Visit the farm to feed the sheep

해석_ M: 수진, 컴퓨터로 그리고 있는 게 뭐니?

W: 대관령 양떼 목장의 설경이야.

M: 아, 너 거기 갔었구나. 어땠어?

W: 아름다웠어. 양들에게 먹이도 줄 수 있었어.

M: 재밌겠는데. 그거 진짜 해보고 싶다. 그건 그렇고, 너 그림에 소질 있구나.

W: 글쎄, 그냥 재밌어. 컴퓨터가 내가 그림 그리는 걸 녹화하고 있어. 그래서 다 그린 후에 스케치부터 색칠까지의 전 과정을 볼 수 있어.

M: 와, 그거 정말 재밌겠다. 네가 그리는 걸 보고 싶다.

Q. 여자는 그림을 다 그린 후에 무엇을 할 것 같은가?

(a) 남자를 양떼 목장으로 데려가기
(b) 남자에게 그림 가르쳐 주기
(c) 그녀의 그림을 다시 보기
(d) 양들에게 먹이 주러 농장 방문하기

해설_ 컴퓨터가 그림을 그리는 전 과정을 녹화하고 있어서 다 그린 후에 볼 수 있다고 했으므로 (c)가 정답임을 알 수 있다.

어휘_ sheep pasture 양떼 목장 have a talent for ~에 재능이 있다

정답_ (c)

42.

M: I heard you are searching for a graduate school. What kind of school do you want to apply for?

W: Actually, I am just learning more about them. I need to study for my GRE.

M: Of course you do, because the GRE test is a big part of your application and a high score will make it easy to get in.

W: That's right. I also hope I can get fellowships or grants to reduce the pressure of the tuition fees.

M: If you need some help, I might be able to help you out. As you know I have taken the GRE test before.

W: That's great. By the way, how's medical school treating you?

Q. What can be inferred about the woman?

(a) She is going to apply for medical school.
(b) She will take the GRE.
(c) She won't be able to pay for tuition if she doesn't get a scholarship.
(d) She decided where she wants to go for graduate school.

해석_ M: 너 대학원 알아보고 있다며. 어떤 학교에 지원하고 싶니?

W: 실은, 학교들에 대해 좀 더 알아보기만 하고 있어. GRE 공부를 해야 하거든.

M: 물론 그래야지. GRE 시험은 지원하는 데 큰 비중을 차지하고 높은 점수를 받아야 쉽게 들어갈 수 있어.

W: 맞아. 그리고 수업료 압박을 줄이기 위해 장학금을 받고 싶어.

M: 도움이 필요하면 내가 도와줄 수 있어. 너도 알다시피 난 전에 GRE 시험 본 적 있잖아.

W: 좋았어. 그건 그렇고, 네가 다니는 의대는 어때?

Q. 여자에 관해 추론할 수 있는 것은?

(a) 그녀는 의대에 지원할 것이다.

(b) 그녀는 GRE 시험을 볼 것이다.

(c) 그녀는 장학금을 타지 못하면 등록금을 내지 못할 것이다.

(d) 그녀는 어느 대학원을 갈지 결정했다.

해설_ 여자의 첫 번째 대사에, GRE 공부를 해야 한다고 했으므로 (b)가 정답임을 알 수 있다. (c)는 수업료 압박을 줄이기 위해 장학금을 타고 싶다고 했으므로 맞지 않다.

어휘_ fellowship (연구 지원비로서의) 장학금 grant (일반적인) 장학금 tuition fees 수업료 go for ~에 들어가다

정답_ (b)

43.

W: Wow, look at this place! It's so clean! Did you clean it up by yourself?

M: Of course. That's not a big deal. I feel better when things are well arranged in my personal space.

W: I didn't know that.

M: Honestly, when I was young, my mom always pushed me to clean up and it became a habit to me.

W: That's impressive. So you can't stand if things are a little messy, eh?

M: Well, I like things to be clean. You should give having an orderly life a try.

Q. What can be inferred from the conversation?

(a) The man wasn't orderly as a child.

(b) The woman's room is messy.

(c) The woman will clean her room after going home.

(d) The man has liked cleaning since childhood.

해석_ W: 와, 여기 좀 봐! 너무 깨끗해! 너 혼자 청소한 거야?

　　M: 물론. 그건 큰일도 아니야. 난 내 개인 공간의 모든 것들이 정돈돼 있어야 마음이 편해.

　　W: 그런 줄 몰랐어.

　　M: 솔직히 어렸을 땐 엄마가 늘 청소하라고 시키셔서 억지로 했었는데, 이제 청소하는 게 습관이 돼버렸어.

　　W: 대단하다. 그래서 지저분한 꼴을 못 참는구나?

　　M: 글쎄, 난 깨끗한 게 좋더라. 너도 정돈된 생활을 가져 봐.

Q. 대화를 통해 추론할 수 있는 것은?

(a) 남자는 어릴 때 깔끔하지 않았다.

(b) 여자의 방은 지저분하다.

(c) 여자는 집에 돌아간 후 그녀의 방을 청소할 것이다.

(d) 남자는 어릴 때부터 청소하는 것을 좋아했다.

해설_ 어렸을 땐 엄마의 강요에 의해 청소를 했다고 했으므로 (d)는 틀리며, (b), (c)는 알 수 없다. 따라서 정답은 (a).

어휘_ clean up 깨끗이 청소하다, 치우다   give ... a try ~을 한 번 해보다   orderly 정돈된, 깔끔한

정답_ (a)

44.

W: What are you staring at out the window?

M: I thought that woman around the corner was one of my friends.

W: What does she look like?

M: She has long hair and is wearing exactly the same leather jacket as my friend.

W: There are tons of similar leather jackets worn by people. That is a big trend now.

M: Yes, I guess so. Besides, my friend wears glasses and is supposed to be in school right now.

Q. What can be inferred about the man's friend mentioned from the conversation?

(a) His friend was standing on the corner.

(b) His friend likes leather jackets.

(c) His friend has bad eyesight.

(d) His friend wore a leather jacket today.

해석_ W: 창문 너머로 뭘 쳐다보고 있는 거야?

　　M: 모퉁이 쪽에 있는 저 여자가 내 친구인 줄 알았어.

　　W: 어떻게 생겼는데?

　　M: 머리가 길고 내 친구랑 똑같은 가죽 재킷을 입고 있어.

　　W: 요즘 비슷한 가죽 재킷 입고 다니는 사람들이 얼마나 많은데. 그게 지금 대유행이야.

　　M: 그래, 나도 그렇게 생각해. 게다가 내 친구는 안경을 썼고, 지금 학교에 있을 시간이야.

Q. 대화에서 언급된 남자의 친구에 관해 추론할 수 있는 것은?

(a) 그의 친구는 모퉁이에 서 있었다.

(b) 그의 친구는 가죽 재킷을 좋아한다.

(c) 그의 친구는 시력이 나쁘다.

(d) 그의 친구는 오늘 가죽 재킷을 입었다.

해설_ 남자의 마지막 대사에 그의 친구가 안경을 쓴다는 내용이 나오므로 (c)가 정답임을 알 수 있다. 모퉁이에 있는 사람은 그의 친구를 닮은 사람이므로 (a)는 틀리다. 또 그의 친구가 가죽 재킷을 가지고 있다고 했을 뿐, 그것을 좋아하는지는 알 수 없으며, 오늘 그 재킷을 입었는지 또한 알 수 없으므로 (b), (d) 역시 정답이 될 수 없다.

어휘_ stare at ~을 응시하다 eyesight 시력

정답_ (c)

45.

W: I have a conference this Friday in Texas. So I booked the ticket to leave tomorrow morning.

M: What time do you depart? How long will the flight take?

W: I take off at 11 a.m. and it takes 7 hours to get there. I should be at the airport by nine.

M: What will you do while waiting to board the plane?

W: I'll read the book that Mike lent me a couple days ago.

M: Is that the graphic novel? I heard that was fun to read.

Q. What can you infer about the woman?

(a) She has a conference tomorrow morning.

(b) She is on the way back to Texas.

(c) She will be in Texas at 6 p.m.

(d) She will keep reading the book on the plane.

해석_ W: 이번 금요일에 텍사스에서 회의가 있어. 그래서 내일 아침에 떠나려고 티켓을 예매했어.

M: 몇 시에 출발하니? 비행 시간은 얼마나 걸려?

W: 오전 11시 출발이고, 가는 데 7시간 걸릴 거야. 난 9시까지 공항에 가야 해.

M: 비행기 탈 때까지 뭐 할 거니?

W: 며칠 전에 마이크가 빌려 준 책 읽을 거야.

M: 그거 만화 소설이지? 그 책 재밌다고 들었어.

Q. 여자에 관해 추론할 수 있는 것은?

(a) 그녀는 내일 아침에 회의가 있다.

(b) 그녀는 텍사스로 돌아가는 중이다.

(c) 그녀는 오후 6시에 텍사스에 있을 것이다.

(d) 그녀는 기내에서 계속 책을 읽을 것이다.

해설_ 비행기는 오전 11시에 출발하고, 텍사스까지 7시간이 걸린다고 했으므로 (c)가 정답임을 알 수 있다. 금요일 아침에 회의가 있어 내일 아침 텍사스로 떠난다고 했으므로 (a), (b)는 내용에 어긋나며, (d)는 읽을 가능성은 있지만 정확히 알 수 없으므로 정답이 될 수 없다.

어휘_ graphic novel 만화 소설

정답_ (c)

Part 4

46.

Pierre Bonnard was born in Paris. At the insistence of his father, Bonnard studied, and graduated in law. But he attended art classes in his spare time. A practising lawyer, his focus remained primarily on art. He was one of the first artists to use pure colour in flat patterns enlivened by decorative linear arabesques in paintings, posters, and designs for stained-glass windows and books. In the late 1880s, Bonnard was a founding member of the Nabis whose works were influenced by the paintings of Paul Gauguin and Claude Monet.

Q. What is the talk mainly about?

(a) The contribution of Pierre Bonnard to modern art

(b) Pierre Bonnard's passion shown through his paintings

(c) The conflict between Pierre Bonnard and his father

(d) The life of Pierre Bonnard

해석_ 피에르 보나르는 파리에서 태어났습니다. 아버지의 강압으로 보나르는 법대에서 공부하고 졸업했지만 틈틈이 미술 강의를 들었습니다. 개업 변호사를 했지만 그의 초점은 주로 예술에 맞춰져 있었습니다. 그림, 포스터, 그리고 스테인드글라스 유리창과 책에 쓰일 디자인에 있어서 장식적인 선 모양의 아라베스크로 생동감을 준 단조로운 패턴에 순수 색상을 사용한 예술가 중 한 명이었습니다. 1880년대 후반, 보나르는 폴 고갱과 클로드

모네 작품의 영향을 받은 나비파의 창단 멤버가 되었습니다.

Q. 주로 무엇에 관한 담화인가?

(a) 피에르 보나르의 현대 예술에 대한 공헌

(b) 그의 그림을 통해 보여진 피에르 보나르의 열정

(c) 피에르 보나르와 그의 아버지와의 갈등

(d) 피에르 보나르의 삶

해설_ 글 전반적으로 피에르 보나르의 삶에 대한 내용을 담고 있으므로 정답은 (d)가 된다.

어휘_ insistence 주장, 고집 practising lawyer 개업 변호사 flat 단조로운, 평범한 enliven 활기 있게 만들다, 생기를 주다 decorative 장식의 linear 선 모양의, 선적인 arabesque 아라베스크 founding member 창단 멤버

정답_ (d)

47.

Welcome to The Metropolitan Museum of Art. This program enables participants to explore the "living encyclopedia of world art", that is, The Metropolitan Museum of Art. Participants have the opportunity for close study and informal discussions with distinguished educators and curators in the galleries of the Museum. We will be starting our tour soon, so please use this time to look around the lobby and take care of any last-minute preparations.

Q. What is the purpose of this announcement?

(a) To introduce a lecture on world art
(b) To explain the diverse opportunities provided to participants
(c) To invite people to a program
(d) To welcome program participants

해석_ 메트로폴리탄 예술 박물관에 오신 것을 환영합니다. 이번 프로그램은 참가자 여러분들이 메트로폴리탄 예술 박물관, 즉 세계 예술의 살아 있는 백과사전을 탐험할 수 있도록 해줍니다. 참가자 여러분들은 박물관의 여러 전시실에서 저명한 교육 전문가와 큐레이터들과 함께 면밀한 연구와 스스럼없는 토론을 할 수 있는 기회를 갖게 됩니다. 곧 견학을 시작할 예정이오니, 지금은 로비를 둘러보시며 마지막 준비를 해주시기 바랍니다.

Q. 이 안내 방송의 목적은 무엇인가?

(a) 세계 예술에 관한 강의를 소개하기 위해

(b) 참가자들에게 제공되는 다양한 기회를 설명하기 위해

(c) 사람들을 프로그램에 초대하기 위해

(d) 프로그램 참가자들을 환영하기 위해

해설_ 메트로폴리탄 예술 박물관에 온 참가자들을 환영하는 인사말로 안내 방송을 시작하고 있으므로 (d)가 정답임을 알 수 있다.

어휘_ explore 탐험하다 close 면밀한 informal 격의 없는 distinguished 뛰어난, 저명한 educator 교육 전문가[학자] last-minute 막바지의 preparation 준비 diverse 다양한

정답_ (d)

48.

In 2005, a 15-year-old Canadian teenager named Christina Desforges kissed her boyfriend and died. Her death, reported around the world, was blamed on peanuts. Desforges was allergic to peanuts and her boyfriend had eaten peanut-butter toast hours before their deadly smooch. Sudden death due to an allergic reaction to food is known as anaphylaxis.

Q. What is the main idea of the report?

(a) Juvenile delinquency is a very serious problem in the U.S.
(b) A girl's sudden death occured from an allergic reaction.
(c) A microbe causes the human body to be weakened by allergies.
(d) Many people around the world mourned her loss.

해석_ 2005년에 크리스티나 데스퍼그라고 불리는 15살 난 한 캐나다 십대 소녀가 남자친구와 키스를 한 후 죽었습니다. 전 세계에 보도된 그녀의 죽음은 땅콩 때문이었습니다. 데스퍼그는 땅콩에 알레르기가 있었고 그녀의 남자친구는 치명적인 키스를 나누기 몇 시간 전 땅콩버터 토스트를 먹었습니다. 음식 알레르기 반응으로 인한 갑작스런 죽음은 "아나필락시스"라고 알려져 있습니다.

Q. 기사의 요지는 무엇인가?

(a) 청소년 비행은 미국에서 매우 심각한 문제다.

(b) 한 소녀의 갑작스런 죽음은 알레르기 반응 때문에 발생했다.

(c) 세균은 인체가 알러기로 인해 약화되게 만든다.

(d) 전 세계 많은 사람들이 그녀의 죽음을 슬퍼했다.

해설_ 한 십대 소녀가 남자친구와 키스를 한 후 사망했는데 그 원인이 땅콩 알레르기로 인한 것이었음을 전하는 내용이므로 정답은 (b)가 된다.

어휘_ be blamed on ~의 탓으로 돌리다, ~ 때문이다 deadly 치명적인 smooch 〈구어〉 키스 reaction 반응 anaphylaxis 아나필락시스 juvenile delinquency 청소년 비행 microbe 세균, 미생물 weaken 약화시키다 mourn 슬퍼하다 loss 사망

정답_ (b)

49.

A few lucky people in parts of Asia and Africa witnessed a rare sight last Monday. They watched as the moon passed in front of the sun in a partial solar eclipse, creating a blazing ring of fire in the sky. A total eclipse occurs when the orbits of the sun, the moon and the Earth line up exactly. In a partial eclipse, the moon is farther away from Earth. This stops the moon from entirely blocking out the sun. Viewers wore special glasses to shield their eyes.

Q. What is the main idea of the report?

(a) The total eclipse occurred only in Africa.

(b) The orbits of the sun, the moon and the Earth seldom line up exactly.

(c) People who have poor eyesight should wear glasses.

(d) Last Monday some people witnessed a partial solar eclipse.

해석_ 아시아와 아프리카 일부 지역의 몇몇 운 좋은 사람들은 지난 월요일에 희귀한 장면을 목격했습니다. 그들은 달이 부분 일식 상태의 태양 앞을 지나갈 때 하늘에 불꽃 고리를 형성하는 것을 목격했습니다. 개기 일식은 태양, 달, 그리고 지구의 궤도가 정확히 일직선을 이룰 때 발생합니다. 부분 일식에서는 달이 지구에서 조금 더 멀리 떨어져 있습니다. 이것은 달이 태양을 완전히 가리지 못하게 합니다. 목격자들은 그들의 눈을 보호하기 위해서 특수 안경을 착용했습니다.

Q. 기사의 요지는 무엇인가?

(a) 개기 일식은 아프리카에서만 발생했다.

(b) 태양, 달, 그리고 지구의 궤도는 정확하게 일직선을 이루는 경우가 드물다.

(c) 시력이 안 좋은 사람들은 안경을 착용해야 한다.

(d) 지난 월요일 몇몇 사람들이 부분 일식을 목격했다.

해설_ 지난 월요일 아시아와 아프리카 일부 지역의 몇몇 사람들이 부분 일식을 목격했다는 내용이 중심 내용이므로 정답은 (d)가 된다.

어휘_ rare 희귀한, 드문 partial 일부분의 solar eclipse 일식 blazing 타오르는, 타는 듯한 total eclipse 개기 일식 orbit 궤도 line up 한 줄로 늘어서다 block out 차단하다 viewer 보는 사람, 관찰자 shield 보호하다

정답_ (d)

50.

Britain's biggest coffee shops have promised to take salt and fat out of sandwiches and cakes eaten by tens of millions of customers as part of a new campaign against junk food launched today. *The Independent* has learned that seven chains — Starbucks, Costa Coffee, Pret A Manger, Caffè Nero, Eat, Greggs and BB's — have made public commitments to change hundreds of products that contribute to heart disease and obesity.

Q. What is the report about?

(a) The new campaign against junk food has launched last week.

(b) Coffee shops have held a monopoly on salt.

(c) The Starbucks in Korea have also made public commitments as the similar to those of British Starbucks.

(d) Britain's coffee shops promised to take salt and fat out of their products.

해석_ 영국의 가장 큰 커피점들이 오늘 시작된, 정크 푸드에 반대하는 새 캠페인의 일환으로 수천만 명의 소비자들이 먹는 샌드위치와 케이크에서 소금과 지방을 빼겠다고 약속했습니다. 〈인디펜던트〉지는 스타벅스, 코스타 커피, 프레타망제, 카페 네로, 잇, 그레그스와 비비스의 7개 체인점들이 심장병과 비만에 일조한 수백 여개의 제품을 바꾸겠다는 공약을 한 사실을 알게 되었습니다.

Q. 무엇에 관한 기사인가?

(a) 정크 푸드에 반대하는 새 캠페인이 지난주 시작되었다.

(b) 커피점들이 소금을 독점해 왔다.

(c) 한국의 스타벅스 또한 영국의 스타벅스와 유사한 공약을 했다.

(d) 영국의 커피점들은 그들의 제품에서 소금과 지방을 빼겠다고 약속했다.

해설_ 글 첫 부분에 언급된 내용이 중심 내용으로, 영국 최대 커피점들이 소비자들이 먹는 샌드위치와 케이크에서 소금과 지방을 빼겠다고 약속했다고 했으므로 정답은 (d)가 된다.

어휘_ public commitment 공약 hold a monopoly 전매권을 갖다

정답_ (d)

51.

The Amazon rainforest is one of the biggest and most important living stores of carbon on the planet through its ability to convert atmospheric carbon dioxide into solid carbon. But this massive natural "sink" for carbon cannot be relied on to continue absorbing carbon dioxide in perpetuity, a study shows. Researchers have found that, for a period in 2005, the Amazon rainforest actually slipped into reverse gear and started to emit more carbon than it absorbed.

Q. What is the main topic of the talk?

(a) The Amazon rainforest has started to emit more carbon than it absorbed.

(b) The Amazon was one of the most important living stores of carbon.

(c) Scientists are trying to preserve the Amazon rainforest.

(d) The ability to convert atmospheric carbon dioxide into solid carbon is very important.

해석_ 아마존 열대우림은 대기 중의 이산화탄소를 고체 탄소로 전환하는 능력으로 인해 지구상에서 가장 크고 가장 중요한 살아 있는 탄소 저장고입니다. 그러나 한 연구에 따르면, 영구히 이산화탄소를 계속 흡수하기 위해 탄소를 위한 이 거대한 자연 하수구에 의존할 수는 없다고 합니다. 연구원들은 2005년 기간 동안, 아마존 열대우림이 실제로 후진 상태를 보였고 흡수한 것보다 더

많은 탄소를 방출하기 시작했다는 사실을 밝혔습니다.

Q. 담화의 주제는 무엇인가?

(a) 아마존 열대우림은 흡수한 것보다 더 많은 탄소를 방출하기 시작했다.

(b) 아마존은 가장 중요한 살아 있는 탄소 저장고 중 하나였다.

(c) 과학자들은 아마존 열대우림을 보존하기 위해 노력 중이다.

(d) 대기 중의 이산화탄소를 고체 탄소로 바꾸는 능력은 매우 중요하다.

해설_ (b)를 정답으로 생각할 수도 있겠지만 이 글의 중심 내용은 접속사 But 이하에 전개되고 있다. 아마존 열대우림이 흡수한 것보다 더 많은 탄소를 방출하기 시작했다고 했으므로 정답은 (a)가 된다.

어휘_ rainforest 열대 우림 store 저장고 carbon 탄소 convert 변하게 하다, 전환하다 atmospheric 대기의, 공기의 carbon dioxide 이산화탄소 solid 고체의 massive 거대한 sink 하수구 absorb 흡수하다 in perpetuity 영구히 slip into ~에 빠지다, ~으로 갈아입다 reverse gear 후진 기어 emit 방출하다 preserve 보존하다

정답_ (a)

52.

Poverty is what made Alicia Avila an expert quilter. Avila grew up in a family of migrant workers who traveled regularly between Texas and Wisconsin and couldn't afford new bed coverings. So Avila's grandmother would save and sew remnants of cloth to make quilts, and Avila would mimic her, starting first by piecing scraps of paper together and then graduating to real stitches in time.

Q. Which of the following is true according to the talk?

(a) Sewing requires very acute hand coordination.

(b) Avila couldn't afford to buy bed coverings.

(c) Avila sold quilts at the market on the weekend.

(d) Avila's family used to travel between Texas and Wisconsin on vacations.

53.

This year the euro celebrates its tenth anniversary. Since the global financial system is in tatters, the case for Britain going in is now stronger than ever. Britain's business cycle is synchronised closely enough with the condition of the Frankfurt suburban area. This suggests that "imbalanced shocks" — events like oil price hikes that might affect Britain differently from the rest of Europe — are unlikely to be a real problem in making the currency work.

Q. Which of the following is true according to the report?

(a) Britain's business cycle is very similar to Europe's.

(b) Because Britain is not using the euro, Britain's economy is suffering.

(c) The global financial system has fallen into a serious depression.

(d) All countries in Europe but Britain use the euro.

54.

William Lavery, president of Virginia Tech from 1975 to 1987 died Monday. He was 78. The university announced Lavery's death today, lauding his work to grow research at Tech and develop initiatives such as the Virginia Tech Corporate Research Center and Virginia Tech Intellectual Properties. Lavery's tenure also coincided with exponential growth in fundraising at Tech.

Q. Which is correct about William Lavery?

(a) He was President of the Republic of Virginia 1975~1987.

(b) He developed initiatives like the Virginia Tech Corporate Research Center.

(c) He was a sophomore in Virginia Tech in 1975.

(d) He raised funds for the famine in Africa.

해석 1975~1987년 버지니아 공대 학장이었던, 윌리엄 레버리가 월요일에 사망했습니다. 그의 나이 78세였습니다. 대학에서는 공과대학에 연구를 장려하고 Virginia Tech Corporate Research Center와 Virginia Tech Intellectual Properties와 같은 발의를 진전시켰던 업적을 기리며, 오늘 레버리의 사망 소식을 발표했습니다. 레버리의 재임 기간에는 또한 공과대학에서의 기금 모금이 기하급수적으로 증가했습니다.

Q. 윌리엄 레버리에 관해 맞는 것은 어느 것인가?

(a) 그는 1975~1987년에 버지니아 공화국 대통령이었다.

(b) 그는 Virginia Tech Corporate Research Center와 같은 발의를 진전시켰다.

(c) 그는 1975년에 버지니아 공대 2학년생이었다.

(d) 그는 아프리카의 기아를 위한 기금을 모금했다.

해설 1975~1987년에 공대 학장으로 있었으므로 (a), (c)는 틀리다. 또 그의 재임 기간 동안 공과대학에서의 기금 모금이 증가했다고 했으므로 (d) 역시 맞지 않다. 따라서 정답은 (b).

어휘 laud 기리다, 찬미하다 tenure 재임 기간 coincide 동시에 일어나다 exponential 기하급수적인 fundraising 기금 모금 sophomore 2학년생 famine 기근, 기아

정답 (b)

55.

One tractor-trailer driver is dead and another injured following a collision that shut down one lane of Interstate 77 in Carroll County this afternoon. Just after noon today a tractor-trailer heading north near mile marker 22 spun out of control in a curve, crashed through a guardrail and struck a southbound tractor-trailer, Virginia State Police Sgt. Mike Conroy said.

Q. Which is correct according to the news?

(a) One tractor-trailer heading north lost control while turning a curve.

(b) The wrecked car's owner was Virginia State Police Sgt. Mike Conroy.

(c) The car accident injured many people.

(d) The highway collision was caused by a drowsy driver.

해석 오늘 오후 캐롤 카운티 77번 고속도로의 한 차선을 폐쇄시킨 충돌 사고 후 대형 화물 트럭 운전사가 사망하고 또 다른 사람은 부상을 입었습니다. 오늘 정오 직후에 22마일 간선 표지판 근처에서 북쪽으로 향하던 대형 화물 트럭이 커브길에서 통제력을 잃고 가드레일을 들이받아 남쪽으로 향하던 대형 트럭 화물과 충돌했다고 버지니아 주립 관할 경찰서의 마이크 콘로이 경사가 말했습니다.

Q. 뉴스에 따르면 맞는 것은 어느 것인가?

(a) 북쪽으로 향하던 대형 화물 트럭 한 대가 커브를 도는 동안 통제력을 상실했다.

(b) 파손된 차량의 소유주는 버지니아 주립 관할 경찰서의 마이크 콘로이 경사였다.

(c) 그 교통사고로 많은 사람들이 다쳤다.

(d) 고속도로 충돌 사고는 졸음 운전 때문에 일어났다.

해설 충돌 사고로 트럭 운전사가 사망하고 다른 한 사람은 부상당했다고 했으므로 (c)는 틀리다. (d)는 내용에 언급돼 있지 않으며, (b) 역시 엉뚱한 내용이므로 정답이 될 수 없다. 따라서 정답은 (a).

어휘 tractor-trailer 대형 화물 트럭 collision 충돌 shut down 막다, 폐쇄하다 interstate 주간(州間) 고속도로 spin out of control 통제력을 상실하다 crash 충돌하다 guardrail 가드레일 strike ~에 충돌하다, 들이받다 Sgt.(= Sergeant) 경사 wrecked 파손된 drowsy 꾸벅꾸벅 조는

정답 (a)

56.

British scientists are about to mount one of the boldest-ever missions, to search for life forms that have survived for possibly millions of years in a frozen "lost world" beneath an ancient ice sheet. This week, a team of Antarctic scientists has been given the go-ahead to drill through a two-mile-thick sheet of ice that has sealed a sub-glacial lake from the rest of the biosphere for at least as long as Homo sapiens have walked the Earth.

Q. Which of the following is true according to the report?

(a) Antarctic scientists were allowed to drill down through a sheet of ice.

(b) The sheet of ice has revealed a sub-glacial

lake.

(c) British scientists are about to climb a mountain in the Arctic.

(d) Atlantis is buried in a frozen state beneath an ancient ice sheet.

해석_ 영국의 과학자들은 고대 대륙 빙하 바로 아래 얼어 있는 잃어버린 세계에 아마도 수백 년 동안 생존해 왔을 생명체를 탐사하기 위해 가장 과감한 임무 중 하나를 시작하려고 합니다. 이번주 남극 탐사 과학자 팀은 최소한 인류가 지구에 존재해 왔던 만큼이나 오랫동안 생물권의 잔여 부분으로부터 빙하 밑 호수를 봉인해 왔던 2마일 두께의 얼음판을 뚫는 허가를 받았습니다.

Q. 기사에 따르면 맞는 것은 어느 것인가?

(a) 남극 탐사 과학자들은 얼음판 밑을 파헤치도록 허가받았다.

(b) 얼음판은 빙하 밑 호수를 드러냈다.

(c) 영국 과학자들은 북극의 산을 오르려 하고 있다.

(d) 아틀란티스 섬은 고대 대륙 빙하 바로 아래에 결빙 상태로 묻혀 있다.

해설_ 얼음판을 뚫는 허가를 받았다고 했으므로 정답은 (a)다.

어휘_ mount 준비하다, 시작하다 mission 사명, 임무 frozen 언, 결빙한 beneath ~의 바로 밑에 ice sheet 대륙 빙하 Antarctic 남극의 give the go-ahead 허가하다 drill through 구멍을 뚫다 a sheet of ice (극지의) 얼음판 seal 봉하다 sub-glacial 빙하 밑의 biosphere 생물권 drill down through (어떤 것의) 밑(바닥)을 파헤치다 the Arctic 북극 Atlantis 아틀란티스 섬 bury 묻다

정답_ (a)

57.

A 22-year-old Allentown man admitted today that he gunned down two men in the city in 2007. William Torres, who became known for the fuzzy lion slippers he wore at his arraignment, pleaded guilty to two counts of third-degree murder. The plea agreement calls for him to serve 70 to 80 years in state prison. Torres was charged in January 2008 with two counts of homicide in Dec. 12, 2007.

Q. What will probably happen according to this report?

(a) The murders will make people less likely to leave their homes.

(b) The man will deny his guilt of third-degree murder.

(c) The man will request to be released on bail.

(d) The man will likely spend the rest of his life in jail.

해석_ 앨런타운에 사는 22살의 한 남자가 오늘 그가 2007년에 두 남자를 총으로 살해한 사실을 시인했습니다. 심문 당시에 털 달린 사자 슬리퍼를 신고 와서 유명해진 윌리엄 토레스는 3급 살인에 대한 두 개의 기소에서 유죄를 인정했습니다. 살인혐의 시인으로 그는 70~80년을 주 교도소에서 복역하게 될 것입니다. 토레스는 2007년 12월 12일에 발생했던 두 개의 살인사건 기소에 대해 2008년 1월에 형을 받았습니다.

Q. 이 기사에 따르면 무슨 일이 일어날 것 같은가?

(a) 살인사건으로 인해 사람들이 외출할 가능성이 더 낮아질 것이다.

(b) 남자는 자신의 3급 살인 혐의를 부인할 것이다.

(c) 남자는 보석 석방을 요청할 것이다.

(d) 남자는 그의 남은 인생을 감옥에서 보낼 것 같다.

해설_ 살인 혐의를 인정함에 따라 70~80년을 복역하게 될 것이라고 했으므로 (d)가 정답임을 알 수 있다.

어휘_ gun down 총으로 쏴 죽이다 fuzzy 보풀로 덮인, 잔털 모양의 arraignment 심문 plead guilty 유죄를 인정하다 count (기소장의) 소인(訴因), 기소 조항 third-degree 3급의 plea agreement 유죄 합의[인정] serve 복역하다 state prison 주 교도소 homicide 살인 be released on bail 보석으로 풀려나다

정답_ (d)

58.

The bomber detonated his explosives near a side entrance of the police academy, which is in a mainly Shiite area of eastern Baghdad. Extremists have increasingly targeted Iraqi forces as they try to prove they can take over the country's security so the American troops can go home. Baghdad's main police academy has been hit by several bombings. Another suicide bombing there killed at least 33 people and wounded dozens on Dec. 1.

Q. Which is the most likely reason for the bomber to have detonated the bomb?

(a) To kill American troops
(b) To free imprisoned Iraqi forces
(c) To destroy hostile forces
(d) To prove that they have the power to drive out the American army

해석_ 폭파범은 바그다드 동부의 주요 시아파 지역에 있는 경찰학교 측면 입구 부근에 폭약을 터뜨렸습니다. 극단주의자들은 그들이 국가의 안전을 떠맡아 미국 병력을 철수시킬 수 있다는 것을 입증해 보임으로써 이라크 병력을 점차적으로 목표로 삼고 있습니다. 바그다드의 주요 경찰학교는 몇 차례 폭탄 공격을 받았습니다. 12월 1일 그곳에서 또 다른 자살폭탄 공격으로 인해 최소한 33명이 죽고, 수십 명이 부상당했습니다.

Q. 폭파범이 폭탄을 터뜨린 이유로 가장 가까운 것은?

(a) 미군을 죽이기 위해
(b) 수감된 이라크군을 석방시키기 위해
(c) 적군을 죽이기 위해
(d) 그들이 미군을 추방할 힘이 있음을 증명하기 위해

해설_ 미군을 철수시킬 수 있다는 것을 증명함으로써 이라크 병력을 목표 대상으로 삼고 있다고 했으므로 정답은 (d)가 된다.

어휘_ bomber 폭파범 detonate 폭발시키다 explosive 폭발물, 폭약 Shiite 시아파의 extremist 극단주의자 take over 떠맡다 troops 군대, 병력 bombing 폭격, 폭탄 투하 hostile forces 적군 imprison 수감하다, 구속하다 drive out 쫓아내다

정답_ (d)

59.

As International Women's Day was being celebrated, the Vatican had a novel message for the women of the world: Give thanks for the washing machine. This humble domestic appliance has done more for the women's liberation movement than the contraceptive pill or working outside the home, said the official Vatican newspaper, *Osservatore Romano*.

Q. What can be inferred from the report?

(a) The Vatican thought that household appliances had contributed to women's liberation.
(b) Contraceptive pills have not contributed to women's liberation.
(c) The Vatican urged for a women's liberation campaign.
(d) International Women's Day is celebrated only in the Vatican.

해석_ 세계 여성의 날이 경축되고 있었을 때, 교황청은 세계 여성들에게 기발한 메시지를 전했습니다. 세탁기에 대해 감사하라고 말이죠. 이 작은 가정용 가전제품이 피임약이나 직장생활보다도 더 많이 여성 해방운동에 기여했다고 교황청 공식 신문인 〈오세르 바토레 로마노〉가 전했습니다.

Q. 기사를 통해 추론할 수 있는 것은?

(a) 교황청은 가전제품이 여성 해방에 기여했다고 생각했다.
(b) 피임약은 여성 해방에 기여하지 않았다.
(c) 교황청은 여성 해방 캠페인을 촉구했다.
(d) 세계 여성의 날은 교황청에서만 경축된다.

해설_ 세탁기가 여성 해방운동을 위해 피임약이나 직장생활보다도 더 많은 것을 했다는 내용으로 보아 (a)가 정답임을 알 수 있다.

어휘_ celebrate (식을 올려) 경축하다 novel 새로운, 기발한 humble 시시한, 작은 domestic appliance 가전제품 liberation 해방 contraceptive pill 피임약 contribute 기여하다

정답_ (a)

60.

A calendar is a system of organizing days for a social, religious, commercial or administrative purpose. This organization is done by giving names to periods of time — typically days, weeks, months and years. Periods in a calendar are usually, though not necessarily, synchronized with the cycles of some astronomical phenomenon, such as the cycle of the sun, or the moon. Many civilizations and societies have devised calendars, suited to their particular needs.

Q. What can be inferred from the talk?

(a) Calendars have been devised by many civilizations satisfying certain needs.

(b) Calendars have been mainly made for political purposes.
(c) Periods in a calendar are frequently in discord with the cycle of the sun.
(d) The system of organizing days is done by dividing certain periods of time.

해석_ 달력은 사회적, 종교적, 상업적 또는 행정상의 목적을 위해 날짜를 정리하는 체계이다. 이러한 정리는 전형적으로 일, 주, 월, 그리고 년과 같이 기간에 이름을 붙임으로써 이루어진다. 달력에서 기간은, 반드시 그렇지는 않을지라도, 대개 태양이나 달의 주기와 같은 천문 현상의 주기와 일치한다. 많은 문명과 사회는 그들의 특정한 요구에 맞춰진 달력을 고안했다.

Q. 담화를 통해 추론할 수 있는 것은?

(a) 달력은 특정한 요구를 만족시키면서 많은 문명에 의해 고안되어 왔다.

(b) 달력은 주로 정치적 목적을 위해 만들어져 왔다.

(c) 달력의 기간은 종종 태양의 주기와 불일치한다.

(d) 날짜를 조직하는 체계는 일정한 기간을 분류함으로써 이루어진다.

해설_ 마지막 부분을 통해 (a)가 정답임을 알 수 있다. (b)는 첫 부분에 언급된 내용에 비추어 맞지 않으며, (c)와 (d) 역시 글 내용과 다르다.

어휘_ commercial 상업적인 administrative 행정상의 synchronize 동시성을 가지다 civilization 문명 devise 고안하다 in discord with ~와 일치하지 않다

정답_ (a)